New Green World

By

JOSEPHINE HERBST

HASTINGS HOUSE   PUBLISHERS   NEW YORK

for Jessie

This was the sun come dandling down
Green Babylon in the thronged sheaves—
Shelled such dingles, tan such bloom
By the roved brooksides, all the day long.
Lightly like music running, our blood
In and out of the cloud's woven pastures,
It was all in the shade of the vines and meadows
Where Adam delves, in the green fables
Of the dogdays, in early youth.

—Jean Garrigue
from *The Monument Rose*

ILLUSTRATIONS

BETWEEN PAGES 148 AND 149

New Green World

FOREWORD

J OHN BARTRAM, Eighteenth Century botanist and explorer of the wilderness, lived his long, good life in the State of Pennsylvania, some thirty-five miles from the place where I now live, and where a little plant called the Star of Bethlehem, thought by Bartram doomed to perish, continues to flourish. He was not merely a botanist nor is this study of certain phases of his life made from any specialized viewpoint. In his day botany was an open field; a new species cause for a shout of joy. Each specimen was carefully studied in its natural habitat; it was related to a universe. The little coterie of men who devoted their lives to what was then known as natural history, for it included stones and turtles as well as trees and flowers, were whole men confronting a whole world, not human beings floating in a culture medium. When a man

1

said "I" he meant exactly "I," not an ego or a super-ego lost in a soup of determinants. The mistake about the "I" only came later when by saying "I" one meant nothing but one's own fragmented self alone in a world divided into pieces, abstract and aloof.

Who knows the exact origin of a book? A book begins with a writer's "I" even when the matter involves lives that seem disrelated in time and space to his own. If in the beginning the flowers that enchanted my own childhood seem to have pointed to the seedlings discovered by Bartram on this continent, it soon became clear that the ingredient I wished to recover from that vast wilderness so passionately pursued was not only a botanical specimen but the confident lost "I" of whole men. In Bartram's day the individual could be an individual with a better conscience than today. These men whose lives I began to explore as Bartram had explored his wilderness seemed closer to stalks of growing grain in the field than we are. They were flung about more violently by storms and pestilence but even the plague that fell mysteriously upon Philadelphia in that century came as a collective woe. War and fire might shake the collective field of stalks but what was left standing could be answered for. It could be defined. Today the point of gravity for responsibility has shifted from the small community to relationships between *things*. Experiences have even made themselves independent of men. They are to be found by turning the pages of a pictorial magazine or in the cozy isolation of one's living room by staring at a television screen. Over the airways, in movies, experiences have come to be dogmatized to certain kinds of experience at the cost of all others. If experience does not come from one's actual work who can say from whence it comes? With so many people interpreting experience who is even entitled to his anger? The world comes second hand—fifth hand—to us and the illusion that it is fresh because it is shown as a picture of an actual place or is given as a "true account" by some reporter who claims to have been "there" divides man into incalculable parts without any true center.

But when you go back to Bartram and his coterie you begin to realize that here was culture coming to men who were at their work. It was not at an expense of life but an exaltation of life itself. Botany came to Bartram through his eyes and hands as he ploughed a field or searched the woods for wild honey. Books were cherished; learning did not make a man a "highbrow" but equipped him with tools for living. Nor did Bartram speculate with the wilderness when he made his long marches into it; he never staked out a claim to resell at a profit. What he took in by the eye, he proved by the deed. Plant life forced him away from home, compelled him to break with parochial ideas, made him give up all dogmas, in defense of a mystical connection with an illimitable universe. When he was accused by his own Quaker brethren of exalting God, the Almighty Father, and denying God, the Son, he paid no attention to the reprimand, but time after time sat proud and indomitable, his own "I" in the same seat, asserting his right of belief among people who would deny him.

Of course he believed in the future. He believed in progress for mankind. But he saw the flaws and dared to criticize and to warn. Toward the end of his life he even began to suspect that the gains of progress might bring also a severance from the wholeness of things. In a county in Pennsylvania not remote from Bartram's old home there was once a park where children had lavish picnics; circuses put up their tents and country fairs displayed prize cows and women prize loaves of bread. All this has vanished in recent days under acres of hard cement and a housing development showing a thin streak of bald lawn. One can no longer find the old swimming hole; it was caged and trapped and diverted elsewhere. Under the hardened body of the town it doubtless runs, lost to minnows and boys, as Minetta brook continues to bubble under the pavements of New York. But the water is a threat, no longer a joy. And under the growing body of facts and discoveries the present-day mind must look sharp for a chink if it wants to scrutinize any question closely. Countless views, opinions, ideas, from all sorts of sick and sound brains, waking and dreaming, congeal and form a hardness which the inquiring mind must break through. Man comes to feel he is dangerously close to the stage where he will suffer the fate of certain prehistoric animals. The ground streams away under his feet and in the dark realm where he is rooted he lacks the friendly mediation of words that once spoke with authority to him.

It was not like this with these men. They were not overawed by conventions of their day. They were out to challenge. They even believed that it might be possible to comprehend the universe by devotion to the minutest creatures whose laws of life might shadow the greater design. They were not so inundated by the latest happenings always pushing ahead first that they had no chance to feel the flow from the source. The source was everything. You can call what they felt "wonder." You can call it "love." But the little twig, the light on a hill, became an experience sunk deep in essential nature, an experience not even possible to transmit into words. Like the simplest and deepest of all emotions in love where two human beings take pure delight in each other—the natural origin of all the other more complex emotions they come to feel—their delight in the world about them became for these men the source for their exploring minds. The wonder of a plant and its fabulous parts. The wonder of fish gliding in troops, of deer in herds, of birds migrating in tribal harmony. The wonder was geared to a profound respect for

4

facts, harmonized by a rational mind functioning in proportion to the extent of the love. In those days, matter-of-factness was a fire on the mountain. It showed the way. It proclaimed the virtue of clear scrutiny. Dizzy from centuries of contemplating the heavens, Eighteenth Century man sat down and in contact with solid ground gained his strength through a new law of gravitation. Madly intoxicated with his new-found powers, he saw it all with a too hopeful eye. But the delight and certainty to be gained from facts, the need to be free from traditional scruples, inhibitions; to possess courage and initiative and a dogged endurance made a climate in which thought became deed. That this also included a veneration for measure and number amounting to a dangerous distrust of the imagination was only perceived by a few. The poets saw the danger; Blake, Wordsworth, Coleridge proclaimed it.

The Bartrams understood that changes were due in the world. But such an idea was not soul-shattering. Had they not observed the mutations in a plant? And solid matter-of-fact John Bartram with his ingrained sense of awe and his rapture for the green world was followed by his more sensitive, often difficult son William. And William's account of the birds and Indians of Florida, wild glorious creatures all, was transformed in its turn into the poetry of Coleridge and Wordsworth, carrying imagery and idea far beyond the primitive forests through which the father and son had wandered. For it does connect up; the matter-of-fact zeal with the imaginative flight, before the Nineteenth Century came in ponderously, portentously.

CHAPTER I

ON JULY 3, 1743 John Bartram set out from his home on the Schuylkill River, three miles from Philadelphia, to travel through the wilderness to Onondaga, Oswego and Lake Ontario in Canada on a mission for the British government to the Indian tribes of the Five Nations. He was already forty-four years old and for nine years had been ransacking virgin forests for seeds and seedlings to go to England. He had two noble patrons, the Duke of Richmond and the Duke of Norfolk, and an influential friend, a prosperous London merchant in the woolen trade who was an ardent amateur botanist, Peter Collinson.

This was an important venture for John Bartram. In nine short years he had made himself, through Collinson's assistance, the man most qualified to make a true report on

7

the wilderness. It was a touchy mission. Many factors were involved which could not be openly discussed. Trade was at stake and territory. The French and the British had already set Indian tribes at each other's throats in their efforts to gain control of the fish and fur trade. There were tribes like the Delawares who were to side finally with the French, and there were the Five Nations that had, so far, been friendly to the British. Bartram would, in effect, be the personal representative of the Crown, and he had to measure up to the Indian conception of a friend. In that respect he had an advantage. He was a Quaker and, up to that time, the Quakers had the confidence of the Iroquois, siding with them in their quarrels with the Delawares.

On the surface, the mission to the Indians was to negotiate between the Delawares and the Five Nations in order to make peace between the tribes and to assure tranquillity along the frontier. But the territory to be covered on the trip was virgin; no maps had been made, no reckoning computed of the resources to be found. Bartram's function was to take notice of everything that grew and to make a report that would be useful for the development of the region. Different parties undoubtedly had opposing views concerning the nature of any development to take place. The evidence seems to show that certain New England merchants were already secretly plotting with the British government for the future control of Canada and the fur trade, now in the hands of the French. But Bartram was not a plotter. He knew the wilderness and had already tackled it on solitary ventures. Bark, seeds, soils, rocks and mosses. He was their merchant and could make an inventory of his findings. His eyes were keen for a seed, a bird; he knew bad soil from good and could taste its quality. This was new country he was to travel, Indian country now, but the settlers were pushing into it, following the trader. If, in the long range plan for the control of the fish and fur trade, Bartram was a useful pawn, he did not know it. He was too much his own man to be aware of scheming.

At base Bartram was a sound practical American farmer. But at the time of the Great Lakes Expedition he had already veered away from total preoccupation with his farm. From the moment that he had settled with himself that botany was his chief and burning interest, his life had begun to expand. He had become an explorer, a gatherer of seeds, the maker of a garden already unique for its cultivation of rare native plants. If his outer life had altered to suit his now determined intentions, his inner life had undergone no less a change. His mind was open and experimental and he was as eager to explore new ideas as he now was to enter the unexplored wilderness.

This man whose native abilities were to emerge with so much distinction, does not seem to have had an exceptional background. No great names shine among his forebears. His grandfather, also a John Bartram, came to America from Derbyshire, England, in 1682 "before there was a single house in Philadelphia." He had three sons and one daughter. The only son to marry was William, the father of John, the botanist. He married Elizabeth Hunt and they had two sons, John and James. Bartram was only two years old when his mother died, leaving the little boy to the care of his grandmother. In relating what he knew of his family history John Bartram was curiously reticent about his father, mentioning only the fact that he had made a second marriage with Elizabeth Smith by whom he had a son, William, and a daughter, Elizabeth. There must have been painful memories associated with his father who moved to North Carolina with his new wife, leaving young John with his grandmother in Pennsylvania.

William, the son of John Bartram, was not so reticent

when it came his turn to relate the family history. He tells the story told to him by his uncle, William, the child of his grandfather and Elizabeth Smith. He heard it during a year's sojourn in North Carolina when he would have had ample time to get the story straight from his uncle. The story goes that after John's father moved to North Carolina he was killed by the Indians at a plantation called Whitoc. His widow and two children were carried away as captives but were later ransomed and returned to Philadelphia. William, one of the surviving children, afterwards returned to North Carolina and remained there the rest of his life. The reason he gave for John Bartram's father migrating from Philadelphia was a long involved row with his fellow Quakers of the Darby Meeting. He complained of "wrongs and abuses" received from men and women Friends which seem to have led to a postponement of his second marriage. When an investigating committee appointed by the Meeting could find no cause for complaint, he refused to accept their decision or to appear before the Meeting. His name ceased to show in the records after 1709. Though John was not taken to North Carolina by his father and stepmother, he was well guarded and cared for by his grandmother in Pennsylvania, and his father's brother, Isaac, kept a protective look-out for the child. When Isaac died he left his small farm to John's grandmother with the proviso that it was to go to John after her death.

William's story, dubbed "romantic" by some commentators on the Bartrams, has all the earmarks of veracity. It was written by William in his maturity when he was a full-fledged scientific man and it bears witness to the kind of imaginative perception he assuredly had. It accounts for certain factors in John Bartram's development which appear on the surface to go against the grain of his Quaker upbringing. Though Bartram had not yet taken a belligerent stand against the Indians at the time of the Great Lakes trip, he was to become most un-quakerlike in his final judgment toward them. William's own development took an opposing course; he became one of the few American colonists who staunchly defended the Indian position, and condemned the white man's approach to the Indian problem. The source of these opposing attitudes is relevant to the entire development of the father and son, but, for the moment, it is sufficient to state that father and son took opposite stands on one of the most vital questions of the day and that John Bartram's position may have sprung from the murder of his own father by the Indians.

But there is a second factor in the character of the father of John that has an even more important bearing on the nature of the man who became not only an internationally known botanist but one who was prepared to defend the most advanced ideas of his day. Both father and son were embroiled with their fellow Quakers. Both men were called up for an accounting before the Darby Meeting. Both men refused to alter the position which they had taken. In the case of the father, the contested question involved personal matters relating to his second marriage. His son, John, defied the Darby Meeting on more serious grounds. While proclaiming his adoration of God, the Father, he denied the divinity of the Son, and thus allied himself with many of the scientific thinkers of his day rather than with his Quaker brethren.

When the overseers of the Darby Meeting on 5 mo., 5, 1757, "entered a complaint against John Bartram for disbelieving in Christ as the Son of God and having been desired to attend this Meeting to account for his disorderly belief," he answered with silence and a refusal to put in an appearance. A committee was then appointed to visit with him and "to treat with him on account of his said unbelief and put him upon attending at the next Monthly

Meeting." Nothing happened. The case dragged on for fifteen months. A new committee appointed to visit Bartram and "to labor with him, in the spirit of meekness to turn from the spirit of unbelief" reported that they had visited him but could not prevail upon him to believe in the divinity of Jesus Christ, but on the contrary, he had stated that although Jesus was endowed with the power of God he was no more than a man. The society was reluctant to proceed. Members of the committee who had been appointed to draw up an accusation against him did not even show up at the Meeting. Finally testimony was written out and approved. Bartram was given the right to appeal but refused to make a move. After a delay of two months, the Darby Meeting drew up a final letter of disownment. Bartram's answer was to pay no attention to the entire proceeding and to continue to take his seat in the Meeting house as if nothing had happened. In his eyes, the action of the Quaker brethren could only be discreditable and childish. He would pay no more attention to it than he would to the antics of a mischievous infant. His well known sentiments were emphasized for all visitors to see in 1770 when he affixed over his study window a stone slab with the words cut deep into the rock:

It is God alone, Almyty Lord,
The Holy One by Me Ador'd
John Bartram 1770

His clear mind and firm will thus asserted itself. In stone. It had to be stone, longer lasting than mortal man, more enduring than the congregation of the living who had made a puny attempt to abase his deepest convictions.

This man of independent character never had more than a meager education at the Friends School at Darby where they taught reading, writing, arithmetic and spelling. His early letters show bad spelling, poor grammar and penmanship below half-a-dozen or so of his neighbors who kept the records of the Darby Meeting. He was sensitive all his life about his handicap but in spite of his limited education he soon became a person of consequence in his community. And he never stopped studying and learning.

Bartram's first wife, Mary Maris, also a Quaker, died in 1727 after four years of marriage, of an epidemic then raging. At twenty-eight, Bartram was left a widower with two small children. A year later he bought at a sheriff's sale a tract of land of one hundred and two acres, with another piece of five acres, on the banks of the Schuylkill River near Kinsessing. Nearby was Gray's ferry which carried most of the southern and western traffic into Philadelphia and was an important place. The road gave easy access to the city which Bartram frequently visited to transact business, visit libraries and friends, and to attend meetings of the Philosophical Society.

The sole building on the land was a small Swedish house but when he married again in 1729 he began at once to build a larger house around the nucleus of the original structure. His second wife, Ann Mendenhall, was a Quaker who belonged to the Chester Meeting. The new structure was big and roomy. It had to be, for the couple were to have ten children, among them twins. William, the most notable of Bartram's children, and his twin sister Elizabeth, came third in the row of many births.

Like many men of his time, Bartram combined intense practicality with a passion for book-learning. He was an expert stone-cutter and proud of it. He not only built the house on the Schuylkill but in the course of his lifetime erected three more stone structures. Later in his life he boasted to his friend Jared Eliot that he had been used to "split rocks to make steps, door-sills, window frames,

13

pig and water troughs" and that for the purposes of his
house he had split rocks seventeen feet long with his own
hands. By boring holes and applying wedges he found he
could split a rock almost as true as sawn timber. There
are slabs six to eight feet long in the house, still standing
today. Carvings in the stonework around the windows and
doors show loving care. On one slab a date is hewn, indicating the time it must have taken to complete the structure:

John-Ann Bartram
1731

The house was built on a site of land facing the river
with a fine view. Terraces and walks comprising about an
acre of land were laid out between the house and the
river. It was Bartram's only attempt to formalize the
grounds of his property.

His first efforts were directed toward practical farming. In 1738 he bought an additional one hundred and
forty acres and the next year added forty acres with another plot of ten acres. He then sold off some parcels of
land and consolidated the rest into a farm of two hundred
and sixty-one acres of excellent farm land. But by that
time, his real life was outside farming.

Travelers attested to the success of his methods of
farming which were not the ordinary practices of the day.
His acres yielded twenty-eight to thirty-eight bushels of
wheat an acre when other men, less knowing, were glad
to get twenty bushels. Flax, oats and corn thrived equally
with him. Crèvecoeur, who visited Bartram when he was
in his sixties, imputes some miracles to the botanist-farmer.
His hay was beyond anything. Though the description
may be just another myth, it is certain that Bartram
contrived ingenious schemes. He brought the water of

a spring down to a reservoir on his farm and into this dumped old lime, ashes, and horse dung. This brew was allowed to steep and then it was let loose twice a week during the summer over his meadow land which in winter got a good bed covering of old fodder, rotting straw or whatever he found about his barn. Thus enriched, petted and tended to fertility, the ground that had formerly grown little more than five-fingers (a plant resembling the wild strawberry) bore fifty-three hundreds of excellent hay per acre.

Peter Kalm, the Swedish explorer-botanist, who came to Philadelphia several years after Bartram's expedition to the Great Lakes, agreed with the American farmer about the bad state of agricultural practices in the New World. Few men used the conservation principles which allowed Bartram to outstrip his neighbors. Most men bought a piece of land which had not been ploughed since Creation, cut down the timber, tore up roots, ploughed and planted to corn. First season, a fine crop. But in several years the land lost its fertility. The settler's answer was to chop down more trees and repeat the process, allowing the first field to lie fallow. Soon he had a number of little fields, all corn, depriving the land. Then he returned to his first field, now somewhat restored. But he will never give the fields anything. It's not so easy to find fertilizer as the cattle roam the forests. Then there is the weed problem; they grow to gigantic size in fallow fields. Kalm believed it was a great waste and that such habits sprang from nothing less than a profusion of riches. In his own more restricted country, they could not afford such practices.

Excellent though his farming methods were, it was Bartram's botanical garden that was the prize attraction. Started in 1729 on a five-acre plot running down to the river, it became so unique that his many visitors failed to register more than sketchy impressions of his household. It is known that Benjamin Franklin came to sit with Bartram beside his Franklin stove drinking cider drawn from his garden mill and that the Frenchman, Crèvecoeur, liked to bask in the tranquillized assemblage, sharing the "honest country dinner" to which Bartram's own freed slaves sat freely down. At the end of the meal an Aeolian harp called the guests to the broad slope, the terraced river, and a view of the watering trough cut out of solid rock by Bartram. In 1760 he added a greenhouse with a proud inscription of Pope's lines hewn in stone above the door:

> Slave to no sect, who takes no private road,
> But looks through nature up to Nature's God.

Whatever richness lay about the house came from lavish nature schooled by Bartram. Within the house all was Quaker plainness, even frugality. The fashionable chairs from Seddons, London, with their lyre backs which figured in wealthy Philadelphia homes had no place here. For such furbishings Bartram seems to have had only refined disdain. By the middle of the century he was even expressing himself emphatically against the wallowing in luxury of the Philadelphia citizenry, an attitude that was to be echoed by Chateaubriand on his visit to America at the time of the French Revolution when he was scandalized to witness luxury on all sides, frivolous conversation, gaming tables, theaters galore, ballrooms with protocol as fiddling fine as any at Bath or Boulogne. What he had looked for was the noble austerity of early Rome. Joseph Priestley too was shocked when in 1794 he fled from England after his house was burned to the ground by Tories in retaliation for his sympathies with republican France. He also had expected to find noble Roman austerity in the New World and when he could not discover it in Philadelphia, he retreated to a village on the Susquehanna where he tilled his fields, wrote his books and drove to market in his Yarmouth wagon.

For the plain food on his table, Bartram made no apologies to folk whose palates might be accustomed to delicacies. He boasted good garden stuff, pitchers of milk and cider, and once a year spread a feast for relatives and friends to gather around in praise of the good harvests and Nature's blessings. Good food was surely cooked in the big stone ovens that had often to accommodate themselves to birds and turtles drying out for the voyage overseas. Cupboards for drying seeds were close to the fireplace where the warmth could suck out the moisture and prevent mildew.

The atmosphere of the Bartram home was of simple piety and reverence; the Bible was read regularly and religiously. God was everywhere, in the simplest flower, the most astringent weed, in a bird's wing, in the endless sky. And for the Bartrams, God was joy. To the very end of his life, John Bartram exhorted his children never to forget to love, not only one another, but to let love go beyond one's family circle into the world. "Love God," he wrote in a manuscript addressed to them, "and love one another; extend charity to the necessitious and mercy to the distressed." He did not speak in vain. His son William was to echo his sentiments in the years to come.

How this plain American farmer was deflected from farming to the new science of botany was already a subject of speculation and myth in his own lifetime. In his *Letters from an American Farmer* Crèvecoeur gives a sentimental account of what he alleged to be the origin of Bartram's interest. According to his version Bartram was ploughing a field when his eye fell upon a daisy. Mechanically pulling it to pieces, he observed its many distinct and curious parts. "What a shame," quoth he to himself

17

(according to Crèvecoeur) "that thee should have employed so many years tilling the earth and destroying so many flowers and plants, without being acquainted with their structure and uses." His curiosity aroused, he hired a man to plough for him and went to Philadelphia to search out a book on botany and a Latin grammar to interpret it. Next he applied himself to a schoolmaster to teach him enough Latin to master the grammar. Then he began to botanize his farm and thence branched out to many pilgrimages.

Bartram once wrote his friend Collinson his own explanation saying that from the time he was ten years old he had been drawn to plants and finally was so taken in he could not do otherwise than devote himself to them. It is certain that both Bartram and Collinson began to apply themselves to serious study in their twenties. Bartram's son William gave a much more plausible account testifying that his father "had a very early inclination to the study of physics and surgery. He even acquired so much knowledge in the practice of the latter science, as to be useful; in many instances, he gave relief to his poor neighbors. . . . It is extremely probable that as most of his medicines were derived from the vegetable kingdom, this circumstance might point out to him the necessity of, and excite a desire for, the study of botany." Bartram was certainly alive to all questions relating to medicinal herbs as Kalm was to testify in his American journal. Such an interest may have been quickened by the death of his first wife in an epidemic, the nature of which the medical men did not then understand.

Conjectures as to Bartram's entrance into botany can only lead to idle romancing. What is known is enough to place him in his time and condition. He was a farmer who never stopped farming and whose exploring mind found most fortunate ground for its development. He was handicapped from the beginning by a lack of funds and an ever growing family. Two children died in infancy but the remaining six sons and three daughters were no small matter. Until they were old enough to relieve him of some responsibility about the farm he had to regulate his explorations to accommodate the needs of ploughing and harvesting. This was usually in the fall when the seeds of wild plants were ripe for harvesting.

The wilderness, for all its hazards and obstacles, was his great opportunity. And it was at his very back door. He was living on the frontier of a botanical and unexplored wild garden covering thousands of square miles, filled with useful and ornamental plants unknown to European collectors. When he came upon the scene it was at a time when systematists in Europe were particularly eager to obtain specimens of American flora and when gardeners and horticulturists were looking for new plants from the temperate zone which could survive a European winter. Big estate owners had awakened to the desirability of ornamenting their property with exotics from the New World.

The chance to use the wilderness for a laboratory for research and further insight into the secrets of botany came through Peter Collinson, the London merchant, who had built up a considerable business in the colonies and had a wide acquaintance among people in Carolina, Virginia, Maryland and New England. In his eagerness to get new plants from America for himself and his friends he tried to inspire his correspondents in the New World to send specimens. But he could find no one with the patience or understanding necessary to handle the job. Tired of his pleas, his correspondents gave him to understand they would buy his woolens but could not be bothered with his plants. The situation was at a stalemate when Joseph Breitnall, a member of Franklin's Junto, got the idea of suggesting John Bartram's name to Collinson. Franklin called Breitnall "a copier of deeds for scriveners, a good natured, friendly man, a great lover of poetry, reading all he could meet with and writing some that was tolerable; very ingenious in making little knick-knackeries and of sensible conversation." Breitnall who did business with Collinson was probably glad to suggest someone who might take Collinson's burdensome requests for plants off his back.

Collinson did not foresee any great amount of business. He was anxious to get plants and knew they must be paid for but in the beginning he fancied that the best they might do was to get a few boxes from the American. At first, a price of five pounds, five shillings was charged for each box of American specimens. Bartram took hold of the proposition as his golden opportunity. From 1735 until the end of his life a steady flow of American trees, shrubs, wild flowers and seeds went to England.

Collinson's proposition started Bartram on his way but his own innate genius soon made him much more than an explorer or collector. Botany was in its infancy. Many plants were unclassified and stones were puzzling even to scientifically minded men. A stone, a seed, a bird, a fall of water—these were all simple manifestations of Nature but to men like Bartram they became a challenge. What did they mean? Where had they come from? How were they made? Where did a swallow fly in winter? The accepted world of trees, rivers, stones and plants was reborn by a new vision. It was related to the metamorphosis that takes place in a work of art when an ordinary chair shows up in a painting in some startling new aspect. Before we had viewed the artist's chair, had we really known what a chair actually looked like? Before Bartram and his group of fellow botanists began their challenge of stones and trees, many of the secrets of their growth and meaning had been hidden from view. Bartram sought to break through the thickets of superstition to find the truth; to touch the wilderness tenderly that all men might understand.

John Bartram, intact, with all his senses lively to detail, had great style. Today we might say it is the style of genius. Then it was closer to the style of what might be called the common man. The pioneers had it. A simplicity and wholeness. Before the Revolution it was not unique to seethe, to want to touch, to know. Bartram was a self-taught botanist but he was not shut up in the specialized closet in which modern science imprisons its victims. He was anything but a victim. Botany's servant and master, he was first his own man, unafraid of humble tasks and yet daring for the rare enterprise. At base, he was a plain American farmer with a farmer's problems. His difference was that he did not stop with farming. Turning rank marsh land to good meadows for grazing cattle was a beginning and a means, not the end. Nature thrust at him and he thrust back, making roots and seeds, rocks and moisture yield the yeast of his living.

This inward looking to the source of things was not uncommon then. Bartram had it to a high degree. Its immediacy, its lack of pretense, its sensual quality made for lively playfulness that did not detract from the passionate, serious intent. To know. To search. It was a time not yet given to boasting of man's control of Nature. Before the Industrial Revolution, Nature's laws were the clue to the order of the universe and compelled awe. Though the vast promise of the unexplored wilderness excited some to dark deeds, some to greedy aggrandizement, to a few like Bartram, the swamps and thorny hillsides, the gloomy woods and fragile wild flowers, were not to plunder or even to civilize, but to see and receive devotion.

History has made heroes of the reckless, the acquisitive

21

and the worldly powerful. The Bartrams have slipped down some crevasse among the mosses to be found only through search or patient listening. For Bartram, beginnings were important. It was the tiny acorn that held the oak tree; the egg, the future bird, and if he crossed a river, he must push through thickets to the source. Or he picked up a stone imbedded with small shells, tiny fragments of some sea, and was given over to wonder. Vast fields of knowledge now clarified for us were then mysteries. And with the sense of mystery went awe and a profound reverence that led to knowledge. Today we accept this sum of knowledge as casually as our cars take gas but in Bartram's day it was a beckoning beyond known boundaries.

What place did notions of fame have in a man like that? I think he thought of fame no more than did Daniel Boone. He was too well tuned to the immediacy and by such tuning sensed what was afar. Not for himself, nor even for his large family, but for the curiosity. The wonder. The word "curiosity" was then good coinage. Men wrote back and forth to one another to relate their precious findings. Seeds, insects, mosses traveled back and forth overseas, pampered in the captain's cabin. A "noble" chrysalis found in Virginia opened in a rich London merchant's garden. A frog made the journey under the captain's bed, in a sailing ship, as a present to the King. Turtle shells were treasures and Lady Petrie put in her bid for a humming bird's nest. The Duchess of Portland, reported as a "great virtuoso in shells and all marine productions" must have drawings of all land, river and sea shells and Billy, Bartram's talented son, promptly set about to execute the order. Think of the scope of it! *All* of them. The naïveté, the wonder, the confidence and willingness to grasp ALL.

Bartram was not the man to be so wrapped up in private affairs or family concerns as to limit his vision of the world. Nor did he sink into botany as in a dream. If he discovered something new he made no secret of it. Knowledge was to be shouted to the heavens not to be hoarded in a miser's den. There was an elasticity about the man, yielding to discovery and eager for it. Not for golden cities. The glitter that beckoned Cortez, Pizzaro or De Soto was not for him. His treasure was an unworldly flower, as yet unnamed. Rattlers were a daily enemy in the wilderness and die they must. But the death of a rattler was only painful necessity; he felt no triumph and brought back no slain trophies. It was his frank admission that there were few animals or insects which he cared to touch. His flesh crawled and rebelled at touching spiders; he loathed the evil smelling opossum. But if his flesh rejected these creatures he yielded to them his compassion. He might not like to touch them but he respected them as living creatures and could not bear to look upon any one of them in their "agonizing mortal pains without pity." It was his opinion that "the creatures commonly called brutes possessed higher qualifications and more exalted ideas than the traditional mystery mongers were willing to allow them."

Knowledge was for the enrichment of all in a world that was just beginning to realize the extent of its material powers. It was so monstrous a vista that knowledge might be cheaply scattered to the winds and not become the prerogative of a closed oligarchy. There lay the genius of the early days! The potential might be extended to every citizen. If Linnaeus, the great Swedish botanist, was a correspondent of Bartram, the farmer, who never went to school beyond his eleventh year, so was a secluded widow in Virginia whose solitary passion for discovery led to the finding of a dazzling new species of lily. To open up the radiant world, to capture the enormous designs that the American forests cast! Seeds were to be found among brambles, in spongy marsh land that sucked the boots from a man's feet, on the side of a shiny mirrored rock where a split might hatch a hairlike wonder; or snatching cones from trees, mountainous with snow, might bring down a shuddering wintry avalanche.

Once Bartram got the seeds home in leathern covered pouches from trips that meant fording streams whose source no white man had yet explored, they were warmed, tended, sorted and some were put in a silken bag to go in a box on the grand voyage to England. Others were planted in the garden, in rocks, among weeds, as nearly as could be to their native habitat. Oxford dons were as eager for this plunder as any Spanish grandee for the jewels of Montezuma. The honor of naming a new species held as high a place in the esteem of this congregation of enthusiasts as the storming of a rich city to a soldier.

In this green underworld, within a bustling, aggressive, expanding, mercantile, ruthless, plundering period of many wars, lived an entire community of men, in tune with one another, living an intensity within quietude. Bartram was their missionary in the wilderness.

His mind was clear, undeluged with innocuous print. He had equipped himself with source books sent from England by the London woolen merchant. Other works he had borrowed from Logan's library. A constant and greedy reader, he was always on the look-out for new soundings that would deepen his understanding. When he made the trip to the Great Lakes he was no longer a novice. Beginning with his own farm he had botanized his surroundings, then pushed off to unknown places.

When Collinson procured the first substantial patron, Lord Petrie, in 1735, Bartram started off at once to explore Rattlesnake Mountain. In the fall of that year he journeyed to the source of the Schuylkill River and went beyond the Blue Mountains. In returning, he visited a cave near Reading, probably what is now known as Crystal Cave, and enchanted Collinson with a report of his venturing. That same year he went to New Jersey to take a look at a "curious tree" as yet unidentified. In the spring of 1738 he got as far as Lancaster County in Pennsylvania but by the end of the summer he had gone back to New Jersey, crossed into Delaware and traveled as far south as Maryland. In 1738 he made his most extensive journey to that date; he covered eleven hundred miles into Maryland and found one of the most beautiful "vales" he was ever to witness. The next few years he traveled many times over east and west Jersey, making excursions into New York state and climbing the Catskill Mountains where he could overlook a "fine prospect of New England."

His name was by this time well known among Franklin's set in Philadelphia, and botanists in London, at Oxford and in Sweden spoke of him with respect. The Great Lakes trip was dignified in Bartram's eyes because he had been chosen among other possible candidates to do a survey and give a responsible accounting to the Crown. The objective was not only a touchy one—the great Five Nations—but the territory was a vast expanse of wilderness which might contain fabulous natural resources. Trappers and hunters had penetrated these gloomy regions but no man properly equipped to describe what was to be seen had as yet made the journey.

In his journal of the Great Lakes trip he tells the truth, not making more than is, not striking fictitious terror. He is not a marveling poet; yet, though he is on business for the Crown, he is saturated with a poet's wonder of the world. The King will get his practical observations of the country; a reckoning of soil, rocks, timber and potential dams. But for himself and his friends, Bartram will note every springing thing that grows. The rich bottom land is interspersed with spruce, white pine, oak, beech and plane

25

trees. Along a good trout stream is good rich soil, now sown to wild nettles. This he notes for future farmers. Birch, maple, oak and poplar are for the King. But for whom are hepatica, maidenhair, gooseberries and red currants? These choice bits he finds along a lively branch of the Susquehanna pouring down over rocks with sufficient force "to turn a mill." Though he gathers few seeds on this trip, he is packing a bag of morsels for more than he knows. The poets who will be nourished from this source are all unknown to him; many unborn. Pope is his man in that line and it is a line from Pope he has carved in stone above his house door. But future unknown poets will dip in the same sack that he dips into now with his chants of joy in mere enumeration of the miracle of profusion. His use may be a sober one, but he has a son, and that son stems from such a father that he will not be able to tend a store, will not add up to a merchant or a printer, will get the itch to wander and to repeat in more luxuriant language and with more meticulous praise the Nature his father adores.

This cataloging has begun its ascent. If Bartram is not the founder, he is one whose steps are bent toward the fountain. From the beginning of time Nature has presented a chameleon challenge; in one period, a temple for sacred gods, in another, a sinister dwelling for fearsome spirits. A subject of awe, of worship, of dread, Nature was about to enter a dual role; scientists would attempt to scale her rules and habits; they would seek to tame her to man's uses. But in the Eighteenth Century, their language would leap the dry gap of calculation to an awed wonder of Nature's revelations. The echo of their wonder would re-echo among the poets. Coleridge, Wordsworth, Whitman and Thoreau; a host of writers and poets would become saturated with the new outlook, the fresh observations, the eternal discovery. Nature would become the source of the original—and the banal. It would bring forth style and appraisal; it would produce platitude and loose raptures. Poe would revolt from its abstractions and cutting loose from the misty green branches, start a new style, intent on the rocks and dank ground. Goethe would insist that Nature does not feel; the sun shines upon the good and wicked alike, and the moon and stars upon the criminal as upon the best of men. Sade and Swinburne would insist that evil was the Natural Law and be contradicted by other men who struggled to hold to Nature and Nature's laws as the divine good.

Bartram has no notion of the mysterious ascent of language. He has no premonition that his son will be plundered by the poets-to-come to the advantage of all. He is one of a band of men whose emotions are profoundly wrapped in wonder of the creation and whose duty it is to scrape away superstitions, dissipate evil born of witchcraft obsessions, reveal the germ of actuality and precision as it lies wrapped in awesome mystery. Bartram would begin with simple, tested facts. He would study a stone and search to read its beginnings. His pockets were weighty on this trip with specimens he could not bear to leave behind. What do the scratches on the smooth surfaces mean? Where did the shells imbedded in the rock come from? Was this once a great sea or covered in the Deluge? Noah's tale was history for the man of that day.

CHAPTER II

T
HE TRIP TO the Great Lakes, made on horseback, began on a hot July day, 1743, at Bartram's house near Philadelphia and reached to Lake Ontario, then called Lake Candarakin. Tough, hearty, confident, Bartram makes the journey in good stout boots, wears a rough suit of woolen woven in London.

If one looks at a contemporary map for comparison with the course outlined by Dr. Lewis Evans, a surgeon, surveyor and map-maker, who accompanied Bartram, there is little to hold the two versions together except the shape of a general outline indicating mountains and rivers. Many names then in use have vanished. Dr. Evans's map is inclined to narrow the territory covered and his tiny dots indicating the path the travelers took become lost like grains of sand in a modern version of the same country.

Where are the Endless Mountains, the Impenetrable Mountains and the Dismal Vale beyond what was then known as a famous Licking Place for deer? The Blue Mountains were as blue then as now and the name holds, but the wonderful descriptive allusions to places reminiscent of Bunyan's *Pilgrim's Progress* have altered to sedate nomenclature. Some of the creeks seem to have held to their original names; Perkimony, Swatara, Tulpehocken; the rivers were then as now, Schuylkill, Susquehanna, Allegheny. Manatony, a town, has become Manatawny, and perhaps was at that early date when travelers were none too sound as to spelling. The Indian villages are tiny crosses on the old map resembling tepees; they are few and far between. But the old map with its imaginative names suggests more of the voyage Bartram took than the modern one now thick with roads and towns, veined with rivers and brooks, each with a definite location.

The long reach of the Allegheny Mountains could well have seemed impenetrable to these travelers and before they came to that impassable point, there were the Endless Mountains in sharp short ranges to cross. Neither the Endless Mountains nor the Impenetrable Mountains were crossed on this journey; they were indicated as part of the rumor enveloping those regions. Stories told by trappers and Indians. But the Blue Mountains lay in a beautiful loose sprawl in several parallel chains before any approach to the Endless Mountains began and over the Blue Mountains they must pass to reach their journey's end.

Between the western edge of the Blue Mountains and the eastern branch of the Susquehanna was an open plain called St. Anthony's Wilderness by the exploring Count Zinzendorf. Where the Dismal Vale is today would be hard to say. Its location on the old map is somewhat to the southwest of the Impenetrable Mountains, now the Allegheny range. There is a mythlike quality to this old map that conveys both the peril and the wonder of the wilderness. The old names bear the stamp of emotional grandeur. The shock of encountering the strange and the terrifying stimulated the nerves. To a man on horseback, scanning a ridge of rock for a gap to break through to the territory beyond, every crag, each steep declivity was a menace or a promise. Each step was an either-or question. Nothing could be ignored; darkness itself was thick with unseen dangers. No wonder the Indian war whoop became a symbol of terror among early colonists, springing as it did from the midst of the dark cataract of forest trees where the naked bodies drifted in firefly array behind black trunks and branches, or seemed to sink into the phosphorescent glow of swamps with a piercing echo of wild cries that preceded the arrow.

Riding horseback over country new and strange, the travelers gave themselves up to joyful impressions. They were not out to conquer or to clip land from anyone, to hunt gold or stake a claim, they came in peace to the Indians and gave them the benefit of good intentions. Their alertness tipped toward grass and rocks, rivers and springs. They stopped to smell, to pluck herbs and flowers, and to view. The first sight of the Blue Mountains brought them to a halt. From the top of Flying Hill they could see beyond the vale of the Tulpehocken the long blue range smoking in wisps of mist.

The first day, July 3, they got no further than beyond Perkimony Creek, a branch of the Schuylkill. The second day they passed Manatony at dawn and crossing the Schuylkill ascended Flying Hill where the wild turkeys used to make their flights to the plain below. Used to! In a sense, Bartram must have enjoyed this historical reference. So this vast wilderness has already a past, something to reckon from. The descent from Flying Hill was steep and stony and they rested for the night. On the third day they crossed Tulpehocken Creek and the Swatara and entered a fine limestone valley many hundred miles long and ten to twenty miles broad toward the north where it was broken by a rise of the Blue Mountains. A man who was to help them carry provisions to Shamokin could not go because his horse was not properly shod.

On the fourth day they ascended the first ridge of the Blue Mountains and made observations. The top and south side of the ridge was middling land and lush with wild grass, fern, oaks and chestnut. But descending on the north side it was poor stuff, steep and stony. After they passed the first branch of the Swatara they found good low land, the five-leafed pine, poplar and white oak. They "dined by a spruce swamp."

It took six days to reach Shamokin. The approach was through a fine oak grove where eight cabins by Shamokin Creek were the only indication of a settlement. They had been joined by Conrad Weiser who was to act as interpreter to the Indians. Weiser's name pops up again and again in the old accounts. At the pow-wow he seems to have been indispensable. The Indians trusted him and they had good reason for their trust. For a period of years he had lived among them. As a child he had been one of the Palatinate fugitives who had found refuge in England from the persecutions of Louis XIV. Queen Anne sent them to America where Weiser's father placed the young boy in charge of an Indian chief of the Maque nation to learn the language. When the boy returned home a new stepmother made his life so miserable that he preferred living with the savages. At one time a monk in the Seventh Day Baptist cloister at Ephrata, he became a trusted ambassador to the Indians. From 1731 to 1760 he was active in many councils and his own account of the Great Lakes trip is one of the best records of an Indian council that exists. This lively, versatile man had built himself a homestead in the mountains west of Reading and south of Womelsdorf in 1729 where it stands today as a landmark in that region. Then it was an isolated house in a little clearing in the wilderness.

Shamokin itself was an embryo. Coal had not been discovered and the settlement was a dreamy village, shiny bright. In the hot July, the travelers shucked their heavy clothes and went for a swim in a pool chin deep with water so lucid "a pin might have been seen on the bottom." But their camping spot was thick with fleas and at night Bartram slung his blanket like a hammock from trees in the hope he might escape them.

By the tenth day they had picked up an Indian guide, Shicckalamy, and his son. Actually Shicckalamy was a Frenchman, the chief man in a town of Delaware Indians, who had been born in Montreal and adopted by the Oneidas after being taken prisoner. Early settlers and venturers often came upon white men, and women too, who had first been captured by Indians, then reconciled, did not want to return to the old white environment. Did not want to be liberated but preferred Indian enchantment.

The enlarged party had now turned north and following the main eastern branch of the Susquehanna continued to stick to the valleys of its tributaries. The account begins to read like a mariner's chart with directions, N.E., then N.N.E., marking the journey. Then the travelers bore toward the west with every advantage taken of runs and hollows.

Bartram is not a man to break out into rapturous language. His account is choppy, spaced with remarks on stones and trees rather than on the view. He is a surveyor making a stiff reckoning for the Crown. Land, sites, timber and useful plants must be noted for future development. He does not see eye to eye with other reporters of British make who are interested only in the exploitation of America for England's profit. Reporters with their interests firmly based in England are also wandering along the seacoast reporting their findings, in glee that this fine, rich country can raise so much food stuff, yield so many furs and fish, and opining that never, never, can colonists be expected to manufacture. That should be England's prerogative and this England's market for manufactured goods. So far, the colonies have had to look to the old world for manufactured commodities; pins, needles, sewing silk, tools and books all come from overseas. But Bartram is one of the first true colonial reporters, looking toward the future from the colonist's slant. When he crosses the upper reaches of the Susquehanna he marvels at the power residing there.

Though his point of view reckons the future for the benefit of the colonies rather than for exploitation by England, he is not deflected from his duty to make a true report to the Crown. When he comes to a narrow valley, he examines the soil: "It is moderately rich, the hills hung with lofty timber, the stones generally flat, then a steep hill, where I found fossil steel in many stones, the soil middling oak land, and here had a view of a Bluff pointing North by the river's side; then descending down a steep hill N.E. we came to a rich bottom by the river, hence N. after N.W. to a creek and so through a grove of white walnut and locust, and exceeding rich land, half a mile broad, and now some higher level land, affording oak, hickory, walnut, locust and pitch pine, our course generally N.N.W.; riding over a hazel nut plain we met eight Shawnee Indians on horseback coming from the Allegheny River."

They ate together. Bartram, like all the early travelers, had a hearty appetite. His account is sensitive to food; he writes out many of the recipes with a keen relish for their goodness. But on this particular day, the food was venison

33

and it fell to his portion to consume the neck and the throat. Etiquette demands that he eat all of it, but it is hard to get down. What cannot be eaten must be burned and it is certain he will not go against the Indian customs on this delicate mission.

Are they moving or does the land take flight under their feet? It seems to run away in Bartram's account and to be some great animal, now covered with a pelt of pitch pine, now with white pine. He is always stooping to touch the soil; to say, stop and wait for me. The soil is brown, the stones flat and gritty. He is always stuffing his pockets with specimens. Brooks are the veins to follow even though they lead through the damp dark where rattlers lie in wait. The bottom land was all rich, the trees a mingling of chestnut, oak and pine with laurel thickly banking the hillsides. Bartram kept his eyes alerted for smaller growth, too. He spies ginseng and gathers some roots to send to Peter Collinson in London. Toward the north the timber grows higher and their course leads not only through swampy land but spots deep in bog. Chestnut, linden, ash, sugar maple, poplar, spruce and some white pine tower above them and beneath, around the roots, the soil is brown grit. Trees have fallen to rot, turned up roots project anguished decay, moss spreads over the surface of the ground where it is perpetually shaded. The earth is spongy with ancient damp but yellow wasps flitter brightly through the gloom. It takes hours to go through this dismal wilderness but when they break out, the rich bottom land sprouts delicate flowers. Some of the tiny blooms nest in clusters of maidenhair fern.

The night is warm. A glow of enchantment leaks into Bartram's sober account. One of the Indians begins to sing in a "solemn, harmonious manner, for seven or eight minutes." Bartram, who cannot keep figures out of his journal, even in an account of a song, is swept away by the voice.

It is no common Indian tune, he believes, but must be a hymn to the Great Spirit. Almost—almost, he catches something, is fused for a moment with this tuneful emanation from the Indian nature, but in the end, he too, will succumb to the Indian dread, and stand off, refusing to touch, to know.

At dawn on the fourteenth day they make their way up a little hill, picking a path through groves of oak and chestnut where the ground is sprinkled with huckleberries and honeysuckle. Some white pine, spruce and laurel darken with deeper green the lighter hardwood growth. At half-past seven in the morning after hours of hardy travel since dawn, they enter a great swamp of giant white pine and spruce where the wrecks of fallen trees lie prostrate in the soggy soil or lean helplessly against live trunks which crowd so close it would be impossible, the party calculates, "to shoot a man at a hundred yards distance, let him stand never so fair." The straight bodies of these trees are so thickly set that a bullet must hit one before it could fly a hundred yards in the most open part. Here all is hush and gloom; their voices sound small and faint as if spoken into a cabinet lined with plush. A great dead tree slides slowly from its embrace of a living trunk, collapses with a faint squeak and long whine, and with a hollow groan sinks into a clutter of rotten chunks and broken branches. From the gored heart beetles begin to stammer and run.

From out this vast arching darkness the party emerge gratefully into lighter open ground and trace once more a wandering branch of the Susquehanna. Flat whetstones are cast recklessly about the ground like playthings of the forest gods; some of the stones are four feet long. Practical Bartram salvages some to take home to whet his ax, scythe, chisels and knives. He stoops to pluck a leaf, root up a plant, taste soil; his pockets are heavy with bits of rocks in which lie mysterious traces of fern and shells.

There are few human encounters on this trip. Now and then a trader pushes along their path, bowed under his pack. Or in a jeweled clearing, set deep among countless trees, a settler lounges in high grass, worn out with the toil of clearing land and planting corn. Apathetic, sunk in a gloomy boil of inertia and the restless itch to kill something, he yawns and stretches, offers hospitality. His miserable hut provides only a bare earthen floor for a traveler's bed. Bartram and his friends make a try at the floor; it is thick with fleas and soon they quietly get up to find a bed of sweet grass under the night sky.

Where is Bartram now, exactly, on the map? Who can say? This record is bereft of precise locations. It is presented in terms of time. This is the sixteenth day. He might be a Noah keeping track of an ark sailing a trackless waste of water. For the wilderness was an uncharted sea to these early explorers. Rivers were safe channels; mountains their unnamed buoys. But with his mariner's compass, Bartram is moving steadily northward where the trees grow higher, denser. It is mostly a vast silence. No shrill cry of a wildcat. Not the sign of a bear but some indications of bear tracks. Only once did he hear the howl of a wolf in this untenanted wilderness. The snap of a twig, the sigh of top branches of trees stirring in some breeze of the upper air, the spongy suck of swamp underfoot; these are their sound accompaniments. Deer are fairly common, stealthy and mostly distant. But they shoot one for eating, at dawn. Brooks and rivers are filled with fish but it takes an Indian to snare them. Bartram notes with satisfaction their long poles spiked at the end to strike the fleet trout and yet on the day Bartram watches, the Indians miss a catch. There is an old beaver dam but no beaver.

He is a man sensitive to death; the death of a rattler, the death of a tree. Death in the wilderness gives a dismal cast to a bright sky. And a real storm descends.

"In the afternoon it thundered hard pretty close to us, but rained little; we observed the tops of trees so close to one another for many miles that there is no seeing which way the clouds drive, nor which way the wind sets; and it seems almost as if the sun had never shone on the ground, since Creation. About sunset it cleared up, and we encamped on the last branch of the Susquehanna; the night following, it thundered and rained very fast and took us at a disadvantage, for we had made no shelter to keep off the rain, neither could we see it until just over our heads and it began to fall."

He must stop where he is, moored under trees, and make some shelter. Poles are settled slantwise in the ground and others tied across them. Over these they spread a blanket. They make a fire in the wetness. An Indian guide crawled inside *his* hut made of four sticks, five feet long, stuck in the ground at a two foot distance and over which he spread what Bartram calls his "match coat." He crept through and fell to singing. Mosquitoes were troublesome. On nights when there are no mosquitoes there are fleas. Yellow wasps abound in the dismal wilderness that stretches for endless miles.

On some days, fog steams up through the valleys in long streamers that hide the world below. Then Bartram contents himself with the feel of the hill beneath his feet. It is a little sandy with pines growing upon it. They have come out of the dismal dark pocketed growth to a spot where they may look about them. What jubilation to see what lies below and overhead when for two whole days they have been wandering in a darkness as thick as in a cave. Now they get a prospect over the vale of the mountain they have just crossed and which differed remarkably, so Bartram says, from all he had ever seen before "in its leafy and fruitful ascent and descent, in its great width, everywhere crowned with noble and lofty woods, but above all, in its being entirely free from naked rocks and steep precipices."

Indians are collecting salt. Boys fish in a lake as women fetch water and gather wood. Now they make fires, while their lord and master basks on the sand under the bushes. When the women have filled a gallon keg of water, they boil it to about a pound of salt. But the Indian male—a lazy brute in Bartram's book! His own native industry is overriding his sensitivity; he begins to show his distaste for the Redskin. But the next moment, he responds with admiration to the Indian's quick precision. He has watched him use his arrows, made of reed and down, to shoot small birds. And again, he is struck by the skill with which several Indians harpoon eels. He notes the procedure carefully. How they use shafts eighteen or twenty feet long, pointed at the end with iron. Two splints of wood, spreading at each side, direct the point to the fish which, at a great depth, it would otherwise be difficult to hit. He saw one canoe with a large piece of bark spread across and on this lay gravel and sand for a bed where fire might burn to allure the fish. When the eels are caught, they are cooked over embers and eaten with Indian boiled corn and watermelons. The Indian guide chewed cornstalks, spitting out the substance while sucking the juice.

The Indian will never become a source of fresh knowledge, not even for Bartram. His skills are listed; they may be useful. The great plenitude had its victims. There was too much. Too many gnats, worms, wild pigeons. All crowding the trees. Indian and worm are tossed into a chanting catalog, no one better than the other, and crowding upon them, come the fossils. Then he must drop everything to observe a glitter in the bushes like flakes of ice or snow on a sunshiny day. He thinks it is from the vapor of an intense salt brine that congeals to trees and bushes.

Each observation is tossed in as it comes to him. Here is a finding of leather bark; there a sudden burst of statesmanship. He envisions the country opened wide by navigating belts along the Great Lakes which "a good Englishman cannot be without hopes of seeing one day accustomed to English navigation." He sees rivers joined to rivers by canals and the southland penetrated with a waterway. He is running ahead of himself, ahead of time, and outdistancing the Indian, doomed to be outdistanced. Yet he comes as a conciliator to Indian tribes.

Near the lakes, they abandon horses and travel on foot. Finally they paddle down Onondaga Lake to the lower end called by the French Ganentaba; thence down a river a mile north, big enough to carry a large boat if the trees fallen into the stream were carried away, and finally, to the river of Cayuga country, near one hundred yards wide, very still and so deep, they could see no bottom. The land on both sides is enticingly rich and low to within a mile of the Oneida River where the stream begins to run fleet and the bottom becomes visible to a good depth.

Albany traders come down this river to barter with the Indians for fish and furs. The first thing they do, notes Bartram, is to tempt the Indian with spirituous liquor, another kind of snake in the wilderness. Then the traders cheat the Indian. The French deal more fairly with these savages. The word "savage" is Bartram's, but tempered by a certain admiration, by a sense of justice. The Indian is wronged by the British traders who come impersonally, wily, pushing the way for the encroaching settler. The French do better; they deal man to man. Bartram sees it. It is his business to see. And he will make the effort for this strange specimen. Politics and scheming have entered into this wild Eden and the natural man that Rousseau was to exalt appears in Bartram's eyes as disorderly, drunk, but strictly honorable in his promises.

Bartram scribbles in his journal, kept religiously each day before he breakfasts: "Here I cannot help observing, it was scarcely ever known, that an Indian chief or counsellor, once gained so far as to promise his interest, did break his promise, whatever presents have been offered to him from another quarter." Here is incorruptibility, but the trader mentality won. Even now, this early, the Indian is becoming a symbol, hounded out, to emerge with time in curious innerly unconscious workings of imaginative minds.

The seams of Bartram's Quaker personality burst at the vision of the Great Lakes fed by so many tumbling rivers. His imagination by-passed the Indian to soar along a bounding line to an immense future. The Indian bark canoe will be replaced with English ships. The settler and trader will make of Oneida, now a tiny settlement set up by the province of New York as an outpost, a bustling hive.

At the conference with the tribes, Bartram is torn between involuntary admiration and irritated parental reproof. Now he grumbles at the Mohawks. Then he amends that their morals have not been bettered by intercourse with Christians. He thinks the fault is not with our religion but with our "professors." Yet in spite of their deterioration in morals, he notes that the Mohawks, though dwindling in numbers, have shown a "most steady affection for us" and that whites live among them. But the women, oh the women! They torture him with their racketing. "Squaws got very drunk and made a bad noise all night." His guide is sullen, ill natured, and talks to himself. In the night, Bartram hears him "at an incantation or a prayer. It was certainly no song." The bawling, good humored women, the touchy braves. And in the midst of all, another feast! Hominy with dried eels and other fish boiled in it. One kettle of squashes and their flowers boiled in water and a little meal mixed. Lastly, a bowl of Indian dumplings made of new soft corn, scraped from the ear, then with the addition of boiled beans, lapped up well in Indian corn leaves. Menus crowd his pages as he rounds off his trip. Wild huckleberries and hominy boiled in venison broth. "Noble entertainment," quoth Bartram, "too good to leave any."

Bartram sees the Indian, but not quite. He is not the man to live here, to give himself over to an understanding of Indian life. It will take years for his son to come along to do that and then it will be among another grouping of dwindling Indians, not here, but in Georgia and Florida. It will take his son, with his shyness, his introverted nature, his rejection of the bustling hive, to give himself up to a revealing study of the Indian nature. Bartram has made his own descent to the ground of his desire. The Indian is one bit of nature to elude him. But he tries. He is thrown off the track by his own sobriety, by their drunkenness and howling. But in council, the Indians stand high with Bartram. He sees them as subtle, prudent and judicious. In war, they are indefatigable, crafty and revengeful.

Bartram put it down. He was impressed by the Indian townhouse, thirty feet long. Upon long grass, cut by the Indians and spread upon the floor, the travelers lounged and watched as their hosts smoked their pipes. One brave held a pipe six feet long with a head of carved stone. At Onondaga there is even a greater house; eighty feet by seventeen feet. Bartram's precise way of pinning down an impression is to give a dimension. Measurements and time he handles with ease. This is the twentieth day.

He is vague when it comes to what actually transpired at the council. It was set up by the British in the hope of winning friends among the Indians and settling disputes among the Indians themselves. To win the Indians from the French was no small undertaking. Pow-wow after pow-wow haggled over Indian rights to hunting and fishing, set boundaries beyond which white settlers should not pass, but all in vain. The Dutch, the French and the English had used the Indians for their rival purposes. Indians were set against Indians; British plans to lull the storm came too late, fell too short. Everything agreed upon at the Great Lakes meeting was ratified at a meeting with the Indians at Lancaster, Pennsylvania, a year later. Tribal differences were for the moment pacified but only for the moment. Nothing could stop the march of events and the shattering of the Indian dream.

But the Indian had already degenerated to an anti-white symbol in the colonial mind, even in a mind so generous as Bartram's, so little preoccupied with grabbing off pieces of the wilderness for himself. For he was enchanted in a different world and in that world the Indian was to prove a hindrance. Unlike the settler, Bartram did not wish to plunder or to hunt. But when the Indian troubles stirred up a fracas all along the border of the wilderness, deep into the forests, he could no longer tread exploring paths, and the way made treacherous to him, turned the Indian to a treacherous foe.

His journal is actually more pliant with grasses and stones than with Indian life. His words begin to bounce when he comes upon a petrifying spring trickling over leaves to harden into rocks as big as one can lift. But when he comes once more to that dismal wilderness under the dome of interlocking branches his stout heart quails. One walks here with a ghostlike tread. Then he is cheered by the sight of an old log which the bears have cunningly turned to pick up snails, beetles and grubs under it. Now he has his clue; to *see,* and he will proceed with watch-fulness, spying fresh wonders.

Rewarded! Rewarded at last. Here is a magnolia tree in a clearing towering in a spasm of green. One hundred feet, he calculates, and three feet in diameter. A god of a tree, something to write about to London, something to reckon from. Mark well this tree, it is a great outpouring of what a tree can do. Here is the true green fountain.

His horse is lame with the hardship of the journey and for the final stretches, Bartram walks to spare the horse. Weary though he is, he is filled with satisfaction. He has been recognized from afar; the Crown paid for this trip. It gives solid professional standing to the man who, on his own, has already explored much and brought precision to the myth of the wilderness. Of all exploring botanists of the New World, he is best equipped for fur-ther adventuring to a purpose and he knows it. This trip will fire him with the urge to penetrate more remote places. His passion to spy out strange plants in Louisiana, Ken-tucky and Florida will make shifts in his Quaker nature. He will be brought to such a pitch of frustration, through Indian warfare, that he will come to execrate the Indian, now seen with Quaker compassion and some inkling of what the alien personality sums up to. The Indian will come, at last, to mean only another rattler.

Now in a gentle, speculative frame of mind, he pon-ders the origin of the Indian tribes. From whence did they arise? How did they come from the cradle of the old world to here? William Penn, too, was fond of this kind of specu-lation and thought the Indians very like the Jews. He even classified them as one of the flock of ten Biblical tribes. Penn thought the Indian countenance not unlike the Jewish and contended that Indian children bore so lively a resemblance to Jewish that one "would think himself in Duke's Place or Berry Street, London, when he looks upon them."

Bartram's wife, his children, his cattle, his stone house with oven specially built near the fireplace for drying seeds, his meadows and fields, ripening to harvest will be waiting for him. And he will get off good stories in his own circle, remembering for years to come details that have escaped his journal.

CHAPTER III

PETER KALM, the Swedish explorer-botanist, made his trip to the Great Lakes and Niagara at least three years after Bartram's expedition. Kalm's venture to America had been inspired by the great Linnaeus of Upsala, Sweden, whose force of personality and serious enthusiasm for exact observation stimulated a prodigious amount of ardent and careful research on the part of others. Kalm came to America to see and to learn and to make a report of his findings to colleagues in Sweden. After a stay in the neighborhood of Philadelphia, he explored the territory along the Hudson, crossing Lake George and Lake Champlain to Quebec. On his return trip he took in Niagara and then crossed the Blue Mountains on the trail earlier followed by Bartram.

When he went back to Sweden in 1750 Kalm stopped

over in London, and Peter Collinson let him read Bartram's journal, recently recovered after being lost for years. The ship carrying the captain who was entrusted with the manuscript had been captured by the French but when the captain finally got his freedom he showed up in London with the sheets of Bartram's journal, kept safe on his own person all that time. When Kalm had visited Bartram he had been so impressed with the American's rich store of lore, scientific fact and humorous observations, that reading his journal, after so much good talk, was disappointing. "Why he has not filled it with a thousandth part of his great knowledge," he told Collinson. In his own account of his American trip Kalm even made the flat statement that exposing Bartram's journal to the public did him more harm than good. In his opinion, Bartram was rather backward about writing down what he knew. He even thought that the journal contained few new observations. His views do not seem to have diminished Bartram's growing reputation, though, at the time they upset Collinson considerably. When the account appeared in print it was deprecated in a foreword implying that publication was made without Bartram's knowledge; had he intended it for public view "he would have made it more interesting." Collinson may have thought the journal needed some padding or that its contents might be enhanced by including a few remarks by a writer whose style was more in harmony with the travel accounts of the day, for Kalm's impressions of Niagara Falls were added as an end-piece to the little volume.

Bartram's journal dealt with the green world, solidly rooted in the earth; Kalm's with water. In Bartram, fountains of green so deep the sun is shut from sight; in Kalm, such cascades of water that in the elemental roar, fog blinds, birds lose their way; beasts, birds and Indians fall in broken fragments under tons of granite water. A chaos of profusion calls to Bartram for the guiding principle; he would invoke the rule, penetrate to the secret of Creation. Kalm, more detached, is the poet of the fact.

The birds, the birds! Kalm sees them flying in thousands in the fog of vapor rising above the roar of the falls. Broken bodies of swans, teal, ducks and geese are scattered each morning in such numbers below the falls in the months of September and October when the great flights were thickest that the garrison of the fort lived chiefly on them.

Kalm speculates; have the birds become confused by the roar? Are their wings heavy with spray so that they fall? Does the terrifying noise astonish them into immobility as the snake may hypnotize? He witnesses entire flocks ride blithely to their destruction. First, the birds seem to be enjoying an airy swim in the river above the falls. It is such a treat to ride delightfully with the current, floating rather than swimming, that, imperceptibly they let themselves drift nearer and nearer to the cataracts. Indulging themselves, idling, joyful, they glide toward the pitching downpour, and too late, stunned by the roar, frantically try to rise into the air. Drenched with spray and fog, their feet clogged with the mighty rush of waters, they tip dizzily over before they can save themselves, progenitors of the daredevil man who will later ride the falls in a barrel.

Enough feathers to stuff a number of feather beds are found each morning, reports Kalm. Broken bodies of birds, of fish pitched headlong, are spewn upon the rocks below where sometimes a deer lies in pieces. And the great shabby paw of a bear. Pieces of things; fragmented wildness; the wilderness magic is breaking up before this watcher's eyes. Here among the grey limestone, at the base of the falls, it is not uncommon to come upon the torn parts of a human body. An Indian body. Some unknown savage tried to cross above the falls. One of those who were paid twenty pence for carrying a pack of furs, chiefly of deer and bear, a distance of three leagues, for a white trader.

Kalm's enthusiasm for America had begun in Philadelphia where he had arrived from London with a letter of introduction from Collinson to Franklin. He admired the town of ten thousand souls with its well laid streets at least fifty feet wide, and Market Street, all of a hundred feet wide. He liked the neat brick and limestone houses and in the market place couldn't keep his eyes off the stacks of boxes and pails, made of buttonwood bark. There were even little dishes made of the bark for holding whortleberries.

When he visited Bartram's farm, three miles out of the city, it was his first view of rural America and he was stunned at the variety of plants. "I found I was now come into a new world," he wrote. "Wherever I looked to the ground, I every where found such plants as I had never seen before. When I saw a tree, I was forced to stop and ask how it was called." The first plant to strike his eyes was a kind of grass called *Andropogon*. "I was seized with terror at the thought of ranging so many new and unknown parts of natural history. At first I only considered the plants, without venturing a more accurate examination."

He describes the plain around Bartram's dwelling where all kinds of trees flourished. The tulip tree grew to a great size and was used for canoes, dishes, spoons and doorposts. White oak was in abundance. He reels off a delirious list of trees and plants—"fifty-eight varieties growing spontaneously"—and gives special recognition to the persimmon, walnut, hickory, maple, chestnut, white elm and laurel. Little houses stood in clearings with a meadow before the front door. Vines clambered to the tops of trees in the walnut and chestnut groves.

The blissful prospect was slightly marred by the croaking of thousands of frogs all night long. Mosquitoes attacked Kalm from dark to dawn and stung him so badly that he was ashamed to show himself. Gnats hung in suspended balloonlike clots in unexpected places. Locusts and grasshoppers made such a racket that it was hardly possible for one person to understand another. But the trees were crowded with birds of such variety of song and plumage as to dazzle the foreigner.

When Kalm walked in the orchards of Bartram and his neighbors, he could pick as much fruit as he wanted. As for the ground itself, it was covered with flowers in mid-September; gentian, goldenrod, fox gloves, asters, dandelion and yellow sorrel. The simplest householder had an orchard of peaches; they were free to eat or to be trod upon and even the swine were fed peaches. Why, exclaimed Kalm, in Sweden the people guarded their turnips more carefully than the Americans did their most exquisite fruit! Peaches in Sweden were so rare that only the rich could taste them.

When Kalm admired the fine growth of trees there were old settlers, even in that young country, who could shake their heads and tell him it was nothing to what it had been. Why the country had been covered with thick tall trees sixty years before; now most of them had been cut down, the swamps had been drained, the land cultivated to cornfields, meadows and pasture. The old people could remember when the woods had been thick with grass and herbs that grew to the height of a man but grazing cattle had destroyed them. Wood still seemed so plentiful to Kalm that he could not understand why it cost so much in the Philadelphia market. Labor was dear. With mulberry trees in abundance, it was strange that the colonists did not raise silkworms. He had heard that a governor of Connecticut had raised silkworms so successfully that everyone in the family, including the servants, had silk garments. Bartram explained that to raise silkworms cost too much as labor was costly; a man got eighteen pence to two shillings a day, women too; corn, flax and grains were more advantageous as they did not require so much care as feeding silkworms. The same was true for the cultivation of grapes. Cider and beer were the popular beverages.

The richness of the country was only surpassed for Kalm by the wealth of Bartram's knowledge. He could not imagine from what sources he drew his voluminous information. His fountains of fact and lore astounded the Swedish botanist who was by no means reluctant to praise. What was especially admirable, in Kalm's opinion, was Bartram's generosity in communicating everything he knew, not only willingly, but eagerly.

This Quaker had an exploring mind that soaked up everything he saw and tracked down what he observed to its source. His mind speculated about origins; origins of rocks and soils, of plants and trees. Was the peach tree indigenous or brought to this country by early settlers? Bartram's lore on the subject of the medicinal uses of herbs and barks so mesmerized Kalm that his own journal is saturated with recipes gleaned from Bartram. Alder bark boiled makes a good suffusion for wounds. The Indians made a great dainty from Wake Robin by boiling spadix and leaves. For a bad stone bruise there was nothing better than a leaf of Pokeweed laid upon the sore spot. Bartram had tried it. But the leaves of this plant, delicious to eat when young and tender, are deadly when tough. Life-everlasting should be stewed in a decoction of flowers and stalk and then used to bathe any painful part. Or tie the plant up in a bag and rub the sore place.

As for plants that produced dye, Bartram knew a long list. Hickory bark gave a beautiful yellow color for woolen and linen. Red maple made a dark blue dye for linen and worsted. Maple bark made ink. If you needed a glorious red color, try Deadly Nightshade. Sassafras flowers were good for tea; the bark yielded a rich orange dye. How they discovered urine should be used in making sassafras dye instead of alum is a mystery, but the recipe must have evolved out of trial and error, and required as well a brass boiler not an iron pot. Sassafras berries were a good medicinal if you could get them before the birds devoured them; they should be boiled and the rich oil skimmed off and rubbed into any painful part. Bartram even knew of a "traumatic"; a plant called by Kalm, *Sarothra genitianoides,* growing in fields and under bushes in dry sandy soil. Once when Bartram had been kicked by a horse he boiled this plant and applied it to his bruises; his pain was "appeased."

If Bartram could supply all the answers to practical questions his speculations on the subject of mysteries was even more intriguing. What did it mean to find oyster shells in the ground and also snails and shells belonging to the sea one hundred miles from shore? Bartram was as confident that the greater part of the country had once been under water and that the rich valleys had been lakes as he was of his known facts, such as the reason for using different kinds of wood on the Hudson River boats. That part always under water was made of black oak; the upper part, now above, now below water was made of red cedar. The black oak was tough and resilient and made a good bottom able to withstand the wear and tear of stone bruises without cracking. Red cedar was good for the upper part but it was too hard and brittle for below.

Bartram was continually playing around commonly accepted notions to find the facts. "People said thunder was caused by rocks breaking loose in the mountains and rolling down hill." Nonsense, of course, but not to everyone.

Kalm was as impatient with credulity as Bartram. "People said that the Delaware Water Gap was made by the Devil when he wanted to get out of Pennsylvania to go to New York." Bartram was to spend a lifetime refuting "what people said." He explained to the eager Kalm his notion as to the formation of the "giant pots" or great holes found in the mountains along the banks of rivers. "People said that they were made by Indians to hide their corn during war time." But Bartram's observations began at home with his own small creek where he had noted several little cavities in the rock possibly generated by a pebble dropped into a cleft and then turned around and around by the violence of inrushing water until it ground out a larger cavity and wore itself round as a marble. The mountainside "giant pots" had been formed in the same way, in his opinion. When the winter ice settles, many pebbles stick in it. In spring when the snow melts, the river swells so high as to reach above the place where these holes are found on the mountain side. The ice will float as high as the river rises. As it melts the pebbles fall out of the ice upon the rocky bank and are carried to a cleft by the rushing water where they grind and boil until they form a hole. Water churning around polishes the stone and helps round out the cavity. New stones are added each spring as the old ones grind to smaller stones and finally to sand. Both Kalm and Bartram agreed that not all mountain cavities were formed in this way.

Peter Kalm was to return to Abo, Sweden, where he taught in the university, with his journal crammed with observations about America and many references to all he had learned from Bartram. His remarks about the fabulous New World would be pored over by Linnaeus who seldom left Upsala, Sweden. But in 1736 he managed to make a trip to London where he met Peter Collinson. A brisk correspondence followed. Many botanists quarreled with the system Linnaeus had constructed but in spite of their protests they trailed after the master as he continued to hold his position through the years. The Earl of Bute could not forgive Linnaeus for the number of "barbarous Swedish names" he gave to plants, "for the sake of which he flings away those fabricated in this country; witness the Meadia, and the Azalea that has become Calmuck or Kalmia."

Collinson was grateful to Linnaeus for naming the Horsebalm, originating in America and sent to London by Bartram, *Collinsonia candenis*. He felt that naming a plant for him was only his due in recognition of the great number of plants and seeds he had annually procured from abroad. "You have been so good," he wrote to Linnaeus, "as to give me a species of eternity, botanically speaking; that is, a name as long as man and books endure." Still his conscience pricked him; should the plant not have been named for Bartram who discovered it and sent it to him in 1735? As for the Horsebalm itself, Kalm thought very little of it as he never failed to get a headache when he passed a growth of this plant in America. But Bartram swore by it as another excellent remedy for aches and pains. Conrad Weiser had even cured an Indian of rattlesnake bite by boiling Horsebalm and making the wretch drink the mixture.

Collinson's appreciation for his bit of eternity did not prevent him from taking Linnaeus to task for changing the good old English names to meaningless new ones. "It gives all botanists pain to see the Pinax sink into oblivion and lost forever . . . if you will be forever making new names and altering old and good ones for such hard names that convey no idea of the plant, it will be impossible to attain to a perfect knowledge in the science of Botany."

He quarreled with Linnaeus also on the subject of swallows. Linnaeus insisted that these birds wintered under water but in spite of his reputation, already world-wide, Collinson boldly disagreed with his watery hibernation theory. The best way to test this notion would be to put the swallow in a tub of water. Just try it, suggested Collinson, and see if this bird has any organs to survive the plunge. Swallows were migrating birds, he asserted, and quoted Sir Charles Wagner, first lord of the Admiralty, who had witnessed on one of his voyages home to England a great flock of swallows descend and settle on his rigging as his ship came into the Channel. Every rope was covered with birds clinging to one another like a swarm of bees. The decks and carvings of the ship were crowded with their spent and famished bodies. Though they appeared to be little more than a bundle of feathers and bones, after a night's rest in the rigging, they took flight the next morning. Captain Wright witnessed the same thing on his ship sailing from Philadelphia to London.

The point to be settled agitated them; did the swallow hibernate under water or migrate to a warmer climate? It may sound ridiculous today, but it was still in the speculative realm at that time and the correspondence between the two men waxed hot. Neither man was upset by the disagreement nor did Linnaeus seem to object when Collinson reproved him for never returning the favors bestowed upon him by collectors all over the world, including Collinson, who sent him plants and fossils without a sign of a specimen in return. "It is the general complaint," he wrote bluntly, "that Dr. Linnaeus receives all and returns nothing."

Letters were important in the Eighteenth Century. Busy men thought nothing of sitting down of an evening to a long bout of letter writing to a host of distant friends. In spite of wars and ships seized, regardless of mice and insects that frequently chewed off corners of the paper or bit holes into the most important sections, the letters flowed back and forth, around the world, with the certainty of the tides. They were another kind of seed and solitary men who tended gardens in isolated spots were in rapt communion with their fellow enthusiasts beyond anything the modern radio can dream up.

Now and then a traveler darted forth from his country as Linnaeus did to London and Kalm to America. Foreigners were later to come in streams to Bartram's garden, and Bartram more than once turned his horse toward the mountains to visit Cadwallader Colden at Newburgh, New York. There he once met another enthusiast, Dr. Alexander Garden, of Charleston, South Carolina. "What congratulations, what salutations passed between us! How happy I should be to pass my life with such men . . . in whom the greatest knowledge and skill are united with the most amiable candour," wrote Dr. Garden to Linnaeus, unable to keep the thing to himself. There was a constant leakage of good feeling, enthusiasm and ideas from one man to another, from one country to another.

They were all busy people, thoroughly engaged. Botany was for most of them a side-line. Cadwallader Colden had started as a physician, then turned Surveyor General of New York. He still had the leisure to make botany a subject of serious research, and was one of the first Americans to master Linnaeus's system. He even had time to write a book on the Five Indian Nations. Dr. Garden, for whom the gardenia was named, went in for fishes and reptiles as well as botany during the thirty years he was a practicing physician in Charleston; he lived to side with the British in 1775.

If a man discovered a rare plant in Virginia, he was apt to end up corresponding with Dr. Gronovius of Holland, Buffon or Jussieu of France, and he was certain to tangle with Peter Collinson in London and to find himself involved with John Bartram who was likely to show up on horseback at his front door. Before he knew it, a host of unseen friends would transform his life, one by one, through the pages of letters from this enthusiast or that. Dr. Mitchell of Virginia might casually mention Mr. John Ellis of the British Museum who had already made the discovery and complete demonstration of the animal nature of corals and coralines. First, Mr. Ellis would be only a name but bit by bit, Ellis, the unknown, would materialize from a misty background. The Virginian would eventually discover that the dynamic Ellis had begun as a merchant, wrote letters to correspondents all over the world, especially to China, India and the West Indies. He would find out that Ellis was the man who learned about coffee in Brazil, varnish in Japan. How he had managed to master corals might never be revealed but Ellis, the man, would gradually take on size and proportion.

In the network of this busy group there were very young men and very old. Sir Hans Sloane of London, the President of the Royal Society, was ninety when Dr. Daniel Solander, a favorite pupil of Linnaeus, was a mere stripling. A new arrival to England from Sweden, Solander began as an assistant to Ellis at the British Museum. His instructions regarding the classification of plants brought order and system out of chaotic confusion. The English did not hesitate to utilize imported men as well as plants; Dr. John Dillenius, born at Darmstadt, Germany, was brought to England by William Sherard, the greatest English botanist of his day, who succeeded in founding a botanical professorship at Oxford and appointed Dillenius as first professor. There were some odd numbers among the group, like Sir John Hill, who was more noted for toadying to the Earl of Bute than for scientific accuracy. Linnaeus put him in his place by naming a plant *Hillia parasitica,* in allusion to his obsequious habits. But for all that, he drew appreciation for his industry from the group; they more than tolerated his foibles.

56

It was not only the age of "reason" and "order" but of "man." Mankind had not yet been scaled down to the common man or the industrial man, mass man or man in transition. He was simply man, a wonder, with the same right to grow as a tree. The tree was a wonder to these particular men; they were in awe of its beauty, its uses and its history. A snail or bit of moss were mysteries to be solved. Many flowers were as yet nameless as drops of water and to name a plant, to place it, was reward enough. Nor did they stop at plants; stones and shells, birds and beasts were objects of marveling wonder.

Once Collinson sent two trumpet shaped leaves of the *Sarracenia* of the Pitcher Plant family, wrapped in moss, to Linnaeus, describing it as one of the wonders of the vegetable kingdom. He wrote of the plant with the delicacy of a painter, alert to every characteristic. "If you could only see," he told Linnaeus, "how the many leaves grow around the center bud which makes a pretty appearance with the mouth open to catch rains and dews; many poor insects lose their lives by being drowned in these cisterns." The correspondence between Collinson and Bartram was a long duet of discovery, rapture and a dash of vinegar when it came to disputed questions.

Peculiarity in plants and men was welcomed with the delighted eagerness which a naturalist feels for the least hint of a mutation. When Dr. Gronovius became somewhat miserly in his old age and resented paying postage for specimens sent to him, Collinson reminds Bartram of his palmier days when he was magnanimous. Dr. Solander may be an ingrate to his great patron, Linnaeus, and even refuse to open the letters of his doting mother, but no one forgets his solid virtues. There were no pariahs here. There were simply differing varieties, not easy to classify, perhaps, but all with a right to be what they are.

The discovery of a new world, with all the astonishment, the widening horizons and the alteration of the world picture was operative in this century as it had been in the Renaissance. But the new world of this period was to be ushered in, not by navigators, but by scientists, and the horizons were to include an ever brighter prospect for mankind. The theme which had served as a lever toward political, religious, economic and philosophical revolution in the Renaissance was to work in new fields, engineered by men who believed they had only to discover the laws of Nature in order to bring order and sanity to the earth. The vision compelled men to actual tasks and the tasks dimmed the old preoccupation with guilt and despair. Old conceptions, blurred by superstitions and dread, were to be brushed off, turned about in the light of day and named. The name, the name! It becomes a chant, almost an invocation.

The times called forth originality, courted diversity, called upon men to think and roam and to stand up for their conclusions. Love of country did not exclude the world. During wars, English botanists continued to correspond with Frenchmen and mourned for vegetable cargoes lost at sea more than any merchant for his wares. Russia, China, Italy and Greece were chums and brothers of the blood. The blood flowed around the world in sacred wood sap and in the seeds of pine cones. For there was a grand design at work; respect for the glory of mentality.

If men could not conquer death, they might manage life. All the monstrous, unmanageable things that men put outside themselves and named God because they had not known what to do with this side of their experience, how to tame it, how to face it, this group accepted in its most benignant aspect of sheer wonder, unsolved miracle, potent might which might be bent to man's salvation. It was a period auspicious for such a breathing space; a time, for once, of decision and calm, a hopefulness casting a ray so strong that all the violent, the incomprehensible, was for a brief spell kept at bay. Things to be classified and understood were innumerable and the duty of this little band of men seemed to them to lie in solving this from that, in keeping problems solved from those that must be temporarily passed over, and thus, in a restricted form, bring a sense of order to what might be at base only chain stitches in a vast disorder as yet undefined.

The joy of discovery, pregnant with possibilities, was in their very bones. They talked joy and walked it and in a mood of ever hopeful expectation were ready to try anything. Seeds went around the world; a new kind of shot for another kind of revolution. Nor were the seeds thus cast just seeds. To cast their meanings meant more than to solve their practical use. Wide inquiry into the why and wherefore accompanied all this voyaging of the plants and transfigured voyage of plants to voyage of mind. Philadelphia was a lively spot; the practical Franklin had more sides than his pinch-penny one. As a bookseller he had introduced the challenging works of his time and thus helped shock men's minds to a world beyond their own narrowness. Information traveled by word of mouth, leaped across brooks, crossed mountains. The gulf between the language of science and the spoken word did not exist to the extent it does today. There was no incommunicable jargon to shut the new discoveries off from ordinary understanding.

John Bartram began on the fringe of this magic circle of devoted men. The mental climate was fortunate for his kind of inquiring mind. Like Bartram, many of the men prominent in scientific research were Quakers and non-conformists. In England the ban against non-conformists had shunted many bright young men to business or scientific research as positions in the government were closed to them. They were lucky to be shut out also from the Oxford and Cambridge of that day. Their own academies, springing up from a denial elsewhere, were unhampered by the moribund classicism that prevailed, and produced men of original mind, thoroughly alive to the new and strange.

After Bartram began to correspond with Peter Collinson, he saw a future for his seeds. England wanted them. A correspondence and a barter of seeds and plants sprang up between the two men, to last for forty years. There is no better way to become acquainted with Bartram than through this long duet with his friend where the stiffness of his two surviving journals breaks down to playful amiable freedom. Bartram was to carry on a correspondence with many people but in his letters to Collinson he reveals more and betrays more of his secret self. Collinson was to make Bartram's explorations possible by finding the means to pay for them, but that was only the half of it; the other and greater half was the enthusiasm engendered which stimulated the American to become more than a gatherer of seeds.

His quest for seeds in the wilderness led inevitably to the formation of a garden spot especially prepared to receive them. His prize was not well tended land so much as a tangled piece of soil, half rocks, half weeds, where he laid out his precious wilderness seeds and plants. Some seeds were fine as golddust and must be pressed into a vein of damp sand. If he found them under briars, they were nurtured under briars in his garden. Or if in a cranny of a rock, then a split rock cradled this wild child. He was no mere nurseryman. He and all his band plotted for more than themselves. They sifted ashes, bruised earth to make a finer dust; mixed rotted leaves with sand to make the stranger feel at home. They saw themselves as snatchers of the rare from oblivion; the savers and schemers for a future green earth. They deplored the ravage of the woods and streams; both animals and plants, birds and bees, were their sacred trust. They had no lust for waste in days when waste seemed harmless and men killed for the kill. Nor were they idle sentimentalists exclaiming over mere prettiness.

Bartram's shaggy garden was not for show but to perpetuate the species. From plants grown in this rocky tangled spot, he gathered seeds to replant in his own garden or to send to England. Though his garden became famous for the variety of its native species, rivaling all other American gardens in that respect, it was not the first botanical garden nor the only one. Probably the first botanical garden belonged to the brotherhood of German mystics, led by Kelpius, who in 1694 built their steep-roofed cloister, Das Weib in der Wüste, on the banks of the Wissahickon. There they studied mathematics, experimented in alchemy, and, while they read the sky with telescopes, awaited the second coming of Christ. In their forest refuge, gardens ran down the glen, with a mainstay of herbs for medicinal purposes. Dr. Christopher Witt, who lived in Germantown, must have taken fire from Kelpius's garden as well as imbibing strong drafts of alchemy. A painter of sorts, he even made an oil portrait of Kelpius shortly after their acquaintance in 1704, the first year of his residence in America. Kelpius died that same year but some of his plants must have found their way to Dr. Witt's garden and were then passed on to Bartram. Dr. Witt's neighbor, Pastorius, cultivated herbs and plants, also, and in his *Medicus Dilectus* wrote of herbal remedies. In his *Hortenses Deliciae* he celebrated the beauties and virtues of rare plants, among them Dr. Witt's fig tree.

Early gardeners were exchanging plants and seeds before Collinson and Bartram speeded up the practice. James Logan, the brilliant secretary of William Penn, was another botanizer who may have had specimens from Kelpius. He certainly exchanged plants and ideas with

Bartram. His garden at Stenton was a workmanlike place, a laboratory for experiment. As early as 1735 he reported an experiment with maize to prove the theory of sexuality of plants, then in question. There were other gardens; Fair Hill, estate of Isaac Norris, was founded as early as 1705. The fame of Isham Randolph's place in Virginia had spread northward before Bartram was established.

The English had brought to America an enthusiasm for gardening that was already well established as early as the reign of Queen Elizabeth when bulbs from Holland were being planted in the English countryside. At that same time Italian gardens were imitated in France. In his *The Civilization of the Renaissance in Italy,* Jacob Burckhardt has stated that "Italy claims to be the first creator of botanical gardens, though possibly they may have served a practical end, and the claim to priority may be itself disputed." But it seems to have been a fact, that the Italian princes and wealthy men, in laying out their parks, made a point of collecting the greatest possible number of different plants in all their varieties. In the Fifteenth Century, the grounds of the Medicean Villa Careggi would appear to have been almost a botanical garden from the existing descriptions. Burckhardt also cites the villa of the Cardinal Trivulzio at the beginning of the Sixteenth Century with its hedges of roses, trees of every description, twenty sorts of vines and a large kitchen garden. This is the sort of thing that the English began to accomplish on a truly expansive scale in the Eighteenth Century when big estates sought plants from all over the world, and especially from the abundant wilderness of America.

The Italians had not stopped with plants but also collected foreign animals, even some human species. Cities and princes vied with one another for a live lion with as much persistence as Peter Collinson was to show when it came to possessing a huge American tortoise. In Italy the condition of the lions was held to be ominous of good or evil and their fertility a sign of public prosperity. By the end of the Fifteenth Century "to keep horses, dogs, mules, falcons, and other birds, court jesters, singers and foreign animals" was considered an obligation of the great. King Emmanuel knew what he was doing when he presented the Pope, Leo X, with an elephant and a rhinoceros. It was under such circumstances that the foundations of a scientific zoology and botany were laid. The mental climate of the Eighteenth Century was electric with the same sort of wonder and curiosity that had transformed the Renaissance.

Grounded in the selfsufficiency of that period, Bartram took upon himself burden after burden. It was no small matter to raise so many children, cultivate an extensive farm, raise cattle, plant a kitchen garden, cultivate the study of botany, risk life and limb in the awesome wilderness, pack and send case after case of plants and seeds, weighing hundreds of pounds, to England, to say nothing of writing innumerable letters. Yet he seems to have managed all these diverse themes.

His immediate necessities had compelled him first to study Nature as she is related to the farmer, simply to satisfy a want of the human body. There must have been times when he was irritated at the hens clucking in the barnyard when he wanted to follow a bird call to the western side of the mountain. There must have been moments when he despaired of ever getting down in his journal the complexity of the wilderness; sterner, savager than any town man could know. When he looked at an old tree he could see the cuffs it had taken. If he plucked an herb and crushed it in his fingers, it was for no idle whim. Brute necessity was also here. What to do for an ache? For the perpetual bruises, the gashes from an ax, the ailing child? We have forgotten all that, all the source of his wonderment, but in his day the need and the astonished vision were both clear and strong.

His gifts were suited to his time and he made the most of them. When he was troubled with too much farming and no money to carry on ventures into the wilderness, the resourceful Collinson stepped forward with a scheme for financing his American friend. It wasn't lavish but it made the project possible. Among the owners of the big estates in England, Collinson found patrons who were eager for seeds and plants from the new world and would pay for them.

CHAPTER IV

John Bartram, like some poets of the Eighteenth Century, needed patrons. For ten guineas a year, a gentleman in England might expect to enrich his estate with quantities of seedlings from exotic American forests. He could put in his bid for strange insects, birds and even turtles. In English parks and in the estate of men's minds, the new world vegetables, as Bartram called them, were to find a flowering continuity.

The seed from the great magnolia tree found by Bartram on his trip to the Great Lakes will be nursed up in his garden for future emigration. But it will be a year too late to adorn the plantations of his first patron, Lord Petrie, who died of the smallpox in 1742. A find of Peter Collinson's, there will never be another patron to enthuse the woolen draper. His ten guineas may be duplicated by the Duke of Norfolk and the Duke of Richmond, but none, except Petrie, had "so noble a nature or so rich a mind."

Collinson bursts from his merchant shell as he writes the dreadful news to Bartram, and one is reminded that this little circle of enthusiasts was as enclosed in shared devotions as any secret society. "Oh friend John! I can't express the concern of mind I am under, in so many accounts. I have lost my friend, my brother. The man I loved, and was dearer to me than all men—is no more. I could fill this sheet and many more: but oh! my anxiety of mind is so great, that I can hardly write; and yet, I must tell thee, that on Friday, July 2, our dear friend, Lord Petrie, was carried off by the smallpox, in the 30th year of his age. Hard, hard, cruel hard, to be taken from friends, his family, his country, in the prime of life; when he had so many thousand things locked up in his breast, for the benefit of them all; now all lost in embryo. I can go no further but to assure thee I am thy friend, Peter Collinson."

A moment he must have sat there, deep in woe, in chaos of grief and anxious concern. What will happen to their projects without this hand? He picks up his pen and adds tersely, "All our schemes are broke."

The grand view opened to the Quaker Collinson by his dead friend had been lavish. There is not a grain of envy in the rapturous praise he bestows upon his friend's good works and splendors. In earlier letters to Bartram he had chanted the wonders of Lord Petrie's undertakings. Seeds of trees from the continent, from Asia and from America had been planted in his great park to come to maturity in English soil. Collinson reels off the list; 10,000 Americans; 20,000 Europeans. Asians in not quite the same profusion. With great art and precision, Lord Petrie had studied the rate of growth of each variety and had blended his greens like any fine landscape painter. Dark green was laid against bluish green with a shading off to soft yellow.

In thickets and clumps, flowering shrubs filled the out-
skirts in a vast border and when Collinson wandered
among them, he fancied that he was walking in North
America for only there could such abundance have been
duplicated. Lord Petrie kept his nurseries stocked to re-
furbish his plantations and one might easily lift 20,000
trees without missing them.

If Lord Petrie's woods raised Peter Collinson's spirits
to a glow, his table brought him to a pitch of fever. For
here exotic foods rioted. One would think South America
had been transplanted overseas. He confessed he was quite
cloyed with pineapples from Lord Petrie's table. It was
nothing to see a servant come in with ten or a dozen pineapples every day. He begged Bartram not to think he was
speaking figuratively when he said that the "stove" which
reared this fruit was sixty feet long, twenty feet wide and
high in proportion. And further, he must add to pineapples, guavas, pawpaws, ginger and limes in such plenty
that yearly Lord Petrie made an abundance of wet sweet-
meats, of his own growth, to serve his table and to present
to his friends. Finer Collinson had never seen or tasted
from Barbadoes, nor better cured. Petrie exotics grew in
beds of earth, in glass houses; trees stood twenty to thirty
feet high. Wonderful, wonderful, says Collinson—always
a little given to platitude—how Nature is helped and imitated by Art. As for Lord Petrie's collection of West and
East Indian plants, why, this beggars the imagination!
Beyond the imagination, too, were the endless ingenious
contrivances to maintain such a garden and to help bring
every plant and fruit to perfection.

Lord Petrie was in the mode about to be born. The
Romantic Age was to be delivered, and, even this early
in the century, the marks and signs were bannered in the
trees. The innovators in gardening, like Lord Petrie, abandoned the scissors for the grand line. Literary men, ever

sensitive to the significance of things, had been ridiculing the fashion of cutting noble trees to cones, globes and pyramids since the early *Spectator* made its appearance. "Adam and Eve in Yew; Adam a little Shattered by the fall of the Tree of Knowledge in the great Storm; Eve and the Serpent very flourishing; St. George in Box, his arm scarce long enough, but will be in a Condition to Stick the dragon by next April; a pair of Giants, stunted," were some of the items ridiculed even in an age when fashion decreed that natural form was vulgar. And Pope, a formalist in his own line, railed against trees cut to statues, statues thick as trees. Travelers were bringing exotics to England; Chinese wall-papers and painted calicoes from India suggested lightness and grace. The pomp of kings and the pomp of artificiality were soon to shatter to great changes and later in the century, Coleridge could write that "it is an honor to poets and great men, that you think of them as parts of nature; and anything of trick and fashion wounds you in them, as much as when you see venerable yews clipped into miserable peacocks."

The rigid control of space, the reliance on precedent were going out with the improved stagecoach, with the vessels plying to and from America. Merchants tirelessly combed foreign lands for fresh wonders and a revolution in gardening was a portent.

Ten guineas a year does not seem a great sum for such a splendid patron as Lord Petrie, yet the truth is, that Peter Collinson, more than once, had to apologize to Bartram for its delay. He is almost plaintive as he related how hard it seems to be to get money of great people. Though he is willing to give his labors and his pains, take all the shipments and see to their safe delivery, yet there is dilly-dallying. "They are glad of the cargo but are apt to forget all the rest." Giving good words will not always do, and there are moments when he would abandon the patrons in their parks if it were not that his American friend depends upon this source of income. To encourage Bartram's ingenuity is the great thing. He does not mention his own eagerness and the itch of his perpetual curiosity. He must at any cost keep his friend afloat in that fascinating wilderness. But there is the mortgage on Bartram's house and land and his many children. He cannot be expected to risk life and limb for nothing. Though Lord Petrie became a patron in 1735, it was years before Collinson was able to assemble a larger group to help subsidize his friend's operations.

But Lord Petrie. He may have been dilatory in his payments but Petrie dead is a glory over. Collinson picks up his pen to add to the letter he brokenly thought finished and pours forth laudations of the man whom he loved. "Send no seeds for him," he writes and the tone is as if he had written, Oh weep for Adonais; he that gave motion is motionless. But his native spirits soon find ingenious leaks to his sorrow. This will be a great disappointment to Bartram and he is already trying to find a patch for woe. Send the seeds, is his next injunction. "I will endeavor to dispose of them for thee." Perhaps the Duke of Norfolk will take the batch assigned to the dead Petrie. But oh! and again he burst with praise, "he was a fine, tall, comely personage, with the presence of a prince. His affability and sweetness of temper were beyond expression, without the least mixture of pride or haughtiness. If his smile engaged, oh, how much more enchanting were the endowments of his mind!" Few or none could excel him in his knowledge of the liberal arts and sciences, and when one adds his gifts as a great mechanic and as a mathematician, ready at figures and calculations, with elegance in his every taste, it is enough to make even Collinson wonder at the wisdom of the Great Architect for

69

allowing this shapely vessel to have been broken. Here is a paragon gone down.

Who knows when this news will reach John Bartram? It is July 3, 1742 when Collinson writes and three days later, in America, Bartram has only received his friend's letters of March 3rd, 20th and of April 25th. He sits down at once to answer. Embedded in his family, caught up by fascinating occupations, he yet yearns for letters. The wilderness is not a complete paradise; it cannot nourish the whole man. If his mind longs to speed news of his finds, he must wait for ships and obliging captains or make toilsome treks to remote dwellings where men like himself, the passionate few, are of a like aspiration. He frets a little at the more patient Collinson.

Yesterday, he writes Collinson, the ship arrived from London. Their dear friend, Captain Wright, who carried all their precious cargo in his cabin, "hath been left behind, asleep in Neptune's bosom." Such a mortal sickness is on board that the ship is ordered to ride quarantine below Philadelphia. No goods can be got off.

These pestilential torrents! How they pour down. Bartram accepts the end of good Captain Wright without eulogy. Another captain must be found to take his place and Lady Petrie will get her humming bird's nest and eggs if he can find them. She wants a dead pair, too; a hen and cock. Does Collinson know that the fine down composition of the nest is gathered from the stalks of living fern? And has his friend received the bladders of balm which he sent him, gathered on the Balm of Gilead tree on a Catskill mountain? A delicate, fragrant liquor, as clear as spring water. The reference to the bladders calls for a prosaic explanation. The suggestion for the use of ox bladders came from Collinson though he had hardly anticipated they would be adapted to nectar. The bladders were to be used by Bartram on his sorties into the wilderness. If he cut off the neck high, and put a newly found plant with a little earth into the bladder, added a little water, then tied up the neck close around the stock of the plant, leaving leaves and flowers without, he would find it easy to convey his plants, for the bladders could be attached to the pummel of the saddle.

Collinson is something of a general, mapping campaigns for Bartram in the safety of his London study. His notions of necessities for the exhaustive searches went beyond anything Bartram ever managed to rake together. At the start, Collinson spoke of an accompanying servant, of a horse for each man and a third beast to carry equipment. The majority of Bartram's journeys were made alone. Paper was important. With paper sent by Collinson from London, Bartram made little, middling and big bags to hold seeds. He carried two baskets, slung on each side of the horse for plants. It was the most rudimentary equipment imaginable. His compass, too, came from London and a microscope which was nothing at all in comparison to the modern one.

There were moments when Bartram doubted that he could possibly convey to his London friend the difficulties of his expeditions. He cannot refrain from adding to his letter, informing Collinson of his intention to go and gather seeds, that "I hope they will be as much pleasure to you as fatigue and charge to me to get them." He knows he can count on no one except himself. The energetic, competent man cannot help but rail at the incompetent and damn his fellow citizens for their lack of "curiosity." What's more, they have no more trust than they have curiosity. A Colonel Salisbury promised him to gather seeds near York at the propitious season but gathered none. He even claimed he had sent a man on purpose to the mountain where the seeds were to be found but the man excused his failure to return with seeds by blaming the birds. The birds are fond of seeds, was his pitiful excuse.

Some piqued pride leaks through this letter to his kind friend. He is not, it seems, quite satisfied with the response Collinson gave to a map of a cave encountered on an excursion near Reading, Pennsylvania. More than once he has been gently sniffed at for his grammar. Now he apologizes for the map. He is aware it was clumsily done. But then he had neither the proper instruments nor the time. So pressed was he that part was done by day, part by candlelight.

Idle time is something he will never know. More than once he marvels at those benighted souls who complain of boredom. What? In a world bursting its seams, with so much to learn of the wonders of Creation? His passion for the pure vision carries right past Collinson's dawdling with religious ponderings. None too grateful for a volume of Barclay's *Apology*, sent in a package along with a suit of clothes, he cannot resist a mild spurt of sarcasm. The Clothing is just right and generously acknowledged; as for the *Apology*, maybe it was a good thing to send. It will save him time he might have spent had he received books on botany and natural history. A man who must maintain a large family values each second. In case this does not strike home, he drives straight to the point: "I have little respect for *Apologies* and disputes about the ceremonial parts of religion, which often introduce animosities, confusions and disorders of the mind and sometimes of the body; but dear Peter (and he pours on the balm) let us worship the One Almighty Power, in sincerity of heart, with resignation to his divine Will, doing to others as we would have them do to us, if we were in their circumstances. Living in love and innocency, we may die in Hope, then if we don't go to Heaven I believe we shan't go to Hell."

In late July, 1742, Bartram is off to visit Governor Morris at Amboy. He wants to find out about the great horns reported in England a few years back which had excited Collinson to wonder. Beasts, flowers, trees, shrubs, they were all pressing hard for identification. As for the horns, it seems they came from a creature that weighed 1500 lbs. and was excellent eating. The horns differed from those of the moose deer displayed at a meeting of the Philosophical Society at Philadelphia. And everything new under the sun came under discussion there. Bartram can't find a name for it and its horns baffle him but the trip is worth it. He has picked wild flower seeds all along the way, for it is the time of ripening. They have all been well dried and a selection of fifty different sorts of seeds will go off to London with the first packet. Then he hopes to gather cones of Rose Laurel and White Pine, sassafras berries and balm seed during August in the Catskills. After that—well, he tentatively and tenderly refers to a fond dream of following the branches of the Susquehanna to the Great Lakes and encountering the Five Indian Tribes. This will take a backer, and modestly, he does not press the point too hard, but he is certainly counting on Lord Petrie.

He hasn't heard of his patron's death even in September when he comes home laden with a parcel of Balm cones. But he is bubbling over with the good conversation he enjoyed with Dr. Colden at Newburgh. The urge to find a way to make his trip to the Great Lakes is so strong that he cannot refrain from hints and nudges. Dr. Colden recommends the Mohawk country as the most likely spot for rare plants; and there is a proper season which may soon pass. By December he knows, at last, that his patron, Lord Petrie, is dead and that his plans have gone glimmering. He supposes, he writes to Collinson, "that the death of our dear friend will discourage such distant travels and our Americans have not zeal enough to encourage any discoveries of this kind at their own expense." In the mood of his depressed spirits even Collinson appears neglectful. He ends his letter on a gloomy note: "Captain Davis, by whom I sent a box of Red Cedar berries and Maple keys, complains that thee took no care of it, but let it stay on board until he loaded again. Such delays will discourage captains from taking things of that kind unless I pay here."

If a captain complained, Collinson from his side of the ocean sometimes complained of a captain. One unworthy fellow put the cases on deck above the hold and covered them with pipe staves. Mischievous, unruly rats got into it and two nests of callow young rats were kindled there when he came to fetch it away. Above ground, everything was trampled, and below, the roots were ruined by their excretions. Only one root showed any sign of life. John Bartram, too, comes in for some complaints. His cases weigh too much. One weighed three hundred pounds. Better make smaller cases and not send so much sod. On the other hand, from the sod packed around the roots, many pretty plants spring up. Oh, how thick the American woods must be in rare and odd plants! If rats do not attack, beetles, packed in the same case with butterflies and moths, devoured the entire cargo. Such a swarm of pestilent beetles, Collinson never saw! He dreaded to go on board to see the ruin of his friend's labor and pains.

"As we say of an old woman, there's the ruin of a fine face," he wrote, "so I may say, there's the ruin of fine flies." He implores Bartram to divide the precious from the vile, next time. He will send boxes enough. The butterflies or day flies should be kept by themselves, the moths by themselves, and as for the devouring beetles, it would be better to drown them in rum or heat them in a gentle oven to stop their progress. Still, he wants their corpses. Specimens all, he must examine them.

74

He cheerfully admits that "my inclination and fondness to natural productions of all kinds is agreeable to the old proverb: Like the Parson's barn, refuses nothing." As for rattlesnakes, he lets his curiosity roam. Since Bartram meets up with them on every journey, surely he can answer the question as to how the snake wins its prey? Does he dart at it and bite it and then wait for it to die? What about sending a specimen of vegetation called the Poison Stick? Watch out for Lady Slipper and Gentian. Gentian is his favorite flower.

Reading backward in the correspondence covering the years of Lord Petrie's patronage before his death, it is quite evident that this gentleman, too, wanted everything. Wasps' nests seem to have been the rage. Cedar seeds were sent to him by the bushel. He had to have a specimen of the Paw-paw and Collinson sent exact directions; plant and fruit should be gathered when the fruit is ripe and put into strong rum in a jar, corked tight. It is obvious that the two friends cheerfully connived to please the patron: "Friend John," wrote Collinson, "this is only a hint by the way. Lord Petrie is a great admirer of your foreign water fowl. If at any time, an opportunity offers, send him some. Thou will lose nothing by it." And terrapins. They could go in a box with some earth in it and a few tasty pieces of apple laid alongside for them to nibble during the voyage.

Alas, the journey miscarried for these desirable creatures. Some died, some were stolen by sailors. But turtle eggs fared better. When Collinson took the lid off the box with a mind to see the eggs, he saw instead a little head just above ground and while he was looking, the ground moved in a place or two more. In three or four hours, eight tortoises had hatched. Collinson sat glued by the side of the box, all the while, as conscientious as the most faithful midwife, making minute observations. How artfully they disengaged themselves from the shell and then, with their forefeet, scratched their eyes open! He relates with pride that they have had many visitors, such a thing never happening, he dares say, in England before.

He offered them lettuce leaves and drink but the curious creatures would have neither; instead, they crawled about for four days, then buried themselves in the earth of the box. He will take them to Lord Petrie's ponds early in the spring. These ponds are already perfect breeding grounds for a myriad of plants, fish and curiosities.

A lust for turtles seizes the good merchant. He would have all varieties, alive or dead! Then he simmers down to a demand for a shell of each sort, dried, and if anything is remarkable about their head and feet, pray do, include head and feet. And be sure to cure them in a slack oven after the bread is out!

During the eight years that Lord Petrie was a patron of Bartram's botanical explorations, his opinions, his tastes, his yearnings for new varieties were the ground of many of the letters passing between the two friends. But so indefatigable was Bartram that in a few years Collinson had to tell him not to collect any more Tulip cones, Swamp Laurel cones, Hickory, Black Walnut, Sassafras nor Dogwood, Sweet Gum, White Oak acorns, Swamp Spanish Oak, nor Red Cedar Berries, but instead to send all sorts of acorns except White Oak and Spanish Oak; cones from firs, pines, Black Gum or Black Haw berries, Judas tree, Persimmon, Cherries, Plums, Hop Tree, All-Spice. Also all sorts of Ash, Sugar-tree, Wild Roses, Black Beech or Hornbeam and all sorts of flowering shrubs. In particular he would like a locust known as *Guelder Rose*. But after this complicated list of rejections and acceptances, he can't resist adding that there is not anything Bartram may send that will come amiss. And so it goes. Collinson's original admonition to Bartram had been to send any "uncommon" thing he might find, in any branch of Nature, but it soon became plain that almost anything that grew was a temptation.

It was not all one-way traffic. Collinson sent young fruit trees; pears and plum trees. The March before he died, Lord Petrie gathered, "with his own hands" berries of Butcher's Broom and Juniper growing on his estate to send to Bartram. Bartram's request for Spanish Chestnuts and French Walnuts couldn't be filled. Nature's ways were not always propitious; the last ships to America for that season sailed before the nuts were ripe and the first ships to go in the spring after the seeds had rotted. Some of the English tidbits could not stand the more rigorous American winters. Wood sage, flourishing on the high hills of England without suffering frost-bite, dies in Bartram's garden.

Though Collinson, at the moment of Lord Petrie's death moaned that "all their plans are broke," he soon found new ways to keep Bartram afloat. Agitating in his friend's behalf, he stirred up Logan to remember Bartram when it came to the expedition to the Great Lakes, and he busied himself among his influential friends all that winter to round up new patrons for the American shipments. Meanwhile, Nature did not stand still but poured in from America.

Rats are still the bane. They tore into the boxes again and made nests of straw and stalks of shrub. How grieved he was to see the great Rhododendrons stripped clean and the Kalmias lying in mere sticks. Loblolly was chewed up but he intends to plant the roots and to hope. This is one of the most charming evergreens he knows. Bartram's skunk root is in full flower on February 3, 1743, and he begs to be informed how many species of Solomon's Seals he has observed on his travels.

There he sits in his study, late in the evenings, poring

over his treasures. He fancies he has all varieties of American fall flowers, but now he sorely lacks the spring beauties. Come to think of it, he does not even know the spring flowers with which the American woods abound. A vision of woods, thickets, fields and meadows sparkling with flowers makes him reel. What about Bartram's son James making a quire of specimens of ALL the spring flowers for those three months? He recites a drunken list of flowers to be found in England in spring; primroses, daisies, Pilewort, now beginning, to be followed by several specimens of Crowfoot, called Butterflowers. Dandelion make a great show and fields are rich with cowslip, Lady-smocks, marsh marigolds; then come a train of blue hyacinth, daffodils, saxifrage, Stitchwort, blue and white violets, a great variety of *Orchis*—why, exclaims the ardent fellow, "our woods are smothered with anemones, Periwinkle, Woodroof with its white flowers." In his opinion, not one of the English varieties is native to Bartram's country.

Even his contemplation of wonder-haunted spring cannot drive him from his obsession about turtles. If he omits references to these enchanting objects in one letter, he picks up the theme in another with a bubbling enthusiasm. His friend, M. Catesby, has speculated with him on the subject, and he presses hard for any specimens that Bartram may find on his excursions. The Flatter-back, the Red-bellied water turtle, the common land turtle, the Round-back, the Great Black turtle, the Great Red-bellied turtle. Then their eggs. The Red-bellied makes the largest sized eggs of all. Oh how pretty are the long, shining eggs of the Stinking turtle, and this species lays the smallest eggs of all! Eggs or live creatures; send them on. And to urge on his good friend to his devoted labors, he puts the compliment that Sam Chew who recommended Bartram to him, was right when he said that nothing could well escape him.

Let other men invest in gold mines. If he is to speculate, let it be in this sturdy American goods. He grows playful, teasing Bartram for his reproaches that letters do not come as fast as he wishes. Has he no faith? And in the winter following Lord Petrie's death, when the future of their enterprises must have seemed a little shaky, he bolsters up his friend with a present of a bolt of goods called thickset, to be made into a suit of clothes, and for his wife, a packet of silk.

Even more gratifying to Bartram, who yearned for books, was a life subscription to the newly founded Philadelphia Library. Collinson was busy on everybody's business, not only that winter, but for many a year, and not the least of his activities was the stimulus he gave to the founding of the new library for which he was the purchaser in London. "Dear friend," wrote Bartram, "by these demonstrations of thy particular regard for my interests and satisfactions, thee engages to thyself my grateful service and remembrances for such favors."

Bartram undertook arduous tasks that winter and got off three boxes of shrubs on the *Constantine* shortly before he learned of Lord Petrie's death. Some of the plants he hoped to send could not be moved on account of the great snow which fell on the first day of November and the frost and more snow that followed within two weeks after. He had a grievous time to collect the pine cones near Egg Harbour, for the Duke of Norfolk, who never seems to emerge as a very beguiling correspondent or interested party. To get cones, he climbed the tree as rain fell and lopped off the boughs; then he must stand in snow to his knees to pluck off the cones. But if he is brought to some complaining of his toil, he winds up with cheerful predictions. There was a plentiful harvest in Pennsylvania this year and two weeks after his excursion for cones, in deep snow, came a burst of fine weather. By the time he acknowledges news of Petrie's death, there has been a string of spring-like days with the frogs making a noise and birds singing. Bees flew about as in the spring.

Nature will not stop for lack of Patrons and the great push goes on in spite of scarcity in that quarter. For one thing, there is something called a Monack, imported from the new world. Collinson has given one to Sir Hans Sloane and the creature is as tame as a cat and runs up and down like a dog. Sir Hans is delighted with it. It looks like a large gray fox squirrel with long brown fur. Eats green roots and fruits. He understands that in Maryland, from whence it came, it is called One of the Seven Sleepers. It would be pretty to keep one, thinks Collinson, and to watch the provision he makes for his winter's abode, for six or seven months, sleeping all that time without food. By the time Bartram got around to identifying the Monack as a groundhog, Collinson is off on muskrats. Sir Hans wants one.

Though Bartram sends an account of the muskrat which appears very just and natural to Collinson, he takes occasion to read a little lecture to his American friend who is sometimes squeamish. Few can give a reasonable account of their antipathies, he admonishes, and, anticipating modern theories, is of the opinion that such notions are taken in with our nurse's milk. What parents are frightened at, children conceive the same. Perhaps, he suggests, this is Bartram's case with the Opossum. The contemptible creature, in his friend's eyes, has been remarkably distinguished from other animals in the wonderful provision made for the preservation of its young as if it were, indeed, a creature of great consequence. Another wonder, is how the young ones come so very small to the teat. Dr. Mitchell of Urbana, Virginia, is studying the structure of this creature, its marvel of a pouch, its internal arrangements. Collinson doubts not, that in good time, the disputed points will be cleared up.

The handiest word in the language for Collinson is "wonderful." He can tolerate no lesser word. But his immersion in wonders does not dull him to the requests of others. He is like a lightning rod, drawing down upon himself intimations of desires. Mark Catesby, the ornithologist, wants a dried bird. One of a kind of night bird that calls "whippewill" all night long. And what about getting him a specimen of that large piece of polished iron ore that was sent to their friend, Wooley, last quarter? As for the horns that Governor Morris has of the great beast like an elk, wouldn't a broad hint woo these prizes away from the governor?

One marvels where he stored his treasures. And whatever happened to the terrapin and the turtles, the wasp nests and the bird eggs? Did he ever get an answer to the question, "Canst thee assign any reasonable conjecture why your house wasps don't sting in October?"

He had a thriving London business as a wholesale woolen merchant, with quarters at the Red Lion in Grace Church Street, and he had a country house and garden at Peckham in Surrey where his treasures from America and elsewhere were secured. When he changed his country residence in 1749 to Ridgeway House at Mill Hill, it took two years to transplant all his cherished items. Through Collinson, hundreds of new species were introduced into England for the glory of rural palaces and the eternal enrichment of the countryside. The ornamentation of vast estates was only the show window to more elaborate alterations going forward. Since the enclosure of common lands, estates had grown in size and experiments in new methods of farming had become fashionable.

Lord Petrie might go in for trees and exotics, but Robert Bakewell of Leicestershire devoted his efforts toward improving sheep and cattle. The odd looking creature, something between a dog and a goat, weighing 38 lb. in 1710, plumped out its fleece to boast 80 lb. by 1795. Calves upped their weight from a meager 50 lb. in the earlier period to 150 lb. at the end of the century.

Among human kind, it was not so favorable. In the early part of the century, only about one child in four, born in London, survived. Death was a commonplace; the people sought palliatives in drink, gambling and violence. Hogarth's pictures of wretchedness were not bred from fancy. Disease rioted unchecked; smallpox, typhus, dysentery kept the death rate higher than the birth rate until the approach of the Nineteenth Century. Even a Lord Petrie could not escape smallpox.

While England boasted that wheat could now be grown anywhere in England and that even the poor ate white bread, Gay's *Trivia* and Johnson's *London* show London to have been squalid and disease ridden; the contrast between luxury and ugly poverty was intense.

Collinson's letters to Bartram give few clues to the world beyond his garden. In his mild way, he was an enthusiast in a period when Hard Cash was winning, and enthusiasm suspect. Nature became his grand Mistress and by the time he was seventy-five, devotion to her had run him close to financial ruin. In another sense, he was only one of many men with boundless confidence in the future. These vast gardens were laid out for their children's children. The aristocrat traveled with a purpose; studied politics and laws; collected objects for his palace and shrubs for his garden. Improvements in methods of agriculture, in crafts and manufactures were brought home. God, too, suffered a sea change; He became the Great Mechanic.

It's not hard to see why Collinson, seated in his pretty home at Mill Hill, before a cozy fire, with his pens sharpened for a lengthy correspondence with botanical minded friends, valued John Bartram. Bartram took the risks; he was the connective link between this settled spot and an imaginary kingdom. In a century when travel books sold more than any other bookish item outside of works on religious topics, the traveler was a man of distinction. There was a practical side to the subsidizing of Bartram for his pursuit of botanical specimens to glamorize England but that side was less emphatic in Collinson than happy, joyful wonder. Modesty narrowed his private interests down to the small fry of animal and vegetable life. The minutiae haunted him. A butterfly's wing. A snail's eating habits. In a sense, the Lord Petries of his world had overawed him with their wealth of pineapples and glass houses.

Who would ever think, reading Collinson's neat rhapsodic letters, that London streets were a dustbin where the butchers threw their refuse from their slaughter houses! Enterprising gardeners around London and some of the big towns bought refuse and nightsoil to manure their fields and thus helped the growth of cleanliness. But every street and cranny in the first half of the century was a public nuisance; the watercloset was an innovation of a later date. The dead, too, were a nuisance if they were poor and fated to be cast in hideous uncovered graves, called Poor's Holes, dug in great pits and not covered until filled with dead bodies.

Thieving, looting and rioting were commonplace in cities where the housing problem was acute. Most cellars were inhabited, not only by people, but by pigs and fowl. Magistrates seemed to have little control and deportation and death, as De Foe noted, were meted out for trivial offenses. In 1740, the law said that for stealing a handkerchief worth one shilling from a corpse, children could be hanged by the neck until they were dead. Thieving even touches Collinson in his pretty retreat surrounded by his choice rarities. Some of his favorite prized specimens from the New World were raked from the soil during the night. Twice this happened and finally Collinson joked with Bartram on the subject, asking him how he liked the prospect of seeing the thieves, when caught, foisted upon America. And this seems to have been their punishment.

But if there was stench in the streets, the mental climate was salubrious. The dark superstitions of the middle ages that had consigned the workings of Nature to the Satanic order of things had been dissipated by the triumph of Reason. The medieval conception of Nature as the forbidden knowledge was in reverse. The ways of Nature and the ways of God became identical. For an age that had begun to worship the triumph of the machine and to see in the workings of Nature, a superior mathematical mind, it was inevitable that God should become depersonalized, Nature a divine cipher that needed only interpretation. If the dark and irrational problems of guilt and sin were avoided, it was a healthful swing away from a contemplation of Man, the sinful Worm, toward Man with a boundless future on earth, not only in the Hereafter. In a rough, coarse, brutal age where the aggressive and cunning were beginning to interpret Nature's ways as favorable to *laissez faire* in economics, the little group of botanically minded men sought only to discover and rejoice. Many of these men were Quakers, with an ear for the inner voice of conscience and instinctual turning from pomp and ceremony.

Prosperous Collinson was a paradox. His infatuation with the wealthy patrons was partly enthusiasm for the flourishing plant even when it was human. Nor did he indiscriminately admire. His adulation went precisely to those men most profuse in personal talents. One and all, the patrons fretted him in one particular; they were slow pay. It was Collinson, the merchant, who was able to cooperate imaginatively with the toilsome necessities of John Bartram. As a go-between Bartram and the patrons, he undertook heavy burdens.

Bartram provided the Londoner with a peep-hole into a paradise. The quest for a paradisal "other place" that had haunted men's minds since Adam's fall, had temporarily found a home in America. Later, with disillusion, it shifted to the South Seas. Collinson's mission, to aid a pilgrim in Eden, had a sharp practical side. And the times were on the side of sharp practical men. The Benjamin Franklin type of shrewdness was destined to win out over the wonder. The new world men struggled to tame, conquer and possess, rather than to feel, and except for a few men like Boone and Bartram, the great beauty of the wilderness passed unseen.

If the little group of inspired botanists was awed by the mystery of the universe, they were also trapped by the need of the day to particularize and to name. Cold reckoning was needed to dispel the windy mists of superstition. The writers of travel books of the Eighteenth Century sought to be lucid, informative and impersonal. Carteret, Cook and Bougainville loved information for its own sake. Penned up in island England, poets were to find this sober stuff intoxicating. Tipped off to the wonders of the world, they roamed in old accounts of travelers as well of that day; read Purchas and Xenophon, and mixed it up with Bartram's noble magnolia and with his son William's crocodiles and the Florida fountains, mysteriously ebbing to secret caverns. Poetic imaginations were due to soar to Elizabethan scope and filter what they took from travel with the boiling mixture of the French revolution, the new found rights of man and the fallibility of kings. The record is in Coleridge and in Wordsworth. Blake rocketed to the vision of the New World. And plants, now documented for us, but then unknown, unnamed travelers, made their journeys.

The name, the name! To give each plant its citizenship, its ancestry and heritage. With the rising sense of the rights of man went a profound quest for identification of every species. Stones found their ancestors in that exploring period of exploring minds and animals a name and history. Crannies were ransacked for minute growths and a yellow wasp for Peter Collinson had a personality as distinct as William Penn's colt, Tamerlane, brought out from England, sired by the celebrated Godolphin Barb.

All the sciences dealing with life forces were then in an elementary stage where classification and direct description were dominant. Though the earth had been blossoming from the beginning of time, men now demanded the precision of accurate knowledge. The tiny flowers and charming animals of medieval paintings and tapestries, so acutely, so lovingly witnessed, were now to be watched from seed time to harvest, from birth to death. Their habits were to be noted; they would be grouped in families, graded and spaced. Not only their external appearance would be more meticulously examined, but their surroundings would be carefully studied. How were they nourished, how did they breathe, where did they thrive and why? Bartram was even to put challenging questions; didn't animals have more understanding than they were accredited; and what about plants? Only look how sensitive they are; must they not *feel*? The inner tissues of plants and animals would be studied minutely for hidden relationships and they would even decide conclusively in this period that plants, like animals, had a male and female sex.

Today a plant is broken down in a laboratory, impersonally, in a quest for elements. The day is past when its locality is news, but in the Eighteenth Century, a plant was a citizen of the world, seen *whole*. Many medical men of the period, first interested in herbs for the benefit of human kind, caught the fever and not stopping at remedies for disease, rioted among exotics or got off on the track of beetles and stones. Some of the botanical devotees were fussy collectors of oddities, getting in on a fashion. Some verged on the lunatic fringe.

Almost without exception, the scientific men of this period were content with a simple faith in the order of Nature. As early as the Seventeenth Century, the French writer, Pierre Bayle, had complained of the ambiguity of the word "Nature," pointing out that eleven different meanings for it can be discovered in Corinthians i. An American scholar has recently distinguished sixty different senses of the term. But in the Eighteenth Century, the prevailing climate of opinion sanctioned, not the ambiguity, but the universal acceptance of Nature and Nature's laws. The laws of Nature were thought to be the laws of Reason, always and everywhere the same, and like the axioms of mathematics had only to be presented to be acknowledged as just and right.

In his study of the background of this period, Basil Willey has stated that the historic role of Nature at this time was to introduce, "not further confusion, but its precise opposites—peace, concord, toleration and progress in the affairs of men, and in poetry and art, perspicuity, order, unity, proportion." The position held its own seeds of disruption but in the first half of the Eighteenth Century, the unifying elements did their work. Clergymen might continue to wrangle over the problem of reconciling Reason and Faith but the scientists, as had Newton, accepted without question the evidence of a Divine Hand.

If one wants to find a name for the type of religious faith held by the group of botanists, to identify them as

87

Deists would most nearly describe it. They seem to have accepted, without question, one universal God, and to be uninterested in petty differences of religious opinion. Nature was heavenly sunshine to a man like Bartram. He did not want to quibble over religious controversies which he considered "unhealthy exercises." There was too much to be done and the revelation was not to be found so much in a book of the Old Testament as in the wonders around him. Like the earlier Sir Thomas Browne, his mind raced to the altitudes where he might glorify God by glorifying his works.

With the great surge of optimism, the tragic sense of life began a steady decline. In the new world "where the moon looks larger than in Europe," life might be hard in one place but there was always "the other place" offering bountiful horizons. Movement took the place of resignation and repentance. A more hopeful but shallower conception of life crept in. Soil was mined ruthlessly; it was easier to move on than to replenish. Sturgeon were pursued by torchlight in the Hudson and clubbed to death; clouds of pigeons were demolished like so many noisome insects. And to cut off the Indian source of food and thus starve him out, the buffalo was hunted down on the great plains, almost to the last buffalo.

The kind and knowing Collinson had intimations of disaster. In his London home he worried for the day when his cherished tortoises would be no more. He was troubled about the quantity of beaver skins he saw in London markets. What will become of the beaver? His Quaker conscience smarted over the white treatment of the Indians. He asked his friend, Bartram—so un-quakerlike in his belligerency toward the Redskin in his later years—how he would have liked to be served in such a fashion, pushed off, deprived of his land, cheated with broken promises. But such rhetoric was powerless to alter the fateful course.

The centuries that followed the Renaissance had liberated the acquisitive impulses, also in the name of Nature, and severed economic ethics from control by any comprehensive conception of the ultimate purpose of human living. The law of Nature became a sanction for the spoils of the world.

CHAPTER V

WHEN THOREAU began to speak out plainly in the Nineteenth Century, he put into precise language many of the feelings and thoughts, some of the attitudes toward man and Nature, that had ruled Bartram's life. He said, "Man is but the place where I stand, and the prospect hence is infinite. It is not a chamber of mirrors which reflect me." By the infinite, he did not intend the Kingdom of God of Cotton Mather, any more than Bartram did. Such a conception would have been too exclusive for Thoreau or Bartram. For one thing it smelled too strong of brimstone. The Puritan sanctuary had been cleansed of offending Quakers by whippings, finings, burnings of the hands, cutting off ears and putting to death over a ten-year period beginning in 1665. Such treatment had led to the opening up of Pennsylvania to the Quakers by William Penn. Thoreau's infinity had no exclusiveness about it. It included ALL and it was the business of his life to come as close to as much of the whole as he could.

Thoreau's mind wandered freely among the fragments of the past; Buddha was as welcome as Jesus. When he walked forest paths and saw the fallen leaves of hemlock, golden as grain, his mind took flight. Time was not to be measured by work and sleep, by getting and spending. In thought, he could circle the globe and the heavens. Though his steps might haunt Concord, his imagination visited with Socrates or entered the sacred groves where the Vegetation Gods were once worshiped.

John Bartram approaches the same universal embrace. He doesn't seem to have had much chance to pursue old philosophies but he knew the Bible. His inclination was to skirt the whole field. For him, philosophy was to be lived from the center of existence. His acts were prosaic if stripped to their essentials. Digging, hoeing, ploughing, riding, walking, wading streams, making ditches, planting, sorting seeds, packing roots and plants for England. Handling animals and insects gingerly; killing rattlesnakes regretfully. If there was reading to do, other than botanical subjects, it had better be done in winter. But his feelings and outlook were extraordinarily catholic, not hitched to any post. Certainly not to the post of a dogmatic hereafter. It was the grain of realization, of instant life, caught when the seed ripened, that he sought.

His imagination enjoyed backward and forward flights. The tiny shell found hardened in a rock—what had it been once and how did it come here? The small and fabulously constructed living creatures, what might they become in time? A fossil? He believed the day might come when the elk would be as extinct as the dodo or the dragon.

He may never have heard of the Mithraic cult. "The gods were everywhere and mingled in all the events of daily life. The fire which cooked the means of nourishment for the believers and which warmed them; also the air which they breathed, and the day which shone for them, were objects of their homage. . . . The stars in the sky, the wind that whispered in the foliage, the spring or brook which hastened murmuring to the valley, even the earth which the believer trod under his feet, were in his eyes, divine." In Franz Cumont's description, you come close to Bartram's feelings if you substitute the word God for gods. But there is an important distinction between the views of those worshipers and Bartram's views. The independence of his mind could resist the emotional effects of the great impression and set free the reflective faculties necessary for observation.

Man was entering into a new and independent relation to Nature without which no foundation could be laid for science. If man's divorce from Nature had begun, Bartram was not the man to sense it. Science held no terrors for him, only light.

The spirit of his contemplation of the wilderness was not typical. Tough, the early colonists certainly were; they could suffer bitter hardships, contrive and invent. But they were fearful of that wall of green. Its immensity over-powered them; Indians were the very imps of Satan. The enormity of their tasks engulfed them. Who can say it did not take valor to plant corn in a forest clearing? The soil had to be tamed for daily bread. Nature must be broken. They were still at it, breaking nature, up to Thoreau's day and of course, beyond, so that he could say, "The civilized man regards the pine tree as his enemy. He will fell it and let in the light, grub it up and raise wheat and rye there. It is no better than fungus to him." As an inevitable corol-lary to such furious industry, "the Yankee has no leisure to touch his hat to you, even if he were so disposed."

Huddling in clusters along the coast, the early colonists

dug in, where they stood, while the random few pushed on. The great risk—to leave the homeland of Europe—had been taken; afterwards came the urge to stay put, to make safe and to wait. Inadvertently, to destroy; to rush blindly upon the dream and devour it.

At a time when the common passion was to get and to hold, Bartram emerged as one who wanted first to *see*, and after that, to *say*. He did not share the basic mood of the colonists clinging narrowly to their new foothold. He did not speak for them. The voice they listened to was Benjamin Franklin's.

The penny might be taken for Franklin's symbol; *Thrift* the slogan to drive home an uneasy sense of insecurity. Stay put, dig in, hoe, save, be cautious. The advice of a squire gallivanting off to Europe on the next packet. His shrewdness forecast trouble ahead! His preachment, that man must secure himself from the snares of tomorrow, bid the day go! Opposed to this was the beauty and fertility of the wilderness. The forbidden Unknown. They were devoted friends, Franklin and Bartram, and the two names head the list of the founders of the Philadelphia Philosophical Society. No two men could have been less alike in their innerly preoccupations.

Bartram placed his reliance on scientific knowledge as a tool that might help him pierce the darkness surrounding mysteries. In comparison, Franklin appears to toy with its practical manifestations and to foretell the gadget. What did he do with lightning drawn down from the clouds with his kite except to recoil? To fall back upon the safe and solid, upon common sense, which he glorified, sacrificing sensibility. In his own down-to-earth fashion, he did much toward chopping down the flowering wild thing in new world minds that tameness might grow. Thus, he prepared the path for the Nineteenth Century and the conquest of man by the machine.

His advice to John Bartram on the subject of young William Bartram exposes the unresourcefulness of too much practicality. He had another side; he was a wily, accomplished diplomat. But when it came to advice about the future of a young boy, he was as plain as could be. On the knotty problem of launching such a youth, Franklin had stature in the father's mind; he got around, he knew the world. Bartram knew plants and plain farming; he had climbed the tops of our high eastern mountains, had toiled to the fountainhead of rivers. But a boy was not a plant; he had to make his way and Bartram had many children. William was a shy, talented boy in his teens; he had already accompanied his father on his explorations. He was among the first delicately to paint exact representations of American flora and fauna for the delight of Peter Collinson and the London patrons. Foreign botanists of distinction had not hesitated to praise his drawings, but words will not buy boots. Franklin, the worldly wise, can see no prospect for him except to tend a shop or to become a printer. Still, there's not much in printing, Franklin thinks. He's cautious. He is concerned about this boy, and yet, the best he can do is to come up with a crutch. The main thing for William, he thinks, is to get a living, somehow, and then— he can embroider his leisure, if he has any, and pick posies.

William escaped Franklin. He even escaped beyond his father to the refuge of the very Indian whom others feared. Their enemy, his friend.

The solid merchant mentality; how easy for it to dispose of the young fruitful mind! Collinson, too, almost wrecked William's chances. Bartram, tender, touchy, proud, never quite connived at the disposal of his gifted son, and hesitating, loving, allowed the gap for the boy to break through.

He had his own gap to break through beyond the wall of the practical minds of the age. Even Collinson, whimsical, tender, devoted though he was, seems sometimes to be more the solid London merchant than the man of imaginative mind. So young was the study of botany, that tools and precise methods had to be devised; the entire field was open to speculation. Sexuality in plants was a theme for speculation and certitude was still ahead. Books on the subject were few. In 1734 Collinson assures his friend that a complete history of plants is not to be found in any author. He recommends Miller's dictionary of terms and "a few others," unspecified.

The study of botany and the natural sciences was curiously entangled with religious emotions. Some of the enthusiasm of earlier Christian sects—or of the early worshipers of the Vegetation Gods!—crept into the devotions of the new botanists who rapturously embraced the revelations of nature as a first step toward scientific precision. John Ray (1627-1705), usually accounted the founder of modern botany and zoology, was more interested in disposing of the classical arguments for atheism and in proving that Nature was the finished product of Divine Wisdom, than he was in the particularizations which engrossed the Eighteenth Century Linnaeus.

Collinson was among the more conservative; he wrote Bartram that the *Systema Naturae* of Linnaeus was a curious performance for a young man but "his coining a set of new names for plants tends but to embarrass and perplex the study of botany. As to his system, botanists are not agreed upon it. Very few like it. Be that as it may, he is a very ingenious man, and a great naturalist."

From that moment Bartram longed to get hold of this volume or some other work of Linnaeus. Collinson put him off with Parkinson in 1737. He mentions Tournefort and Parkinson as the authorities relied upon for identifying some two hundred specimens sent by Bartram, and in sending him Parkinson, suggests that with this aid and

Miller's dictionary, he can find out any plant with a Latin name. The books were intended as a key to a catalog compiled by Collinson of American plants both acquired and desired.

Dissatisfied with Parkinson, Bartram writes his friend for Tournefort but the too reasonable merchant thinks fifty shillings, the price of the work, too much to lay out. Moreover, he adds what must have been an infuriating bit of complacent advice; "Now thee has got Parkinson and Miller, I would not have thee puzzle thyself with others. Remember Solomon's advice: In the reading of books, there is no end."

It takes five months for this letter to reach Bartram and he answers at once, for he is a man itching to communicate with his friends. With admirable restraint, he postpones answering Collinson's quip on Solomon until he has warmed him with tantalizing bits of information. Panthers, for one thing. They have hotly pursued men on horseback and men on foot. It would be useless to run, for the panther can leap twenty feet. No one has been seized but many are badly frightened. Then he gets down to the business of Solomon and disposes of that gentleman in a few words: "I believe if Solomon had loved women less, and books more, he would have been a wiser and happier man." What's more, he doesn't find that Solomon ever wrote of any plants of humbler growth than the hyssop, so he concludes that he knew as little of mosses as he did of the plants that flourished beyond Mt. Lebanon or in America.

Still he can't get Linnaeus out of Collinson. Nor can he get much satisfaction out of a request for a stronger microscope. James Logan will tell him, advises Collinson, that there is no making a glass to magnify to such a degree as Bartram wants. Besides, he would like to discourage his friend from "too close study." It is a pretty amusement.

"But for me and thee, I think we can't allow it, without prejudice to our other weighty affairs."

Though Bartram sent a phial of spirits containing a flower of sweet gum and one of Pawpaw for Linnaeus at Collinson's request in 1737, he does not seem to have come straight to the man who appears to hold a light to botanical knowledge, until five years later, when, after a visit to his friend, Dr. Colden of Newburgh, he cannot forbear to inform Collinson that the Doctor has a new edition of Linnaeus's *Characteres Plantarum*. He and the Doctor have spent hours in rapturous talk, and, it is evident, that, chiefly through Linnaeus, Colden has come to the greatest knowledge in Botany of any man he has ever discoursed with. And Dr. Colden, quick to sense Bartram's eagerness, has suggested that the best way to get the book is to write Dr. Gronovius in Holland to send it to him.

Dr. Gronovius responded promptly with his own *Index Lapideoe* and he evidently induced Linnaeus to send his *Characteres Plantarum*. But Linnaeus did more; he wrote a "very loving letter" desiring Bartram's correspondence, and like all the other naturalists in Europe, he, too, pines for some curiosities from the new world. Gronovius wants a muskrat skin.

All the curiosities for the eager correspondents had to pass through busy Collinson's hands. He was their postmaster, prying into shipments with a fearful eye. Had the rats chewed up the treasure? Or some tricky sailor made off with a precious root? Would the tumble bug for Sir Hans Sloane arrive alive or dead?

How long did it take him to reach the docks from his office? Then there is his town house, his family, his preoccupied study of his specimens and their arrangements, his moments of rapture when a lily opens. No wonder he occasionally breaks out with annoyance when Bartram complains he has not received a letter as expected. "If my friend, John Bartram, knew better my affairs, my station in life, my public business, many engagements and incumbrances, instead of being in a pet that I answer not the letter he sends by one ship by the next that sails, he would wonder I do so well as I do." But the flow of business cannot dam the desire. He would like six dead wasps to place beside the wasp nest sent earlier. Is there no more Chinquapin? He reproves Bartram: he told him from the first that Chinquapin was wanted. If he had sown it then, there would now be plenty to serve them. It was not to be raised in England for money.

There is the ever pressing need for more patrons. Until the gap can be filled, Bartram is urged to try his luck with four or five of the five-guinea cases, prettily sorted with something of everything; in particular, Pine, Fir, Cedar, Walnut and Hickory. If no one else takes them, he fancies he can dispose of them among London Seedmen. Dr. Dillenius of Oxford has spoken high praise of the shipment sent him and swears that the seeds are so good that he is persuaded Bartram is the only man who ever did things to a purpose.

In spite of his many affairs, he sprinkles compliments generously. He would not have his friend wither for lack of appreciation and all their projects founder. When he reships the specimens intended for Gronovius and Linnaeus, he tells Bartram that he has also advised them "not to forget the pains and travel of the indefatigable John Bartram, but to stick a feather in his cap, who is as deserving as the rest."

Of course, he longs to see the Journal kept by Bartram on his Great Lakes expedition. The brief letter reporting a few observations merely whets his appetite. He is inclined to sniff at Bartram's great magnolia, implying that he has one already. Dr. Mitchell of Urbana sent him a specimen from the stately tree on the plantation of Nicolas Smith on the Rappahannock River, where it was well known and much visited by admirers.

It takes three months for this letter to reach Bartram but he rebounds to its immediacy. His reply is tart. He hopes his find may be different from any that Collinson has yet seen. His friend is sometimes mistaken in specimens. Far from persuaded that his great tree is not unique, he promptly ships a root of it to Collinson, along with several roots of Pawpaw, one fine root of Laurel, full of flower buds, one sod of sweet Persian Iris, one sod of fine creeping *Lychnis* and a sod of *Dracocephalum.* "And pray give Catesby one root of Pawpaw."

Collinson was assuredly mistaken in overestimating the rarity of a *Lychnis* sent to him by Dr. Witt of Germantown. Bartram makes no bones about assuring him he has dignified it too highly. Why, American swamps and low grounds are full of the thing! He had so contemptible an opinion of it, as not to think it worth sending. Nor could he afford it room in his own garden. Possibly the English climate agreed with the specimen sent by Dr. Witt so well that it has now much improved. But if it comes to *Lychnis,* Collinson should see the variety he found in Virginia, growing about five feet high when planted in his own garden, and bearing large spikes of different colored flowers for three or four months of the year. This one is exceedingly beautiful. Then there is another wild one, finely speckled, and striped red on a white ground, with a red eye; the only one of the kind he ever saw.

If these tantalizing, mouth-watering descriptions are not enough to dispose of Dr. Witt and *his* specimen, once and for all, he launches into an account of the "good doctor" whom he visited recently to inquire if he had ever come upon any kind of wild rose that was double. The doctor could not remember finding any. But he did bring out a sample of what had been imposed on him for Snake

Stones, purchased from a great traveler in Spain and Italy. Besides laughing at him, Bartram had taken considerable time to convince him that they were nothing but calcined old horse bones.

As for book learning, Dr. Witt had plenty of it. His library was crowded with a variety of works; Philosophy, Natural Magic, Divinity and even Mystic Divinity! So long as the two men were in the doctor's study, Bartram could not distract Dr. Witt from these fascinating subjects. But there was no denying his understanding of botany and no one could say he was not pliant, facetious and pleasant. But astrology—magic—mystic divinity! Bartram admits that on such subjects he is apt to be troublesome. They will not bear the light. If he handles these fancies more tenderly with Dr. Witt than he would with many others superstitiously inclined, it is out of respect for the man "who has considerable good in him."

Bartram's grip on the world was too close not to recoil from the doctor, who, though a skillful physician and a learned man, yet diverted himself as a "conjurer" and used his mathematical and astronomical learning to cast nativities. Though he might disagree with Dr. Witt and draw aside from his fanciful webs, he did not reject him. A man like Bartram spread the balm of tolerance thick. He saw Dr. Witt, a man twenty-five years his senior, in all his aspects; "the good doctor" was something of a character in his day. He could be solidly practical; he built the first three-storied house in Germantown. He and his neighbor, Pastorius, wrote little poems to one another exalting the beauties of gardening, and tossed them across the hedge separating the properties. When he came to die, at the age of ninety, he left all his property to a family called Wormer, saying they had been kind to him, on his arrival from England as a young man, in giving him a hat, in place of his own, lost on shipboard.

100

What Collinson thought of his friend's summation of Dr. Witt and the rejected *Lychnis,* we shall never know. The men were tactful; some disputed points evaporated in the desert of silence. Collinson could not see eye to eye with Bartram on the question of Linnaeus, but Thoreau, much later, confirmed Bartram's intuitive sanction of the Swedish naturalist by exclaiming, "If you would read books on botany, go to the fathers of the science. Read Linnaeus at once. His *Philosophia Botanica* is simpler, more easy to understand, more comprehensive, than any of the hundred manuals to which it has given birth."

If Bartram ever came upon the little book that Linnaeus wrote to instruct students, it must have been too late to inform him. He had worked out his own techniques early, based on the necessities of his situation. Linnaeus wrote a know-how book for that day, introducing law and order and system, and describing with great economy of words what dress the botanizer should wear, what instruments to carry, what season and hour to observe—"from the leafing of the trees, Sirius excepted, to the fall of the leaf, twice a week in summer, once a week in the spring, from seven in the morning until seven at night"—when to dine, when to rest, whether to go alone or in a crowd; how far to go—two and a half miles at most—what to collect and what kind of observations to make.

This is advice for a saunter not for an assault upon mountains or into virgin forests. In 1738 Bartram traveled 1100 miles in five weeks' time, having rested but one day in all that time, in Williamsburgh. His journey took him through Maryland and Virginia, up the James River to the mountains and over and between the mountains, in many very crooked turnings and windings. He chose to go at the only time for gathering seeds, in autumn, and was lucky in the mild fall which favored the ripening of seeds upon and between the mountains. How he rejoiced at gathering seeds in abundance, many of which had not ripened for several years on account of the early frosts! Beyond the mountains, more seeds in gay profusion and variety.

"The settlers say," he reports to Collinson, "that the ground is covered with delicate beautiful blossoms in the spring which are not to be found after the hot weather comes." Though he carefully put each kind of seed in a separate packet, the roads were so rough that they jolted loose in his saddlebags and hence, by the time they reached London, there was a wild assortment that must be planted at random with no notation except that most of them were perennials.

After such ardent labors, it is not surprising that Bartram came to the sober reckoning and once, at least, protested that he was not amply rewarded for all his pains. Collinson answers him as only a man could who was at such a distance. "Pray, friend John, consider if 21 lb. sterling, returned in goods or money, is a hard case, if it will not make near or quite, or more than 40 lb. a year in your currency. This, I think, will pay for five or six weeks spent annually in thy collection, and hiring a man, and other expenses. Suppose thee art in expense, in thy affair, 10 lb., your currency, per annum, which I don't think, why, to have 30 lb. your currency in circulation in thy affairs, must certainly be a fine thing, and sufficient to content any reasonable person. I know thee art a man of more equity than to desire the subscribers' money for little matters; and on the other hand, thee art so honest to send the most thee can afford to procure for them;—more, they don't desire. Then what reason is there for thee to be uneasy? Pray let me hear no more about it."

What could Bartram answer? He was committed to the passion; give it up, he could not. He had children, a mortgage on his property, but the journeys through the green seas must continue. A plant might be small and mild; it was the unknown and he must capture it. Suppose it should vanish in the rush of colonists at their busy toil of chopping down trees, burning clearings? First to *see,* to bear witness. So that man could say, yes, that fair flower once bloomed. That tree had leaves that smelled of cinnamon.

Though he was trapped and knew he would continue as he had gone, regardless, he answers Collinson and to the point. "Thee supposes," he writes, "that I spend five or six weeks in collections for you, and that ten lbs. will defray all my annual expenses; but I assure thee, I spend more than twice that time, annually; and ten lbs. will not, at a moderate expense, defray my charges abroad—beside my neglect of business at home, in following harvest and seed time. Indeed, I was more than two weeks in gathering the small acorns of the willow-leafed Oak, which are very scarce, and falling with the leaves, so that daily I had to rake up the leaves and shake the acorns out, before they were devoured by the squirrels and hogs; and I reckoned it good luck if I could gather twenty under one tree and hardly one tree in twenty bore any. Yet I don't begrudge my labors; but would do anything reasonable to serve you. But by your letter, you are not sensible of the fourth part of the pains I take to oblige you."

He might have let it go at that. The situation deserved it. But genuine communion between friends was at stake. This too had a value in Bartram's eyes, beyond price. Thoughtfully he added a postscript to his statement of the facts: "Now, my kind and generous friend, I shall return thee my hearty thanks for thy care and pains, and the many good offices thee hath done for me; and further, if thee finds any expressions in my letter a little out of the way, thee will not take it in the wrong sense. I assure thee, I bear thee a great deal of good will; or if thee thinks I am too short and imperfect in explaining any subject, which I give thee any account of, pray let me know, and I will satisfy thee according to the best of my knowledge, for I love plain dealing."

He knew his own worth and stood up to it. Though Collinson was only five years Bartram's senior, he often assumed paternal airs. When Bartram was making his first long sortie into Virginia, Collinson did not hesitate to tell him to get "the drugget clothes made up," that he may not disgrace him or "thyself." He takes pains to add; "I should not esteem thee less, to come to me in what dress thou will,—yet these Virginians are a very gently, well-dressed people—and look, perhaps, more at a man's outside than his inside. Pray go very clean, neat and handsomely dressed to Virginia. Never mind thy clothes; I will send more another year."

What wonder, then, that at a later date, Bartram rejects scornfully the present of a cap from Collinson because it had a hole in it! Collinson muses in his reply, not without fondness for the man who sometimes seems unpredictable; "What very much surprised me, to find thee, who art a philosopher, prouder than I am. My cap, it is true, had a small hole or two on the border, but the lining was new. Instead of giving it away, I wish thee had sent it back to me. It would have served me two or three years, to have worn in the country, in rainy weather."

This little battle in pride fought before the invisible ramparts of the almost legendary Patrons was only a minor flurry compared to Samuel Johnson versus Lord Chesterfield. The pride of ability, as manifested in Bartram and Johnson, dared to stand up to the tradition and pride of place. The Patron was soon to be on the way out; a defunct mechanism in a period of brighter expectations and more flexible arrangements. But at this period, England, itself, stood in the relation of a Patron to the colonists who were already beginning to show their mettle and resentment.

Perhaps the average Englishman showed no more understanding of the perplexing new problems or aspirations of the colonists than Lord Petrie had of the true difficulties suffered by John Bartram when he did not pay up promptly. A modern English writer, J. H. Plumb, in his *England in the Eighteenth Century* seems to think that the majority of the population of England did not think about America at all except as a dumping ground for thieves, bankrupts and prostitutes for which they received tobacco in return.

Even Collinson was of a divided mind. He could fall into raptures on the subject of the new world vegetables but when it came to articles for *trade*, shared the obstinate prepossession cherished in the mother country against anything coming from the colonies. Quick to see the commercial advantages of ginseng for the China trade, he advised Bartram to find as many plants as possible, plant them, and raise what he could from seed. China valued it above everything and Collinson was certain it would prove a profitable commodity. He had compared the American ginseng with the Chinese and found it in all respects the same, but because of his peculiar prejudices, he warned Bartram to keep the transactions between them secret, fearful that if the Chinese learned of the source, it might damage the bargain. He was wrong; such notions were not shared in China and ginseng found a ready acceptance. But it took a long time and a revolution to obliterate the concept of American inferiority in British minds.

Collinson never seemed to grasp the significance of the immense distances that Bartram must conquer to secure the varieties of seeds in demand. Nor could he comprehend that an assistant for Bartram was not to be had for the asking in the new world. Such as were available to Bartram were "certain to deceive him." He came more and more to depend upon himself until such time as his sons

105

were old enough to help him. Once, he hinted to Collinson that a good man might come out of England for this purpose, but Collinson turned him off with an astonished, "An assistant such as thee would like, is not to be had, for none care to leave their native land but those from their bad principles and morals, cannot live in it."

The suspicion finally arises that Collinson wanted sound seeds, good roots, practical observations from Bartram but no more. When it came to speculation, he should leave that, apparently, to the British. More than once, a slight huffiness puffs up between the two friends. But Bartram is not the man to be banged down by opposition. Not when it comes to a subject on which he feels his ground.

As time went by and his own proficiency increased, he was more reluctant to take the word of some botanist in England as gospel truth. He does not hesitate to discount even Dillenius of Oxford who named a plant sent to him by Bartram, a borage. "I think my pretty plant, just in flower, has no affinity to a borage, save only barely in the shape of a single flower," he protested to Collinson. "I believe it as much a new genus as any plant that ever was sent out of America; and not the only one that adorns that spacious vale, 600 miles in length, S.W. by West, in which I have gathered my finest autumnal flowers; and where by report of the inhabitants, it is like as if Flora sported in solitary retirement as Sylva doth on the Katskill Mts., where there is the greatest variety of uncommon trees and shrubs that I ever saw in such a compass of ground."

Philip Miller, author of the dictionary of botanical terms, and the man who developed the ancient Physic Gardens at Chelsea to one of the finest botanic gardens in Europe, also quarreled with Bartram's account of American pines. There is a wrathy note in Bartram's rejection of his quibbling; "As our friend Miller seems to question my account of our Pines, I now tell thee, I generally take care to speak the truth—even to those that I think will bestow no more pains of examination, than to tell me it is not so—to whom silence suits better than arguments, as ignorance doth to their capacity; but as I have a great opinion of Miller's learning and judgment, I am engaged in duty and friendship to inform him the best I can at present."

This is no flabby selfless man speaking. I take it he was the exact opposite: a man all for himself, but gently, with love, unwilling to endure the smallest fracture of his way of doing. His patience allowed him to listen, to question, but to hold tight when he believed he was in the right. He knew his trees; he lived with them, at all hours of the day, at all seasons. In comparison, what is a man in London who merely handles a few seeds, fingers a few specimens?

There are surprises for him and he welcomes a good surprise. For Miller's benefit, he notes that all American pine cones are two summers and one winter in perfecting and casting off their seed, but for one species, the subject of his study, and this opens not until the second or third year after the cones seem perfectly ripe. To his surprise, he has observed upon one branch, all the cones of three, four and five years growth, at one and the same time.

The entire field of pines now began to engross him. He soon found that there was no help to be had from either ancient or modern authors, "they having taken no particular observation worth notice." He must be his own explorer in this uncharted region. The tree draws him strangely to a kind of worship. He yearns to define the perfections of this vegetative growth with its honorable past, lost in myth. Perhaps he did not know that the tree was poetically addressed by men of the middle ages with the title of "mistress," but his deep feelings tangle with an earlier folk. In spite of his rationalism, he would have understood the legends that attributed man's very origin to trees and made a ritual of death by burial in a hollow trunk. Language bears witness, as it so often must, of the forgotten source; in German, the word for coffin became *Totenbaum.*

He soon discovered that whatever he might do along the line of examining the true distinguishing characters of our forest trees would be found to have a flaw, in one way or another, in London. His plan to gather particulars of evergreens in New England and "York," with a further study of oaks and hickories, began with the Hop Hornbean. And he sends as a sample of his endeavors, his account to Collinson, as "a nearly perfect description," to be followed by specimens and descriptions of oaks and evergreens.

The Londoners put their heads together over Bartram's output, and whatever their final decision, their first response wounded him. He replies proudly, "Good grammar, and good spelling may please those that are more taken with a fine superficial flourish than real truth; but my chief aim was to inform my readers of the true, real, distinguishing characters of each genus, and where, and how, each species differed from one another of the same genus. And if you find that my descriptions are not agreeable with the specimens, pray let me know where the disagreement is, and send my descriptions back again that I may correct them, or if they prove deficient, that I may add further observations, for I have no copy, and you have the original. So by all means, send my descriptions back, for I have forgot what I wrote . . ."

It is a despairing conclusion—"I have forgot what I wrote"—and divulges not only his many difficulties but the feelings of a man who has no true audience. But harassed as he was, he never dimmed his light. If London cast shadows upon one observation, he lighted another and raised it high.

The shells found imbedded in rock by Bartram far inland and upon mountain tops on his journey to the Great Lakes had aroused curiosity in Collinson who was constantly airing hypothetical notions as to their origins. He favored the opinion that ocean waves once washed them up, but how, is beyond him. Bartram longed for a better microscope to examine more minutely the composition of the stones he picked up on his travels and lugged, over mountain and across rivers, to his own study. But even without that better eye, he dares to speculate. Typically, the more timid Collinson is inclined to whittle it down as preposterous. "No one doubts," he declared, "that the marble of Tadmor was hewn out of the neighboring mountains; but thy notion of its formation by a mixture of slime or mud with what thee calls nitreous or marine salts, enters not into my comprehension. So thou hath it all to thyself." But he is willing to submit the account to Dr. Fothergill who will pass upon it.

Bartram is so sure of himself that he joyfully accepts the challenge of Dr. Fothergill's verdict. "I hope, if I can stand the test of his trial, I shall come out like gold, well purified," he answered Collinson. "I had rather undergo, now, a thorough purging—a long fusion, than to have any dross left behind." And in full good humor, and as if he knew that future geologists would vindicate him, he added, "My dear worthy friend, thee can't bang me out of the notion that limestone and marble were originally mud, impregnated by a marine salt, which I take to be the original of our terrestrial soils."

At this point, he may have wrapped his letter in dry tobacco leaves for the voyage to England. If he did not, mischievous insects were likely to chew large holes in the most vital parts of his communications.

But better a letter with holes than none at all. Traffic on the high seas was perilous. Bartram's Great Lakes

Journal, lost for years, testified to that fact. Risky or not, Bartram occasionally pined to make a trip to England where he might meet some of his correspondents in the flesh. He was so eager to justify such a journey that he drew up an argument for Peter Collinson to prove how valuable such a trip might be for their botanical projects. For one thing, he could personally escort trees and shrubs that were so delicate they could not safely make the voyage without him. "Only one who understands them, should travel with them, to care for them in the passage," he wrote. But he had hardly put down this inspired thought when he was forced to reflect upon the size of his family. How could he leave so many small children and none of them yet grown enough to take care of his affairs? It set him off on a favorite tirade about servants, who, "in this country, strive to do as little work, and spend as much time as they can in carelessness."

Impatient with unreliable servants, Bartram was contemptuous of the American great who might have stood to him in the same relation as the Patrons of England, had they the foresight or the taste. Franklin even tried to help Bartram by putting an ad in his Philadelphia paper, listing trees, shrubs and plants that might be made available for American customers. Bartram does not seem to have had much response, for his bitterness against the "short-sightedness" of Americans is peppered through his letters for a period of years. Collinson went so far as personally to recommend Bartram to Thomas Penn, the son of William Penn and the present proprietor, suggesting that he allow Bartram to do for him what he was performing to the advantage of the great estates of England. Bartram was hopeful that "he would please be so honorable as to allow me an annual salary, worth while, to furnish his walks with all the natural productions of trees, shrubs and plants, which grow in our four governments." But he soon discovered that Thomas Penn was more interested in land speculation than in conserving nature. "Our proprietor is almost as crafty as coveteous. He won't sell land, because people being necessitated for land to live upon, raiseth its price prodigiously, so that, in a few years, he may sell it at an extortionate ground rent."

The corruption of the man-nature relationship had bitten deep, this early, along the settled border of a continent as yet mysterious, untamed, unbroken. The coastline was hardening fast. This was a new world and the ancient Indian concept of the land was to vanish with the Indian. Tecumseh could not imagine setting a price on land. For him, *the earth lived*. What, sell land! As well sell air and water!

CHAPTER VI

THE ENORMOUS PROFUSION of natural riches of early America did not blind Bartram to the danger of waste. He was over anxious about some small plants. If he found a specimen one year which he failed to discover the next, he seems to have been caught in a panic of despair. This is the last he will ever see of that special bit of goodness! Torn between a farmer's ardent devotion to the soil and what it might produce and the fear that the farmer's ax might chop some rare tree, he was often on tenterhooks of concern. His haste to beat the settler into the wilderness may be accounted for by his fear of that settler's destructiveness. Cattle chewed the tender grasses growing under trees and thus eliminated from a botanical map some species that he would never lay eyes upon again! Or so he was persuaded.

A portrait of John Bartram has to be a kind of tapestry with more in it than the solid figure of the man, a little above average size, with animation and sensibility strongly marked in the rather long face. Like the medieval tapestries there should be animals sporting through thickets and the ground needs to be sprinkled with thousands of tiny flowers. Somewhere there should be a vista of his house, taking the place of the castles, bedecked with banners, in the old tapestries; his solid barn, his greenhouse and certainly his many children. But such a pattern would not illuminate his anxieties even if an Indian were allowed to peer from behind a tree, or a tiny warship indicated in a harbor. Not that there is any suggestion that he lay awake at night stewing in an abyss of worriment. The age was too hopeful to allow for that; Bartram too sure in his grip of his world. But it would be a mistake to imagine that his life was spent in an Arcadian simplicity. The physical magic of the fresh, robust, youthful-minded society of early America is apt to blind us to the changes even then going on, the blunders perpetrated.

Like any character in a good piece of fiction, Bartram's existence was affected by the behavior, the manners, the customs, money sense and unspoken assumptions of his day. He shared the mistake of all the rationalists; their view of the human situation was defective. There was no allowance for the imponderables or for what Freud was to call the "unconscious." Men were supposed to be self-sufficient, upstanding and ripe with integrity; Bartram was. He despised laziness and incompetence; how could he help doing otherwise? But in an age when a good many men were constantly picking a lawsuit with a neighbor, Bartram refrained from ever getting into such a petty quarrel. On the question of slavery, he was among the first to testify against it and to set his own slaves free as an example.

As a colonial reporter he was primarily concerned with the physical appearance of the country he traveled. But the very nature of his calling, a shipper of plants and seeds to big estates in England, forced him also to be something of a merchant. But no one can say that he had the typical merchant's mentality; he wasn't out to buy and sell in the ordinary way. He was rather out to place his plants in an advantageous spot where they might thrive to their full glory.

When he looked at a new plant he really *saw* it. He saw what it looked like and he examined closely the kind of soil in which it stood. Was it in shade or sun? Though he, too, yielded to the rapture of reeling off names of species found and trees observed, he was not chained to mere enumeration. He respected figures but he was not stunned by them.

One has only to compare him to other travelers roaming along the coast to see the difference. They appear to be monotonously of one mind. They can't stop counting. They can't stop reckoning up size. When they look at a hog they see porkchops. They admit, a bit enviously, that the deer are bigger in America than in England.

But what a scene! A thousand buffalo grazing at Blue Licks. Elk the size of a small ox. Fields and woods dyed red with wild strawberries on Manhattan. Cows, sheep, horses and hogs, prodigiously multiplied, sporting in the thick, juicy grasses. Heath hens, by the hundreds; pigeons by the thousand, lying in a welter of dyed feathers at the markets, to be had, as many as you please, for a penny. It is all on a quantitative level; men and women are mere drops of water in an oceanic reckoning, the faceless naught in the 200,000 population of 1700 and the 2,000,000 of 1790.

Say the word "grass" to one of these reporters and out spurts a list of names; cane, clover, rye, pea, buffalo, orchard, spear, blue and crab grass. Venture to mention "Susquehanna" and he hauls in a string of fish; shad, salmon, roach, trout, cub, sunfish, perch. Say "turkey" and you will get forty pounds, the legendary weight of one of these fabulous birds. Ask where he dined and he will reel off what he had to eat, all in one sitting; salmon, veal, beef, mutton, fowl, ham, roots, pudding and one-half pint of madeira. He will add the price, for it is part of his mood to attach value to what he gets. The list above cost five shillings and with it came breakfast, tea, supper and bed. The bed is the sour note; it had bugs in it.

Where is the music in the air, like distant horns, that Thoreau heard? These fellows complain of the deafening noise of the bullfrogs. They carp at the birds for eating peaches before they are ripe; "so long as there are so many birds, there won't be much fruit to ripen." The grass is so rich that the cattle are fed on it without any corn. Forty acres of pasture land fattened forty-one oxen in one year for the Philadelphia market. But one Britisher adds, "The beef isn't so good as ours."

"Mr. Brighton and his father are laying out all the money they can in new lands." They say lands may be sown ten years to rye, ten years to wheat, *without any manure,* and crops never fail to be good. "Mr. Bingham bought land near Philadelphia in 1783 for 850 lbs. and ten years later, it yields 850 lbs. per annum, and *he has never laid out 20 lbs. upon it.*" Three houses were buying up all the land in Pennsylvania they could meet with, giving three shillings six pence to seven shillings an acre. Morris and Nicholson, Bingham and Willings, Cazenove & Co., a Dutch house, were the leaders in the transactions.

If one of these roving reporters is invited to a Philadelphia home, he sees the furniture: "Dined with Mrs. Bingham. Magnificent house and gardens in the best English style; elegant, even superb furniture. Drawing-room chairs from Seddons, London, of the newest taste, the back in the form of a lyre, adorned with festoons of crimson and yellow silk; the curtains of the room, a festoon of the same; the carpet, one of Moore's most expensive patterns, the room papered in the French taste after the style of the Vatican at Rome. In the garden, a profusion of lemon, orange and citrus trees, and many aloes and other exotics." But where is Mrs. Bingham? She is without a face.

Human beings, like cattle, are noted for their fertility. "Dined at the home of Mr. Bridgen at his country house, three miles out of New York on the East River. Top dish an excellent fish called a sheepshead, stewed. Mr. Bridgen is the father of eighteen children. Mrs. Beckman, a guest, is the mother of twelve and still appears capable of producing as many more. In Hanover Square, four families made up fifty-two children." Children were a man's wealth. Thomas Budd was frank about it: "A man that has most children, lives best."

It is all fat and juicy lean. Where is the bone, the gristle? John Bartram was gloomy in 1754 when it looked as if the French might attack Philadelphia: "Our Philadelphia people seem at ease and dissolved in luxury. I think two twenty-two gun ships could take the town, in two hours time."

Pick up a newspaper of the day, and it is filled with "facts." Know-how was getting the upper hand. Here's advice on how to make a burning glass out of a piece of ice. Then come the ads:

> To be sold, a servant man's time, he is a Taylor by Trade, a good workman, and has 3 years to serve.

> Just imported to be sold, by Joseph Marks, a parcel of likely Negro boys and girls. Also good Barbadoes Rum.

Then the imports:

> Recently landed: Brass and iron thimbles, cumberland handkerchiefs, Iron Jews harp, felt hats, women's gloves, and mittens, lawn, Irish linen, ribbons, tapes, nails, iron dogs, shovels and tongs, nutmegs, clouting diaper, diaper tapes.

The torrential recital of things and prices inundates. Memory is borne down by weight; pounds and pence are chanted with the urgency of ritual. Oh for a novelist! There should have been a Jane Austen or a writer of Turgeniev's stamp to do a Sportsman's Sketches for us, filled with sighs and scents, with the whirr of birds on the wing and the speech of a solitary settler in the silent pool of a forest clearing.

The first man in that line to come along was Charles Brockden Brown, the novelist, who was to visit William Bartram in his later years at the family farm. But he comes late in the century and his themes, though American, seem overweighted with matter. He has the distinction, however, of being a novelty for the period. Unless we count the editors of newspapers, no one, literally no one, in the new world, had ever before set up as a writer with the determination to live or die, if need be, by this talent. His dedication was single-minded and complete but he died at thirty-nine of tuberculosis, in the town of Belville on Passaic River, and at a time when a choir of travelers was assuring the world that many citizens lived to be ninety. Seldom, they chanted, were to be seen a blind man or one stricken with gout or palsy. But an asylum for lunatics was firmly established in Philadelphia, filled mostly with women, the majority from Ireland.

A schoolmaster at a college in Flatbush sounded the note: "We do not want to breed up men of deep speculation and abstract knowledge, for a man among us is no more valuable than as he is useful in improving the state of the country."

Here a shoe, there a plough, but seldom a full-sized man to wear the one or to use the other. To think and feel, simultaneously, was not the fashion. In the abundance of material, facts became the property of the man of sense and the aggressive man of sense forced the pattern.

But there were leaks in this practical outlook, all along the line. Robustious high spirits broke ranks. When Bartram was still a child, Madam Knight journeyed in 1704 from Boston to New York along the route now followed by the shore-line train. She was the daughter of a Charlestown shopkeeper who moved across the river to Boston without bettering himself. Marriage brought her little luck. Her husband, an American agent for a London merchant, died abroad, after many long absences from home. The widow kept a little shop on the North side; taught youngsters, copied letters and legal matters. Like John Bartram, she set down her daily observations even when her bones were aching.

Madam Knight let her feelings out; her nose is extravagant; her body luxuriates in its aches. She is as unashamed of her fear of goblin trees on a dark night as she is of her good appetite. There is little to buy on this trip except a miserable meal or two at an inn, so her account is devoid of the fashionable practice of dealing in sums. There was too much spitting and chewing to suit her (Charles Dickens was to echo her sentiments more than a century later). She scolds at the general gawkiness of the inhabitants in the town where she stops and sighs for more education and elegant conversation. When she arrives in New York she falls into the vice of the usual traveler and chants a recital of the dishes served at the table; there was always an array of five or six different dishes and a choice of beer and wine. Food ranks high with her, as it does with all the travelers; it becomes something of a symbol, is colored with sentiment and hints at more complex desires. Bulking against it are the rigors of weather, and water, water everywhere. No journey can be made without fording treacherous streams which seem always to overflow at Madam Knight's approach. Her return journey to Boston crackles with frost and ice, creaking and mushing under her horse's hoofs.

But by the end of the century, comments on America had taken another turn. Mrs. Anne Grant is closer to Bartram's enchanted vision of the universe than she is to the practical, down-to-earth Madam Knight. Writing at a distance, in England, of her childhood impressions in the new world, she is more romantic than the usual commentator and at the same time more reflective. Born in Glasgow, she settled with her parents at Claverack-on-the-Hudson where they lived during the middle of the Eighteenth Century. One may come upon her as an elderly woman in De Quincey's "Literary Reminiscences." Meeting her with her daughter on a journey by stagecoach, he was much impressed with her conversation and her kindness to him, a person then unknown, while she was "an established wit and receiving incense from all quarters."

When Mrs. Grant wrote her book on her early years in America, she was at a safe distance, both in time and space. She had no ax to grind. Unlike many travelers in the colonies, she was not out to acquaint her government "with the true state of the dominions." Like the poets, Blake and Wordsworth, she felt her childhood keenly; all was freshness, all was beauty. Under the burning glass of that early vision she places a rural idyll.

There is no misspelling, no crudities. But the frank explosiveness and gusto of Madam Knight have vanished. Here is a reflective woman of seventy, looking backward.

Her memory has become dream and the dream partakes of the perennial quest for paradise. She is in the company of the seekers for the "Western Isles," the same that started Columbus on his voyages, and that, forever sought, moved ever westward, and became myth. Flickering as light, haunting as music, the dream of a magic place became the pulse of a people. So seldom *here,* so inevitably, *there.*

She catches the dream for a brief moment in time.

The birds and water. Water to bathe in, in the inverted dome of a rock pool where it houses the small brown minnow, the pale trailing mosses, the curious bright stone. Water to drink, bursting from the hillside to tumble into the shell of one's hand. Water to replenish the earth, in rivers, boiling over fallen trees, oozing out over meadows. Water to feed from, dense with urgent salmon and sturgeon, layer on layer, fin to fin.

The continuity is in the water; it embraces, erases, renews. Its innocency purges the valleys; the crimes are for the gloomy woods. The birds fly along the hopeful routes of water; they funnel up from the terror-struck woods in a fountain and spray, lightly as falling leaves, upon the bushes and the trees. On their great migrations they move in thunder clouds that shut out the sun; they are the eclipse. Their slaughter becomes ritual, seems to partake of some ancient rite, a sacrifice to the worship of the sun, the God of Plenty.

The fruitful little town is caught in the arms of water; it seems so tranquil, so still, it is hardly real; more a reflected image in motionless water than something of the land.

The little town she pictures is a toy, sharp with crisp newness. It is the universal image of a green fresh place, the same that Wordsworth wrote of in *Lines composed above Tintern Abbey*:

> . . . these pastoral farms,
> Green to the very door; and wreaths of smoke
> Sent up, in silence, from among the trees!

Every house has its garden, its well and every family owns a cow; every cow has a bell. In the daytime, the cows congregate in a common pasture; in the evening they make a tranquil return with their bells chiming in the evening air. All the more hardy plants grow in the common field, in rows, amidst the hills of Indian corn, on a fertile plain three miles long. Each family hoes its share. Cabbages, potatoes, succulent roots and gourds grow to great size in the sheltering corn and are excellent eating. Strawberries are wild in the woods; family gardens, neat but small. "A woman in very easy circumstances and abundantly gentle in form and manners would sow and plant and rake incessantly." The women also raised flowers, "worthy of Paradise."

Life in the town goes with the rhythm of vegetation. A little girl of eight may read Milton and Bailey's Dictionary in the morning, sew in the afternoon, and in the evening, when company arrives, be sent upstairs to the "waste room." Boys are grave and gay; they would astonish you with their knowledge of plants and soils. A twelve-year-old could point to a wood of red oak and inform you, that, when grubbed up, the earth here will be loam and sand and make good Indian corn ground. This chestnut wood, abounding with wild strawberries, is the best soil for wheat. That poplar grove will not be worth clearing; the soil is wet and cold. But the soil of a hickory wood is rich and deep and certain not to run out.

Wide views of nature were laid open to all, from infancy. Children bathed in water and lore. They knew the uses of wintergreen, Solomon's Seal (a purifier of the blood), and Gold Thread, a small vine with roots like thread, that made a fine dye and was a good wash for sore mouths. The use of these was learned from the Indians.

Boys, unpampered, rooted in the soil, bred to hunting and fishing, sowing and reaping, set about life's business early. They married young. Marlowe's "love at first sight" was not the rule; boys and girls knew one another from birth, tested each other through years of acquaintance and married "in noble simplicity, dignified candour." The pleasures of the young people were shared in a group. Skating and sledge runs were diversions in winter; in summer, the picnic began at sunrise. The whole party took to canoes for a trip "up the river." Until nine or ten o'clock they dipped their paddles briskly until they came to a spot judged suitable. The boys then made fires and went after fish and game. The girls occupied themselves with workbaskets while the boys foraged. They brought with them tea, sugar, rum and fruit. After a big meal, boys and girls gathered wild strawberries to add to the game and fish. It was "counted a reflection to come home empty handed."

There is more tribe than town here. Being together, working together made for a safe harvest, safer journeys, and Mrs. Grant would have us know, joyful communion. Not until one comes upon the descriptions of William Bartram, during his sojourn among the Indians of Florida, will one find so idyllic an image of group living. The old lived to be 90 or 100. Beggars were unheard of. Orphans were never neglected. Maidens, bachelors and childless couples adopted orphans and treated them as their own children.

But in this Homeric world of sterling virtues and simple tastes, Nature was lavish; its wasteful profligacy courted wanton habits of destruction. The honking of geese arouses the hunting blood; carnage and high revelry follow the migrations of birds. The hoe and the spade are dropped for the gun. A drunken gaiety ripples through the town and beyond its borders. When a bright morning darkens with a vast sultry cloud of pigeons, spiraling down to feast at dawn "on a plant more luxuriant than the wild carrot," the inhabitants of the village pour out of their houses, running, shouting, firing madly. Only a windy morning can save the birds from carnage; then they fly so high no shot can reach them. On a cloudy windless day the "slaughter was incredible."

Up until the last great killing at Petoskey, Michigan, in 1878, the pigeons offered an apparently endless plenty to this continent. Alexander Wilson reported them in Kentucky early in the Nineteenth Century, "flying with great steadiness and rapidity, at a height beyond gunshot, in several deep strata. From right to left, as far as the eye could reach, the breadth of this vast procession extended, seeming everywhere crowded. It was then half past one. About four o'clock in the afternoon, the living torrent above my head seemed as numerous and extensive as ever." Wilson reckoned that in this one torrent there were two billion pigeons. Audubon witnessed a flight in 1813 that lasted for three days.

Anne Grant tells of pigeons in pies, roasted, stewed, broiled and used in every fashion that the ingenuity of the cook might devise. She had witnessed the broken stride of the birds and two weeks later the chase turned to the sturgeon. At the height of the season every canoe was launched, at night, for the pursuit over the dark water. Torches flared and the great run was followed for two days until the canoes rode low with the catch and the men returned. Fish ruled the table as game had earlier. Feast followed feast; what could not be eaten was dried and salted.

What appeared to be endless quantity in the new world

became enduring fable. The fable mesmerized men's minds, challenging the individual to a pure and strong affirmation in one direction; in another, leading to wild egotism, anarchic, destructive exploitation. The wasteful predatory industries of the Nineteenth Century had their beginnings in the lushness of the earth as the migratory Europeans, pinched in their forsaken homelands, found it. In the contest, more than the swan took chances. More than the wild pigeon perished. What became of the Indian whom Sir Francis Drake, in an earlier century, had described as "an Arcadian people, whose natures could hardly be told save through the language of music, peoples joyously hospitable, who seemed as free as birds, whose speech and colors were like the warbling and plumage of birds?" In Anne Grant's day, the Indian had become a menace, judged frightful by some, corrupted and treacherous by others, a creature fallen, who, according to Mrs. Grant, "must be seen in his natural state to have any idea what a noble animal man is."

It was an age of raw new settlements, and of wanderings. Here appeared brawlers and boasters, a wretched wrangling class of frontiersmen and Indian killers from whom Daniel Boone fled to push alone into the wilderness to the grateful company of Indians. And here also appeared the proud, heroic individuals, touchy in their defiant self-reliance.

After her rapturous account of the village of her youth, Mrs. Grant's final sober summation of the new world is surprising. Unlike Harriet Martineau, she did not despise Americans as low born boors, thus confirming her countrymen in their notions of superiority. But mature years in England did bring her to the point where she concluded that "self-interest, eagerly grasping at pecuniary advantages, seems to be the ruling principle of this great continent. Love of country hardly exists here. An American loves his country, or prefers it rather, because its rivers are wide and deep, and abound in fish; because he has forests to retire to, if the god of gainful commerce should prove unpropitious on the shore." Few Englishmen found this country sympathetic until Leslie Stephen came to America in 1863, but there were exceptions. Joseph Priestley, the preacher and scientist, whose vision of Paradise lay in a conception of the future rather than in any antique golden age or state of Nature, found a refuge in the new world after a mob burned his home and laboratory in Birmingham and though Coleridge never reached these shores, he at one time planned a hopeful colony to be founded on the banks of the Susquehanna which he fondly imagined would be visited by the tropical birds of William Bartram's travels.

Madam Knight and Mrs. Grant had been inspired amateurs, with no compulsion to add or subtract, and no ambition to specialize. But the scenes they describe were very much a part of the world Bartram confronted. The richness they related was all there; the enchantment and the terror were as real as any "fact" a different type of observer might choose to relate. The scenes they coped with were small; the territory confined. Bartram was to cover vast distances, he was to search for definite relationships between plants and the uses man might make of them, but like these charmed reporters, he was never to lose his sense of the whole scene in a petty entanglement with some specific factual bit of information.

He was often sober in his visions of the future and wary of the way men seemed to over-run Nature in a greedy hope of private gain. And when it comes down to it, the most airy of the optimistic travelers were the commercially minded, with their eyes firmly fixed on trade and empire. The more reflective had their doubts and even questioned whether this country was all Arcadia. Even William Penn was to add his own sad comment: "Sobriety and prudence lead naturally to wealth, and wealth to authority, which soon strikes at the root of the short lived principle of equality."

CHAPTER VII

PLENTIFUL THE NATURAL resources of the new world
certainly were but they could not take the place of
money. The young American colony was as needy,
as anxious for financial help for its development as any
impoverished colonial nation of our day. When it came to
patrons for Bartram's project, they were often scarce and
kept a tight grip on the purse string. For other philan-
thropies they were even less inclined. Collinson was
obliged sadly to remind Joseph Breitnall of Philadelphia,
who solicited him for funds from interested parties for the
new library in that town, that "I cannot flatter thee with
hopes of benefactions from hence. The love of money is
too prevalent and we have too few, generous, public spirited men, considering our numbers; however I shall not
fail to impart your design to some likely persons."

127

Nor could Collinson fail to hint that the colonists might well apply for aid to their own men of wealth. He even gives a tip to Breitnall. Complimenting him on the fact that the present Proprietor of Pennsylvania "has generously" donated a lot for the library building, he suggests it might not come amiss to encourage him further by making him the President of the new Library Society.

Collinson was still foraging for likely persons who might back the botanical explorations of his friend, John Bartram, and it is not probable he would turn aside possible benefactors to the lesser project of the library. His concern and weary acceptance of the prevailing love of money and the stinginess of moneyed persons for "laudable works" was echoed by Bartram, who had failed in his own designs to interest the wealthy among his fellow-countrymen in botanical projects.

With or without new patrons, the work of circulating plants went on along the communication line of the ardent lovers of new wonders. Franklin never made a voyage to England without transmitting some new variety to the homeland. It might be seeds of the true rhubarb or Scotch cabbage, or some peas that were "much applauded here, I forget for what purpose." John Clayton, of Virginia, sent "three papers of seeds, natives of Virginia" to Bartram in return for Meadia, Arbor Vitae and Northern Spruce, to be escorted by Captain Bentley on his ship down the Delaware, through Chesapeake Bay to within three miles of Clayton's home. John St. Clair, of Belville, New Jersey, got hickory nuts from Bartram and reported that he had shipped a venture of strong beer and choice pieces of beef to his friend, the Governor of Senegal, who proposed to make a return in African trees, shrubs, plants and seeds. And if Bartram would send someone to his place to bring out a cow for Mrs. Bartram, of the famous Rhode Island breed, she would oblige him by accepting it.

From his little garden nook in England, Collinson drew unto himself seeds and seedlings from all over the world. He was not the man to exclude these treasures but passed them on enthusiastically to his friends. He sends a seed vessel from Russia to Bartram with the news that this species of *Charmaerhododendros* abounds in the woods near the Lake of Baikal in a latitude of fifty degrees in eastern Tartary. And, wonder of wonders, its like is also found near the Euxine Sea in Turkey and appears to coincide with the variety found by Bartram in the same latitude in America. Can one ask for better proof, he demands, of the unlimited power and goodness of the Creator, that such fine plants, so nearly related, should be dispersed in places so remote from each other, to gratify and please mankind!

No traveler of those days returned empty handed. Missionaries to distant places brought back seeds and disturbing ideas. The Jesuits to China brought the China aster to France, and from France seeds were sent to Collinson in England who forwarded some to Bartram in America. But not only seeds, the "noble savage" himself had made an entry as far back as the Sixteenth Century when Pigafetta, voyaging around the world with Magellan, wrote that the Brazilians followed Nature, wore no clothes, lived to be 140 years old and were free from "civilized vices." In the Seventeenth Century, more travelers repeated the tale; merchants, dreamers and Jesuit missionaries to Brazil, Paraguay and China praised the virtues of "unspoilt Natural Man" whose physique and morals surpassed those of Christendom. More moralists and satirists than anthropologists, they accented the absence in savage societies of inequality, coercive government and the Church and concluded that primitive peoples lived in the Paradise lost by Adam.

There were awkward implications in all this primitivism. Good savages, wise Negroes, tolerant Heathen appeared to have escaped the curse of Adam and when the Jesuit Father le Comte declared in 1696 that the Chinese had preserved "the true knowledge of God for more than two thousand years and had practised a purer morality than most Christians," he was condemned by the Faculty of Theology at Paris. But the ban did not stop the flow of ideas which expressed what the age wanted to believe. For centuries, kings and priests had been spreading a dark blight of tyranny over the surface of the earth and people everywhere chose to imagine that once one had passed that shadow it was possible to find Nature, unspoilt, beguiling.

From the time of the Renaissance writers were constantly using the theme of a still new and half-known world because with this uncorrupted subject matter they could construct a purer and more primitive milieu than existed anywhere in Europe. This idealized vision provided them with an effective device for criticizing a status quo which did not allow an outspoken attack but compelled the writer to search for surreptitious means. Thomas More used the theme of a distant country as an example for reform and his *Utopia* was followed by many other similar works. The use of such a theme had a definite revolutionary force, shaking the established order and setting it in a broader context. Travelers moved restlessly, ever westward, and in the Eighteenth Century Bougainville had established the mirage of the "unspoilt Natural Man" as far distant as Tahiti.

But primitive man was glorified only as a theme; in actual practice his fate was quite different. The burning insight of Friar Bartolomé de Las Casas who made a grand attempt to communicate to the world the uniqueness of Indian society evaporated in the rush for conquest. Las Casas, a member of the Dominican order, born in Seville in 1474, accompanied the Spanish commander Ovando to Cuba in 1502. An eye witness of the sufferings of the Indians, he spent the rest of his long life lashing out at the wrongs being done by Church, State and private adventurers. Above all else, he valued the Indian conception of fullness of life within material meagerness; external insecurity as the very basis for internal security. This vision he attempted to transmit to a world panting for material satisfactions. The vision of the impassioned spiritual inwardness he wished to rescue, for the salvation of the world, all but vanished, as the land was tamed, as the armies of jackrabbits traveling with the buffalo, perished, as the superb white wolf disappeared from the great plains.

The Eighteenth Century man could not help thinking in terms of an "unspoilt Nature" which he worshipped and an erring humanity which he condemned. An idyllic concept of Nature was politicized so energetically in France that it created a wish-image for a design of life. Such an image wielded so immense a power of suggestion that it was confidently believed the perfect society could be immediately realized by a revolution. That the wish-image in its conflict with historical reality was destined to miscarry and to lead to immense disillusionment only enhanced the tendency of men not to feel at home in the world and to retreat, as the Romantic Poets were to do, to a world of Nature, pure and undefiled. But in that realm the revolutionary drive was not lost but was to emerge in a different framework at a later date.

Though that development came later than the period we are examining here, it was already clear that the revulsion from the western, the modern and the complex had begun in Europe, and in the passionate preoccupation of the little group of botanists, one may discern, from the middle of the Eighteenth Century, the dual strains: not only the calm rationalism prevailing; but the germ of an emotion which was to prove later in the century, and thereafter, in the Nineteenth Century highly creative. There was already evidence in Bartram's time of the deep disharmony that was more and more to afflict the developing culture of Europe and America. The surface of this culture was to become ever more discordant with its depth, its literate rationalism to outstrip and lose touch with its emotional and imaginative needs.

Even Bartram, so much a whole man, was to suffer from the conflicting views. His love of order compelled him to master the land and to tame the waters, and yet, that very process imperilled the wilderness with its vast store of the rare and the beautiful. His beloved green world was not safe from the settler's axe or grazing cattle. His explorations were not safe because of the Indian; the Indian became a menace. The "natural man" Rousseau was to romanticize, was Bartram's foe.

A frog may appear as the least offensive creature on earth but to Collinson, who longed for some frogs, they appeared as a possible threat to the peace. He reasoned that as he had no big park, he could not hope to keep them alive in his own small pool without attracting the attention of strolling men and boys who were certain to make the frogs a fatal target. A bullfrog with its assertive voice was doomed to become a sacrificial victim.

An entire pattern of social discord is behind this simple tale of the frog. Though the enclosure of common land had been going on steadily since the Fifteenth Century, the face of England began to be radically changed only after 1750. A series of Enclosure Acts had gradually taken the land away from the common use. The technical case for enclosure of land was exceptionally strong; it actually led to more profitable farming for those who had control of their acreage. But it dispossessed many villagers who looked with antagonism upon the parks and privileges of the great. Pilfering and poaching were savagely punished, as Fielding's *Tom Jones* attests, and the landless villager, without privileges, was tossed out to the cities where he was finally driven, after the Industrial Revolution, to sell himself as a poor-paid hand to the rising industries. His impoverishment, his fate, which divorced him not only from the land but almost from a human condition, ties directly into our theme; the more the sky darkened with the smoke of factories, the more certainly did the poets turn toward the sun and Nature.

Collinson was too closely aligned to the owners of big estates, Bartram's patrons, to sense the woes of the dispossessed villagers and he was to die before the connection between the Nature he adored and the poets had become clearly manifest. Probably he saw his world through a haze of trees and flowers; even events were fortunate or unfortunate as they related to the destiny of "the vegetable kingdom." When the Prince of Wales died, he lamented it because the "Prince had been the best friend of gardening and planting." But so incorrigible is his optimism, that he assures Bartram of the impossibility of the good thing dying with the Prince. "There is such a spirit and love of it amongst our nobility and gentry, and the pleasure and profit that attend it will render it a lasting delight."

The dispossession of villagers from the land created a great flux of displaced persons, with nowhere to go, who were already swelling the ranks of emigrants to the new world. Dean Swift cried out against what he termed "fraudulent promises" which pried untried families from their native soil to be turned loose in the wilds of America. "It is remarkable," he fulminated, "that the Enthusiasm spread among our Northern people of sheltering themselves in the continent of America, hath no other Foundation than their present insupportable condition at Home." He chose to believe that on the hazardous journey, many died miserably, and went on to contend, not without some foundation, that "the Truth is this: The English established in these colonies are in great Want of Men to inhabit that Tract of Ground which lies between them and the Wild Indians, who are not reduced in their dominions. We read of some barbarous People whom the Romans placed in their Armies, for no other Service than to blunt their Enemies' Swords, and afterwards to fill up Trenches with their dead bodies. And thus our people who transport themselves are settled in those interjacent tracts as a Screen against the Insults of the Savages; and may have as much land as they can clear from the woods, at a very Reasonable Rate, if they can afford to pay about a Hundred Year's purchase by their labor."

His pessimism didn't stop the flow of emigrants, often pushed by the extremity of their situation at home as much as by hope for a better life. One has only to read Crèvecoeur's account of the contented American farmer to learn they did not all end up in a ditch. Some did take to the wilds, and reckless, lawless, chopped their way into the wilderness, breaking treaties with the Indians and brewing trouble. They refused to respect the conditions imposed by the British Crown in 1754, when in order to quell the constant disturbances between Indians and whites, they made of the Indian tribes, independent nations. Indian lands were to become inalienable except through voluntary surrender to the Crown. Any attempt by an individual or group to encroach upon Indian land was held to be illegal. As well try to stop a raging cataract. What was legality worth in the wilderness? England was beyond the ocean; the policy so enraged the Borderers along the western fringe of settlement that they not only continued to seize lands but to throw themselves with abandon into war against the hated mother country when the time came.

Even Bartram lost his bearings in the complicated mixture of wills and impulses governing the development of the new world. As much as any Borderer he lived to execrate the Indian and to resent British restrictions. Under such circumstances, it was impossible for men in the new world to look upon the Indian as a "noble savage." He became a Devil incarnate, a remorseless foe.

Unless we take into account this intricate design at work altering the social, economic and imaginative patterns of the period, the pilgrimages of John Bartram and the passionate preoccupations of the little group of inspired botanists would be as lifeless as a stately collection of wax flowers under a glass bell. Though they separated themselves from some of the streams of history, they suffered the winds and the rain, the squalls and the drought of the entire climate of the world. Their ardor may even be said to stem, not only in spite of the circumstances, but because of them.

The botanists maintained a continuity of design that passed from rash love of growing things to a scientific appraisal, in one direction; in another direction, to the imaginative flights of creative minds in the latter part of the Eighteenth Century, and continuing Nineteenth Century. For the nature lovers the dead fir twig was lovingly referred to as a "deer's horns"; for Coleridge, the albatross was to become a symbol as inscrutable as the sperm whale's vast brow for Melville.

In the midst of wars, the botanists kept their bearings and recorded their findings, trusting to some enormous intention within the universe, some miracle of design, to which each man hoped to contribute his part. The progress of a plant was studied with the care of a fever chart. Had the patient thrived? Was it persecuted by mites? Then spray it with water in which tobacco leaves had been soaking. An orphan from America might thrive to unprecedented size in England, or it might come up one year to die down in the next. When Mrs. Martha Logan sent seeds of the striped gilly flower to Bartram from South Carolina, he nursed the stranger carefully, only to be disappointed when the variety turned out a uniform red for him. But he would make a second attempt for the striped wonder another season! Botanists from Holland sent a request for American Sweet Gum through Collinson who immediately was spurred to add the item to his own collection, plus Black Gum, Black Haw, in fruit and leaf, Sugar Birch, Black Thorn and all sorts of White Thorn. He never knew when to stop once the top of his desires started spinning, and the list reminds him that his new specimen of White Cedar looks a "little off." Better send another, quick, as, if this specimen stands up, it will be the only one in all England.

The threat of wars that might drag on for years, seems to have spurred the demand for the American vegetables and by 1748, Collinson had rounded up the Duke of Argyle, Squire Hamilton, two gentlemen designated as Smithson and Williamson, and Lord Newhope and Lord Deskford. His old subscribers, the Duke of Bedford and the Duke of Richmond, languished for that season as Bartram had nothing new to send them. Oh, to make a journey to New England, to Newfoundland and to the Mississippi Valley! His heart is wrenched with frustration but it is no longer safe to go beyond the mountains for fear of the "rascally" Indians. There may be an attack from the "rascally" French upon Philadelphia in the spring and citizens from that town are daily drilling and exercising. Forts and batteries are hastily being erected along the waterfront to oppose the invaders, should they attempt to land.

By 1750 Collinson was so deeply engrossed in business that he can no longer go into particulars in his letters to Bartram. But he has time to put in a request for two terrapin, alive, which he hopes to maintain in his walled garden. And in spite of the pressure of his affairs, he has devised a means to facilitate payments from the ever reluctant patrons. Bartram is advised to draw bills upon him for twenty-five pounds, allowing a month's interval between each bill, and payable ninety days from sight. With such a document, he can have the pretext of pressing hard for Bartram's well earned money. In spite of his urgent affairs, Collinson picked a nosegay of flowers at his country place in January of 1751 and wrote the news of it to his friend. Plenty of violets, he recites jubilantly, crocus, snowdrops, polyanthus, single anemones, double and single stocks, all of them surpassingly sweet. There's not a sign of the evergreen *Rhamus,* the berries of which he hopefully planted. This is the little plant growing to five or six inches high among the dwarf pines that Bartram found in a location referred to as the "great plains in the desert." Has it survived for Bartram? A pity, if they were to lose track of this most rare and curious plant.

Collinson's immersion in business might have allowed him to forget, for a time, his interest in turtles, had not Bartram kept his friend's passion alive with his presents. One year he sends a box of four turtles, dried, after their inner parts have been removed, and were well washed, with shell, head, feet and tail entire. His program for that summer was to include the collection of all kinds of turtles, with the eggs belonging to them, together with insects and fishes. As the ocean voyage was more and more precarious, he planned to send by every ship sailing from America to England in the hope that if some were captured by the "rascals" on the high seas, others might escape and come through alive and well. Whether these creatures ever reached England is not disclosed but the turtle to end all turtles was finally shipped to Collinson after his curiosity concerning a certain giant variety reported in New England had reached fever pitch.

To Collinson's eager inquiries concerning this creature, which some correspondent had claimed to be of a variety capable of "barking," if attacked, Bartram wrote a long and sober reply, explaining that the species described appeared to him to be the Great Mud Turtle, "which is much hunted for, to feast our gentry withal; and is reckoned to be as delicious a morsel as those brought from the Summer Islands. They are very large, of a dark muddy color, large round tail, and feet with claws. The old ones are mossy on the back and often support several leeches to suck the superfluous blood; a large head, sharp nose, and mouth wide enough to cram one's fist in; very sharp gums, or lips, which you will, with which they catch hold of a stick offered to them, or if you prefer, your finger, which they hold so fast that you may lift the turtle as high as your head if you have the strength or the courage. But as for *barking*, I do believe thy relator *barked*, instead of a turtle. They creep all over in the mud where they lie *perdu*; when a duck or fish swims near, they dart the head quick as light, and snap him up. Their eggs are round as a bullet and choice eating."

The description whetted Collinson's appetite for possession and six months later a living specimen from America found itself in his garden. Collinson admits that he and his son are awed by the huge size of the creature. A really formidable animal! It bit fiercely at a stick thrust at it and made an uncouth sound. But a living specimen will not suffice. He hopes Billy Bartram will make a drawing of one the same size, and the manner in which he makes the request is practically that of a gentleman ordering a portrait of a distinguished person. Billy is to see to it that the shell is well washed in order to expose all the sutures, and, as if one expressive portrait of one great turtle were not enough, he once more demands drawings of all species of turtles, with some account of their habits. He has made requests for drawings of turtles before, but never so insistently as now, when he is confronted with a living specimen. In fact, it is clear, that he intends portraits from now on to suffice. "Send no more mud turtles," he advises. "One is enough."

It actually turned out to be more than enough. Several years later he was to report: "A day or two agone, fishing in one of my ponds, I caught a perch; the hook swallowed so deep that I cut the fish in half to get it out; then decided to throw in the line with half the perch still on the hook to try what would take it and let it lay all night. When I came to pull it out, up comes the Great Mud Turtle that I had not seen for a year and a half, much grown. By this experiment I know how to catch the devourer of my fish which have much decreased and now I know the poacher, I must transport him."

Though Collinson might be disillusioned as to the desirability of keeping poaching turtles in his ponds, he continued to plead for portraits of the tribe. Billy's drawing of the snapping turtle sent him into ecstasies. He would like to communicate the boy's account of the turtle and his fine drawing to the public but doesn't know how. Editors of publications, he implies, are very careless of these important matters.

Billy's handsome drawings engage more and more of Collinson's approval but the boy's growing skill only arouses deep concern in both the friend and the father. What can his future be? What is he to do with his gift? How will it help him earn his daily bread? Bartram is pleased that Billy's drawings give such satisfaction and only wishes he could get a handsome livelihood by it. "Botany and drawing are his darling delight," he confides. "I am afraid he can't settle to any business else. Surveying may afford an opportunity to exercise his botany but we have five times more surveyors already than we can employ. If he could get a surveyor general's office, for life, it might do."

William had just turned sixteen. It was now time to propose some way for him to get a living. Bartram was explicit in one particular: "I don't want him to be what is called a gentleman. I want him put to some business by which he may, with care and industry, get a temperate, reasonable living. I am afraid that drawing and botany will not afford him one, and hard labor don't agree with him. I have designed for several years to put him to a doctor, and learn physic and surgery; but that will take him from his drawing, which he takes particular delight in." He prays that his friend will let him have his opinion.

The friends consulted gravely over Billy's situation. Benjamin Franklin was consulted. Bartram wrote Collinson that he had reasoned with Franklin about all the difficulties involved in launching a boy in the world. He acknowledged that Franklin was the only printer known to make a good thing of it, in this place, though many had set up, before and since. It took Franklin's extraordinary and superior abilities and close application to make a go of it. Franklin was of the opinion that merchandising was risky and it would be extremely difficult to make remittances to Europe in such troubled times. Pondering, the great man came up with the suggestion that Billy might make an engraver. In his leisure he might still pursue botany. For a time, this seems to have been considered a happy solution by both Collinson and Bartram. But nothing came of it. Collinson, in particular, thought highly of the notion. "It is a pretty ingenious employ," he wrote his friend. "Never let him reproach thee, and say, Father, if thou had put me to some business by which I might get my bread, I should have by my industry lived in life as well as other people. Let the fault be his, not thine, if he does not."

There is no record of what the boy said, or of what he thought. He was drawing, feverishly, out of sheer love. One drawing of the *Tupelo* brought extended praise from Collinson who reported that it was deservedly admired by everyone. "There is a delightful natural feeling through the whole, and no minute particular omitted, even insects on the leaves."

The father and son made some trips together. While they waited for some plan to materialize for William, seeds must be gathered, journeys undertaken. Who could help Bartram more than this son? Here was the long awaited helper who brought to the task more than willingness, a profound devotion and superior talent. Together they made their way to the Catskills in September, crossing three ridges of the Blue Mountains in New Jersey and pausing to rest on a high elevation. While they ate their lunch, their eyes tracked down the different trees, later to be examined more minutely. Here grew oak of several varieties, chestnut, sassafras, maple, black and white ash, wild cherry, persimmon and the three-leaved pine. There were lush growths of sweet fern and in swampy places *Prinos*. The fox grapes were ripe and excellent eating. Instead of taking the road that led to Goshen, they branched off to explore the broken, mountainous part of the country that Bartram had once traversed alone. The alder was flourishing, to a height of fifteen or twenty feet, considerably taller than it grew at home. The under side of its leaves was a fine silver and made a shimmer as the breeze stirred. As they came down from the mountains on a fine sunny rich bank, they found many roots of the Wild Lovage and gathered seeds to plant in the home garden. Here was a plant that Bartram had despaired of ever seeing again, after fifteen years of searching! One hour later, by the sun, they came to a little cottage and ordered their horses to pasture. Their host insisted that there were the strangest plants growing on his land that ever grew anywhere and that was enough to start the travelers off on an immediate hunt. But all the plants surveyed proved to be but common specimens to Bartram, although some, doubtless, were such as might seem strange to the local inhabitants.

At night seven or eight people, including two families already inhabiting the hut where they were to rest, crowded into a space hardly big enough for a hen roost. Bartram and Billy slept on the ground after a musty piece of supper. "Slept but little in this lousy hut," he writes Collinson, "which we left, as soon we could well see our path, in the morning, having paid our host half a crown, which he charged."

By noon of one day, they reached the sequestered farm, near Newburgh, New York, of Dr. Cadwallader Colden. In the account of this jaunt to Collinson, Bartram does not say if he consulted his friend about Billy's future. But both father and son must have looked with a certain speculation upon the man who was then a surveyor general, the very situation that Bartram had indicated gave such latitude to botanical accomplishments. Colden led a life which would have been admirably suited to the talents of Billy; he was devoted to botany and conducted numerous scientific experiments, refusing to abandon them in spite of the danger from Indian attacks. Here was another man of medicine turned botanist. Graduated from the University of Edinburgh in 1705, he had first settled in Pennsylvania. Always busy with original investigations in medicine and general science, he turned more and more to botanical studies. For years he kept a daily record of the weather. In 1718 he was invited to the State of New York and thereafter held many official posts, not only as surveyor general

142

but as a member of the King's Provincial council. He wrote a book on the Five Indian Nations.

This many-sided energetic man was typical of the Eighteenth Century; Billy was not. By nature, he was too much of an artist. Colden had arrived at his recent tranquil situation by exerting his energies and by engaging powerful friends. Perhaps the father realized that the son would not quite fit this pattern. The surveyor-general job was the pot of gold but the way to it was not by a rainbow.

No sooner had they eaten their dinner with Dr. Colden and his family, than the pair sallied forth at once to gather seeds. Until two hours before dark, they kept at it, making a wide search for rare specimens. In the evening Dr. Colden displayed some exhibits showing the botanical skill of his daughter. Bartram accounted them "most curious, botanical observations." The next morning, as soon as they could see, they were once more on the hunt for plants and kept it up until breakfast. Colden's son escorted them to Dr. Jones's place from whence they got a view of a fine growth of pines on a high hill. Then came dinner and a hunt by the river for Arbor Vitae seeds until dark. In the morning, up again at break of day, to gather more seeds until breakfast.

Colden's daughter sent samples of her observations to Collinson, who seems to have made himself a clearing house for the botanical speculations of the day. He wrote Bartram that he had received several sheets of plants, "very curiously anatomized, in a scientific manner, after Linnaeus's system." He believes she is the first lady to embark on anything of this nature. The exhibit will be sent to Gronovius in Holland, but he, poor man, must be in a bad state of health as nothing has been heard from him, not even an acknowledgment, as yet, of Bartram's system relating to pines and Billy's fine drawings of oaks.

Billy was also executing Collinson's order for drawings

of turtles, all kinds of turtles, as he came upon them. Shipped to Collinson as they were completed, the drawings and descriptions were received with rapture. He could not hope to reward the boy equal to his merit but he did send "a small token of his appreciation" and some fine drawing paper. Nothing could be finer than Billy's execution of the Horned Turtle. Such ingenuity, Collinson muses, brings truth to light. What can be the use of its horns? To strike its prey? He would have Billy draw the wrong side of the Spotted Turtle, and come to think of it, better have him paint the belly-side of ALL the turtles. There is always something remarkable there.

Wrapt in his drawings, steeped in the scent of high grass and the dews of early mornings, it is no wonder that young Billy found it hard to come out of his trance of joyful surrender into the dull round of an occupation which would guarantee him a respectable livelihood. Every project that might have been suitable, seems to have failed. He was not put as an apprentice to study doctoring, nor did he become a printer or engraver. No surveying job opened up. He seems to have been lodged, at last, in a dreary store, where the optimistic Collinson chose to see him as a rising star.

"I am glad Billy has a way to rise in the world. There may be at times some leisure hours when he may divert himself in his favorite amusement." The kind man sent some of the best books available to the imprisoned lad with the admonition that through them he might improve himself. But Billy was not out for a "favorite amusement." He had discovered the passion of his life and through the utmost hardship, through continual attempts to "better himself" in the ways his father thought wise, through perpetual denials, he stumbled and persisted toward his own goal. It was a journey that would occupy the rest of his mortal existence.

144

CHAPTER VIII

BILLY WAS NOT the first son of John Bartram's to break away from home. The decade that began with 1750 was to be a long and painful Odyssey for Billy's elder brother, Moses Bartram.

In the summer of 1751 the nineteen-year-old lad showed up at Collinson's office in London. The ship on which he had sailed as a member of the crew had been sold outright upon reaching England and there was no passage to be had back without paying for it. The boy told Collinson he thought it was a hard case and the older man agreed. Willing though Moses was to work his passage home, no ship destined for Philadelphia or New York would have him on those terms. Few ships to America would sail before Christmas, which was too long to linger. Even then, the voyages would terminate in Maryland or the West Indies.

Moses was ready to hire for the West Indies. But Collinson, who knew ships and their crews, as he was always down at the docks either for his own private business or in behalf of the precious American "vegetables," refused to agree with Moses on the plan to ship to the West Indies. In great haste he wrote the father that such a voyage would mean that the boy would have to associate with their London common sailors, "a most profligate crew who would never rest until they made him like themselves." Collinson was taken with Moses who showed a sturdy, cheerful disposition in his misfortune and appeared to be of an industrious nature. But it would not do, counselled the Londoner, "to expose his virtue to severe trials." British wages were very low; the best sailor got no more than twenty-five shillings a month. Better look out for a steady berth for the boy on a ship owned in New York or Philadelphia. The poor young fellow had showed up very bare of clothes. "He would have been contented with his rags," wrote Collinson, "but with his poor equipment I did not see how I could do less than I did." A frugal outfit was purchased for him and even that was considered "too much" by the modest lad. Collinson must have made some arrangements for Moses; three months later he is still in London. He had gone out to look over Collinson's plantings at Mill Hill and reported that "many things were wanting."

What becomes of him then? It was an age when a youngster, not born to the purple, was expected to stand on his own feet early. In the ten years that it took before young Moses found a safe harbor, he must have tossed about on the seven seas. Four years after he first showed up in his rags at Collinson's office, the kind benefactor is inquiring once more for "poor Moses," who seems to have unburdened himself in letters to his father's friend rather than to his father. Collinson had heard from him in Gibraltar after "tumbling and tossing about the world." He encloses a letter Moses sent him to his father. There has been an earthquake at Lisbon and the city is in ruins. As for Moses, the fate of Lisbon is so cruel that it obliterates, for the time being, more precise news of him.

What ports did he make? What sights did he see? Who were his shipmates? We will never learn from the correspondence between the friends. The boy becomes a symbol, committed to the deep oceans by a father who implicitly trusted in his sturdiness and will to survive. Turtles, magnolia, wild flower seeds, pines and firs reached their cherished destinations. But Moses, a youthful Ulysses, must run his risks until such time as fate decrees a safe landing. Ten years after his first voyage to England, Moses seems to have found a berth at Cape Fear, North Carolina, with his father's brother. By that time he had established himself so well that he is upheld as an example of what persistence and industry may achieve. Praise of Moses is now a reflection upon "poor Billy" who had deserted his Philadelphia job to take refuge also under his uncle's wing at Cape Fear. Bartram writes his brother William about his boys: "I and most of Billy's relations are concerned that he never writes how his trade affairs succeed. I should be glad if he could gain credit, as Isaac and Moses have. They began with little, and unexpectedly dropped into a fine business, fulfilling the first proverb, First creep, then go."

During the probation of Moses on the high seas, Collinson worried about the boy but with his perpetual hopefulness, tended to prognosticate a certain dawn following dark. In 1759, toward the end of Moses's troubles, he writes the father; "I am concerned for poor Moses. Now he has to eat his brown bread, his white will come next. I wish he could write a little Journal in his own way and style, from going to sea to the present. Short hints will do.

147

I question if it is to be paralleled. We don't know what human nature will bear until it is tried."

After Moses, it was Billy's turn to bear the brunt of rude misfortune. The requirements of "human nature" would push the more delicate boy to the breaking point in the following decade. It would take a kind stranger, deliberately intervening, to rescue him from despair. He was even to go into an eclipse in the estimation of his father and the good Collinson; to be reproved for carelessness and sloth; to be doubted and given up for lost; to be advised in ways of life for which his nature was altogether unadaptable; to be praised occasionally when momentary skill and high talent broke through the heavy clods of an existence unsuitable to his genuis. He was to become "poor Billy Bartram" for more than a long, long decade.

Not that there was any strain of hardheartedness on the part of this kind father. He was concerned for the fate of his sons but he shared the general complacence of the age concerning the durability of youth. Later in the century, philosophers in England would look tolerantly at the fate of small children who were expected to toil in the mines and at the looms as a part of God's plan. Bartram entered with sympathetic intensity into the whole life around him but he had his blind spots. When it came to the Indian, he was irrational; when it came to his sons, he was any father who both doubts and demands.

One is reminded of certain men of the Renaissance, mixtures of iron will and great sensitivity; in particular, of Leon Battista Alberti, who, when he was ill, was cured by the sight of a beautiful landscape. If Bartram did not shed tears at the sight of noble trees as Alberti is said to have done, he shared the Italian's close and mysterious communion with the world. Yet, though he had learned for himself in the wilderness that neither roof, nor house, nor bed was necessary to existence, when it came to his sons,

*John Bartram, from the Portrait
Painted by Charles Willson Peale* °
Courtesy John Bartram Association

° *The question has been raised as to
whether this is an actual portrait of John Bartram.*

Draft of a Letter from John Bartram to Philip Miller, Courtesy of the Academy of Natural Sciences and the John Bartram Association

*William Bartram, from the Portrait
Painted by Charles Willson Peale
Courtesy New York Public Library*

HYDRANGEA QUERCIFOLIA.

*Hydrangea Quercifolia, from one of
the Early Drawings of William Bartram
Courtesy New York Public Library*

MICO CHLUCCO the LONG WARIOR
or *KING of the SIMINOLES*

W. Bartram Delin. J. Trenchard Sculp.

*Mico Chlucco the Long Warrior, from
the Drawing by William Bartram
Courtesy New York Public Library*

ANONA PYGMEA.

ANDROMEDA PULVERULENTA.

Above: Anona Pygmea, from the Drawing by William Bartram

Right: Andromeda Pulverulenta as Drawn by William Bartram Courtesy New York Public Library

Turtle, from the Drawing by
William Bartram, Courtesy
New York Public Library

Great Yellow Bream called Old Wife of S.t John's, E.t Florida.

Bird Drawing by William Bartram

Below: Great Yellow Bream, from the
Drawing by William Bartram, St. John's,
Florida, 1774, Courtesy John Bartram
Association

he could not prevent himself from falling under Franklin's spell. The boys must dig in and secure sound livelihoods, at any cost. If it was difficult, so much the better, for he believed that "men can do all things if they will." Bartram himself held to what was difficult, seeing in all Nature the truth of his pattern. Every growing thing defended itself in its own way, seeking at all costs to be itself, against all opposition. In the end, William Bartram, the son, succeeded in doing exactly that; going against all opposition to be himself. But at the start, the father did not recognize that he, too, was an opposing force. He would not risk the chances he himself had taken. William won by giving in; in sinking, he rose.

Collinson and Bartram had ample cause for worry. They were to become more and more concerned with the rising generation of youths in the decade following 1750. They worried about their cargoes and they worried about Bartram's sons. They fretted when Bartram's journeys into the wilderness were endangered by mounting Indian troubles all along the border. Wild species of nature might be rescued and made to flourish in home gardens but the wild species of man found on the North American continent became a vile weed, to be rooted out. The intricate tapestry of Indian life was invisible to the eyes of the colonists and rudely cutting through the multicolored web and weave, they were not even conscious of the extent of their destruction. Bartram sided with the blind and ravenous vanguard. On every other subject he was "as calmly tolerant as a potato field in the sun whose equanimity is not disturbed by the Scotch thistles over the wall." But when it came to the Indian, he went on a tirade against "the barbarous, inhuman, ungrateful Indians, weekly murdering our back inhabitants, skipping from tree to tree, like monkeys, or if in the mountains, leaping from rock to rock, like goats." Certainly it went against his

149

Quaker nature to execrate the Indians as he did. Other Quakers in the New World took opposing stands, and Collinson from London, more than once, tried to speak a reasonable language of cause and effect to his friend.

Bartram would have none of it. There was a hidden wave from the depths of life which could override that stable ego. Who can say what was the source of this irrational emotion in an otherwise most reasonable man? Perhaps his father's death at the hands of the Indians had dyed the early emotional pattern with so dark a stain that no Quaker upbringing could quite obliterate it. Once he cited an encounter with an Indian along a forest path to prove the ferocity he had come to believe part and parcel of the "willful" Indian nature. Meeting a savage in the dark of the woods, the Indian yanked Bartram's hat from his head and "chawed it around the border" in token of what would happen to the man daring to persist in going forward. Collinson would have begun to question himself at such an encounter and to ask how the Indian had fared at the white man's hands that he could react so furiously toward a white man and his hat. He would have remembered how friendly the first Indians had been and in his final judgment, he would have taken some of the blame for the desperate course events had taken. But not Bartram. Though he might be solid as a block of granite, tender as a blade of grass, he did not spring full born out of Jove's head into the Eighteenth Century. Unwittingly, he may have been more akin to the ancient hunters of the tiger and the boar than he knew. Those symbols of power, of danger, of beauty and use had drawn men through the ages after them. What does it matter if his pursuit was not for the bear but for the wildflower? The old primordial urge stirred in him. Thwarted in his search, he rebounded with the vigor of the ancient hunter, balked of his prey.

Then too, the rare dispassionate temper of the earlier

decades was vanishing. Complexities in the world were snarling the even tenor of men's minds. Caught in the trap of a raging forest fire, the victim does not ask who set the blaze, but cries out to escape. And there were real fires in American forests; there were real innocent victims, white and red. For almost a decade the French and Indian wars would try to settle the old account between England and France. Which would lay claim to an early stake in the new world? As the century advanced the bright light of a rational outlook upon the world would prove not sufficient to dispel the mysteries. The anatomy of a turtle would not satisfy the imagination. Nor would it be rewarding to link every phenomena with a beguiling Providence.

The very quarrels between the two friends, Bartram and Collinson, amiable though they were, betrayed the divisions in men's minds. On the surface, Collinson's conservatism becomes tedious. He seems forever trying to water down the enthusiasm of his friend's speculations. To be satisfied with rapt wonder. To be content to collect his shrubs, his turtles, his birds and his stones. At times he appears to be saying to his friend, "Let us praise the Almighty and be content with a rapturous connection with his divine plan." It was not sufficient for Bartram for whom enthusiasm was not enough. To find was only a necessary step toward knowing. If the veil was mysterious, it could be pierced with a brighter light. His more scientific mind was closer to the spirit of the age but the warnings against the limitations of pure reason were already sounding. Some of Collinson's replies indicate as much: "My dear John," he once wrote, "says truly, his hypothesis (concerning the origin of certain rock formations) is composed of broken links, for I cannot unite them; but in ingenious conjectures. Suppositions are endless; we are still in the dark relating to many wonderful phenomena in nature. The great Author of our being has set bounds to our reasoning faculty, that we may consider of our Imperfections, yet has permitted us mental excursions—and those the best connected—and to us the most probable—may be nearest the mark."

The letters of the two men might well be studied as a lesson on how to disagree with equanimity. Neither man refrained from defending an opinion held to be sound, no matter what the opposition set up by the other. Collinson's long expostulations on the subject of the Indian did not alter Bartram's irrational hatred one jot. Nor did the Londoner's temporizing on various theories held by the American stop the flow of the latter's speculations. The two men remained strictly themselves, bound by affection and respect, united in a mutual passion.

In 1753 Collinson's wife died. In a loving letter to "his dear afflicted friend," Bartram reminds him that he himself is in some measure qualified to sympathize with "one of his dearest friends, in his close and tender affliction." He is referring to the loss of his young first wife, after a few years of marriage, whose death in an epidemic of the time led to a lifelong interest in medicinal remedies and herbs. It is the first time, and the last, in all their long correspondence, that Collinson's wife was mentioned. They were not the men to find domestic situations sufficient ground for fascinated discussions. Nor did they consider questions of health entertaining matters. Accidents incidental to Bartram's journeys come into the picture only because they relate to their larger interests. Once he fell from a tree on some exploration and with great difficulty dragged himself home. Another time he suffered from ulcers of the leg following bruises sustained in his contest with rude Nature. Colds and sniffles were not worthy subjects to put on precious paper just as indulgences in gloomy frames of mind were also frowned upon with the severity of a Samuel Johnson reproving the languishing hypochondriac notions of Boswell. Tender alarm for mutual friends was more in their line, and, when Dr. Christopher Witt's eyesight dims in his old age so that he can no longer distinguish a leaf from a flower, Collinson trusts in his inner sight, to strengthen and reward him.

With the advancing years, the sons of both men began to make more and more of an entry. Bartram's boys come into the correspondence with something of the shy unobtrusiveness of appealing plants in need of proper soil, yet not requiring the same delicacy or immediate concern. Collinson's son and son-in-law show up almost as spectators in the drama of Flora and Fauna which engrossed the infatuated Londoner all his life. Here delicious specimens of Nature perform as a direct testimonial of God and his providential ways.

Collinson's situation as a widower brought more letters to Bartram's door. At times he breaks into petulance which Bartram does not hesitate to reprove. It appears to Bartram that when he has endeavored to give the greatest satisfaction, his labors have been valued the least. At Collinson's own earnest request, he sent a cargo of a variety of seeds to distribute to their friends; the cargo arrived safely. So what is the complaint? "When I read these lines of thy letter, *What did'st mean to send so large a box of seeds? It made much trouble, and time, to part it,* this answer quite astonished me—to think it is a trouble to part a few seeds, sent ready to hand to one's intimate friends. I reflected what pains I had taken to collect those seeds, in several hundreds of miles travel, drying, packing, boxing and shipping, and all to put my friend to trouble! Indeed, my good friend, if thee was not a widower, I should be inclined to tell thee that old age had advanced as fast upon thee as upon myself! And perhaps these lines may give offense, for, as times go now, we must not complain of either private or public disappointment, no, not to one's particular friends."

But on one subject even Bartram could not forbear to utter a complaint. Collinson reveals a delightful sense of the desirability of these complaints when he writes; "Thee always complain for want of letters, making no allowances for miscarriages. If all my correspondents were of thy restless turn of mind, I would never set pen to paper." There are moments when Collinson, too, grows restless, protesting that "It is long since I heard from my good friend, John Bartram. I hope no illness prevented him from giving me that pleasure. I am sure it was not for want of materials, for those are always ready to a speculative genius like his. For my part, I have been so engaged, I had little time for speculation."

Nor can he resist employing two puppet characters to illustrate his abiding satisfaction with his friend and his dissatisfaction at his silence. For several years Bartram had had a rival. A man known as Alexander had been shipping quantities of nursery goods to London and though Bartram is acquainted with this gentleman, they are cool when they meet and never discuss business. Collinson slyly refers to Alexander's shipments; "Thy seeds came admirably well and gave satisfaction. I heard quite otherwise of Alexander's. My son says, Father, what is the matter? Friend John has quite forgotten you, who take so much pains to dispose of his seeds. What! No *plants* this year! He might have sent them, having two opportunities on ships in which he sent *only seeds*." And as if this hint were not enough, he concludes by throwing the burden of his desires upon his mouthpiece, his son, whom he quotes as declaring himself an enthusiast for Orchis, Lady Slippers, Hellebore, Lilies, and "all new things."

Will Collinson's desires ever run out? Obviously not. They keep him youthful so that he even loses track of his own age. By the time he is seventy, he is reminding Bartram, in case anyone inquires for the number of his years, not to forget that he is "some months older than thee." Actually, he was five years Bartram's senior. Bartram, too, gets lost in the rush of time. Once Collinson petulantly expostulates; "Thou frequently talks of having sent specimens to me and Lord Petrie, of this, and that and the other species, as if it was but a year or two agone; when, alas! he has been dead fourteen or fifteen years. All such items arè but wasting paper and ink."

Perhaps Collinson rested a trifle too cozily in his trust of Providence. It was the vice of the age. Even Bartram did not escape it, in spite of his risks with fortune. But he is forever contradicting that confidence by asserting his reliance upon his own powers. Nor does he refrain from rebelliousness against Providence if it decrees that he can no longer go on rampages into the wilderness, due to the "treacherous Indians." He longs to penetrate the country beyond Pittsburgh. When he cannot, the old seeds begin to look tiresome. His feeling is even shared by some of the correspondents in the Old World who pant for new wonders. Irritation at their complacent expectations which contain no hint of his difficulties burst out to Collinson: "I have just received two letters by packet. *Send double boxes Pine and Powell and Williamson.* Who is this Pine? *Powell and Eddy desire but half the quantity of walnuts.* Who is this Eddy? *But all desire new things; they are tired of the old ones.* Do they think I can make new ones? I have sent seeds of almost every tree and shrub from Nova Scotia to Carolina; very few are wanting; and from the sea across the continent to the Lakes. It's very likely ignorant people may give strange names to tickle your ears with, but, as I have travelled through most of these provinces and have specimens sent by the best hands, I know well what grows there. Indeed, I have not yet been at Ohio, but have sent many specimens sent to me from there. In about two weeks I hope to set out to search for myself, if the barbarous Indians don't hinder me (and if I die a Martyr to Botany, God's will be done; His Will be done in all things). They domineer, threaten and steal most of the best horses they can. None could have worse luck than I with your roots sent last fall and this spring."

No doubt, his reference to "people who may give strange names to tickle your ears" refers to Alexander, who more than once seems to have got under Bartram's skin. He was justifiably proud of his pioneering in botany and touchy, when others, with less capacity, chose to exploit the gullibility of the public with flourishing pretensions. But his temper soon subsides in experimentations. If he cannot find new plants, he will make new varieties. Collinson applauds his efforts, with his usual backhanded praise: "Now I am more convinced than ever that thou art a deep-rooted botanist; for a little enthusiastic turn, probably the effect of your hot weather, has set thy ideas a rambling in the wide fields of nature. She is not so docile as thou imagines and will be put very little out of her course by all thy inventions. However, by thy trials, thou proposes to make, thou will be convinced of the weakness of thy efforts, to produce any settled or remarkable change in her laws. Pray let me know the success of thy experiment."

Did he receive a reply? Probably. Bartram continued "to bang away" at his notions, of whatever kind, with enthusiasm. Blocked from pursuing a course in the wilderness, he experimented with plants, pondering over the problems of how to create new species. It was no chance, but the result of patient experiment, that produced his hybrid, a flesh colored *Lychnis*. In 1755, half-way through the decade that must have been one of the most frustrating he was to experience, he wrote to Dr. Alexander Garden of a brand new idea. Not content to discover what grew on the surface of the earth he proposed a plan by which the layers beneath the skin of the upper soil might be examined and appraised. A series of borings on a large scale might lead to a discovery of valuable mineral deposits and could form a basis for the determination of the constituents of the soil itself. Minerals were not the only treasure; rich marls and fertilizing products might be found deeply imbedded below the surface, which, when raised to the top, could be useful for enriching poor soil. What he clamored for was a "subterranean" map of the earth. It was a bold idea and in proposing such a plan he was at least fifty years in advance of his time. It was half a century before undertakings along this line began actually to be made for geological surveys. His notion of how limestone and marble were formed had been equally ahead of his time. Collinson had laughed at the idea which was essentially the same as that held by modern geologists.

What his correspondent, Dr. Garden, thought of this audacious scheme is uncertain. But Bartram had an opportunity to renew his acquaintance with the doctor from Charleston, when in 1760 he decided to make a trip toward the south. It was not the trip he most longed to undertake. His eyes were turned westward, but better south than staying at home. He stopped on his way to visit John Clayton, an able botanist in Virginia, who had supplied Gronovius with the most of the descriptions used in his work, *Flora Virginica*. In Charleston he met one of the best correspondents he was ever to have. Mrs. Martha Logan, who, at the age of seventy was to write the first American book on gardening, put her knowledge, her skill and her enthusiasm at Bartram's disposal. When he returned home he wrote enthusiastically to Collinson about the elderly widow lady who "spares no pains nor cost to oblige me. I was with her five minutes in much

157

company, yet we contracted such a mutual correspondence, that one silk bag hath passed and repassed full of seeds three times this fall. I desired her to send some seeds of the Horse Sugar or Yellow Leaf. She directly sent me a box with three fine growing plants, mixed with several other sorts that she thought would please, and paid freight, with promises to send any vegetable in her power to procure; and they thrive finely."

The widower Collinson replied artfully, "I plainly see thou knowest how to fascinate the longing widow, by so close correspondence. When the women enter these amusements, I ever found them the best assistants. I shall not wonder if thy garden abounds with all the rarities of Carolina." Bartram picked up the word "fascinate" delightedly and tossed it back. "Now I hope to be stocked with *Padus,* as I have received a lovely package from Mrs. Logan, my fascinated widow. I saw a lovely tree growing in Governor Glenn's garden when I was there. She sent me a young tree from there, but the rats almost demolished it. I have also fascinated two men's wives, although one I never saw; that is, Mrs. Lamboll, who hath sent me two noble cargoes; one last fall, the other this spring. The other hath sent me, I think, a great curiosity. She calls it a Golden Lily. I thought when I planted it to be the *Atamasco,* but the bud seems different."

Dr. Garden seems not to have been so agreeable as Bartram's women friends. He failed to send anything except thanks in return for a package of bulbous roots. Bartram wrote Collinson of his disappointment and confided that he intended to ship a chest of apples to the busy doctor as an enticement to speak to the purpose.

It was a painful, tedious decade. With Bartram making fewer journeys than was customary, Collinson filled up the gap by reading travel books. He spied out the account of John Josselyn (1630-1675) and in letters to Bartram

tends to scoff at some of the specimens Josselyn alleges
to have encountered. What was his bird "Pilhannew"? A
monstrous great bird. Does he not exaggerate? Frogs, a
foot high! His "rattlesnake vapour" shows him to be a
vapourer. Then consider his account of the turkey-
buzzard. Josselyn must have a fine palate and a good
digestion to say a turkey-buzzard was good meat. And
he must surely have mistook a panther for a lion, especially a she-lion. Lions never are found in such cold climates.
"As for his Indian nymphs with whom he seems to have
been enamoured, what sayeth thou to these originals in
their native dress? Have they ever been able to charm an
Englishman, as they do the French, who are not so delicate?" One item in Josselyn's account won his approval:
a list of English plants growing in New England in his
time, which came in shipments of grass seed or by strange
accidents, as the willow and Scotch thistle. Collinson
admired the Scotch thistle and pointed out that climate
and soil could achieve wonders. Only see what happens
to the *Linaria,* accounted a pest by Bartram, but cherished
by Collinson in his garden for its fine spike of orange and
yellow flowers. But he is willing to give space even to the
ox-eyed daisy though it overruns many an English field.

The friends pined for the tonic wildness of Bartram's
wanderings. The cargoes were well and good; all the
plantings thrived but oh, for something new! War with the
French hemmed in Englishmen; Indians on the warpath
kept Bartram at home. Vast changes were in the making
but the friends could not pierce the future, though their
eyes were sharp for birds. "Pray send a sod or two of thy
pretty *Pyrola* with variegated leaves," implores Collinson.
"It flowered last year but I see no young shoots." It seems
to have been a period when "the present situation" was
always "difficult." How to lay out money properly worried
Collinson who seldom mentions his financial problems.

Stocks were falling every day in 1759 and though he had several thousands lying idle he had no idea "how to lay it out."

Even Bartram does not live up to his friend's expectations. Why has he not transplanted the Jersey waterlily to his own garden? Why be ambitious for plants from England when "here, in thy neighborhood, is the most charming plant of Asia, and yet so little is thy curiosity or industry, that thou canst not avail thyself of so great a curiosity." If Bartram would take the pains to gather the seed when ripe and put it in a bottle with a little sand or earth, he might ship it to them. Or a root might do, if packed in moss.

Bartram responded with his customary vigor: "Thee very unjustly reproacheth me for want of curiosity in the article of the Jersey Lily. I made three tries at different times. Twice it miscarried; and the last it grows so slow as scarcely to be seen. It will be very difficult to send roots; they are almost as brittle as glass, and run two or three feet deep in the mud. I hope to send the seed next fall, and perhaps a root. Spring water kills them, and the marsh weeds choke them." Bartram was later to develop this plant in his garden but it took careful tending, study and watchful waiting.

In spite of Bartram's unsatisfied longings to explore new territory he managed to make the best of staying at home; to experiment, to gather plants and seeds, to box and to ship, to plant and to cultivate. At work on his own acres his eyes enviously followed the birds in their flights. It was during this period that he began to watch their migrations with young Billy who made use of some fine drawing paper sent by Collinson to sketch many of the rare birds lingering in Bartram's garden to "fill their bellies" for the spring flight northward. Billy shot the birds, then carefully dried them. Within the bodies of the "hen birds" he found miniature eggs. Neither father nor son realized where Billy's preoccupation was to lead him. For Collinson it was only another "amusement" for the youth, highly appreciated in London. In later life, Billy was to compile the most complete and correct list of American birds preceding Alexander Wilson. Wilson's own study of birds owed its genesis to William Bartram who induced and encouraged the younger enthusiast in his life work.

The father and son must have dropped all other tasks to watch the birds as they came in great wandering bands over the valley, usually toward the close of day. The sky was a deep blue, turning to opal, as clouds of birds, idling in clumps, floated airily as leaves blown upon by some deep mysterious underground breath from the distant horizon to drift lightly and fall softly upon tree, bush and shrub. Clouds of birds plaintively cheeping, descended in fluttering spirals from on high, and as one group settled, another puff blew birds in from beyond the valley, until band after band of birds, cheeping, flitting from tree to shrub, settled to peck, to preen their feathers, to dip joyfully into water and to shake old seeds from winter-bitten pods.

While Billy made his fine drawings which were to draw exclamations of praise from Collinson—oh wonders, oh revelations!—Bartram kept his sober reckoning of the migrations. Many birds, he noticed, migrate in great flocks, as the geese, brants, pigeons and blackbirds. But others do not follow a straight line but flutter and hop about from tree to tree, or upon the ground, feeding backwards and forwards. It takes careful watching to determine their general direction for they appear to be bent upon going *both* backwards and forwards, moving indirectly toward their destined goal. The blue or ash colored herons never make a straight dash ahead but following the banks of a stream, spread their wings and sail from one side to the other, tacking back and forth in a long searching movement, or mooring on a bank "to victual" as they go. When new arrivals find the locality cluttered with more migrants than can readily find food, the newcomers tend, for the most part, to move onward. All these wild creatures of one species, observes Bartram, appear to belong to one great community with a common understanding of their mutual welfare and rather than pick a quarrel with one another, will move to a distance—"like Abraham and Lot" —where there may be food for all. "But most of our domestic animals are more like their masters. Everyone contends for his own dunghill and is for driving off all that come to encroach upon it."

Might not immense flocks of birds fly too high to be seen by the naked eye? Bartram liked to speculate on what went on above the clouds or in blue so deep as to drown the stealthy wandering multitude. Whooping cranes were more often heard than seen. Their cries descended, ghostlike, from far above any low-hanging clouds. A few sharp-eyed observers claimed to have witnessed, on a clear day, distant specks in the sky as the whooping of the cranes heralded their passage. To these witnesses it was clear that the cranes moved in flocks of about half a score as they flew from winter homes in Florida to summer residence at Hudson's Bay.

Bartram's account of the birds enthralled Collinson, but with his usual avidity for the particular, he yearns for a pair of swallows, a cock and a hen. Doubtless, he speculates, American swallows differ from the English among which he has noted four different varieties.

Collinson's optimism can never submerge for long. Toward the close of the decade he reminds Bartram that he has had remarkable luck with all his cargoes during this war. It's true what he took to be dwarf oaks showed up as a bundle of sticks without a root to their name. Didn't this curious sample of American goods get in by mistake? No matter, there is cause for rejoicing by 1759. Collinson trumpets the announcement that "Ft. Duquesne is in our hands. Soon John Bartram can sally forth with some party of traders. That fine country has been unsearched. So rich a soil is certain to be productive of new and rare vegetables, that we are strangers to!"

Collinson's hopefulness was a little premature. It would be two more years before Bartram could start toward Pittsburgh and in the interval he made the trip southward and met Mrs. Martha Logan. But there was no doubt that the next decade would once more open up the riches of the wilderness to the curiosity and inventive genius of Collinson's American friend.

CHAPTER IX

Y ou'd think that in such fruitful surroundings, it might have been fairly simple for John Bartram to console himself at home when traveling in the wilderness got too risky during Indian rampages. You'd think he might have rested with the thought that he was among the first to hybridize and make new species grow. But his was a quickness that ran to a beyond and a static time made him fume in slothful industry about his familiar farm. When in 1761 Indian troubles lulled, he looked his garden over and saw all his recent importations from the Carolinas thriving so prodigiously, he was "set all aflame" to head out into unexplored regions. The grand design to which he was committed laid hold of him so powerfully that he wrote Collinson he intended to venture to Pittsburgh and down the Ohio as far as he could get safe escort.

The very thought of being on the move again enhanced his living. His garden looks so fresh and strong, so responsive and giving, that he could not help boast to Collinson, but not vaingloriously, "I do believe I can challenge any garden in America for variety." The fair prospect of new journeys even limbers up his gratitude for English seeds and he bursts out to his friend that he has a glorious appearance of carnations, "the brightest colors my eyes ever beheld."

Collinson, too, went all in a flame at the journey proposed by Bartram for the rescue of new plant marvels. "Who knows," he wrote ecstatically, "what wonderful productions may be found about the Lakes?" With Bartram's penetrating eye hidden riches are certain to come to light. He foresees his friend, homeward bound, laden with treasure. His weather eye is already alerted for his share, for Collinson is keeper of a Noah's Ark in Britain to succor waifs of every living plant species. Bartram must bring back new members for his colony on Mt. Ararat. He will unpack the dainties with his own hands, careful of each particle of earth from which some unknown wonder may arise. "For I have raised many odd plants out of earth thou would never think to send seeds of." One sod of *Sarrancenia* (Pitcher Plant) nursed a species of *Orchis* with a most singular flower. Wouldn't it be worth while to send sods, just sods, lifted from the wild boggy places where most of the rare and odd plants thrive? Shouldn't they be transported for the sake of the uncommon specimens they produce?

Collinson will take his chance on a lump of earth. It is certain to yield his kind of gold. Nor will he stop at earth clods when it comes to furnishing his Ark. What about that marvelous Great Buffalo whose bones may be seen standing nearby a licking place alongside the Ohio River? The Indians are said to claim that the herd was struck by

165

lightning where they stood. His friend, George Croghan, saw the skeletons with his own eyes and sent him two great teeth as witnesses. But so unaccustomed was this friend to speculation that he never thought to note the hoofs and horns. Now that Bartram may wander in that vicinity may he not verify these particulars and thus make possible some sort of definition of the species? The name, the name! The clue to mysteries.

The appeal for news of the Buffalo leaves Bartram cold. "My head runs all upon the works of God in Nature," he wrote Collinson. "It is through the telescope I see God in his glory." There is a midnight scene. Bartram with his eye to the telescope was carried away. He describes his vision of an illimitable universe, of "orbs beyond orbs, without number, suns beyond suns, systems beyond systems, with their proper inhabitants of the great Jehovah's empire, how can we look on these without amazement, most humble adoration. Esteeming ourselves, with our wisdom, but as one of the smallest atoms of dust praising the living God, the great I AM." How come down to earth from his exalted mood to pick among old bones? He dismisses the picture of the Buffalo, caught in death, standing as in life at the salt licks as childish. "As for those monstrous skeletons on the Ohio. Thee seems to think they stand in the posture of beasts alive. Why the ligaments would rot, the bones fall out of joint and tumble to the ground. It's a great pity and shame to the learned curiosos, that have great estates, that they don't send some person that will take pains to measure every bone exactly before they are broken and carried away, which they will be soon, by the ignorant, careless people for gain."

He was more interested in identifying a species of the milkweed family which he had sent with other specimens to Dr. Solander for the name, the name! Oh, to name the world and hold it tight, to pin it down from vaporous wanderings! The Doctor called Bartram's find *Ascelpias linifolia*. But Bartram disdained the verdict. Why his find was unique and had flowers and leaves different from the genus named by Solander. He indulges in a rapturous minute description of its excellencies; how it casts its long, rough, misshapen seeds, like bits of rotten wood, out of the top of its long, upright pods. The pod contracts as it dries, squeezing the seed out at the top, which slowly opens by contraction below. Oh, most exact description, not only of a plant, but of a living relationship between a man and his object. This is love wholly occupied with the object.

Bartram's way of seeing his pet Milkweed was typical of the Eighteenth Century. Many men and women of the period were content to gather no spoils, but to watch and to wait for the seasons. In England there was Gilbert White, a man of very different antecedents from Bartram, who watched the birds and field mice without disturbing them. Born at Selborne, Hants, he graduated from Oxford and after serving as proctor and dean of his college, Oriel, finally settled as curate in his native parish. His *Natural History and Antiquities of Selborne* raised natural history into the region of literature as the *Compleat Angler* by Isaac Walton did for angling. Like Thoreau he believed in the importance of studying one locality thoroughly and kept a calendar of his observations, ranging from turtles to weather, from swallows to earthworms. Earthworms, he reported gravely, were addicted to venery. Animals loved their kind. Sociality was independent of sexual attachment. A hen might be attached to a horse, a horse to a hen. Close, small watching, unridden by any pragmatic purpose, engaged the hours of this curate who lived on a comfortable estate, pouring out observations about nature in letters to his friends. Like Bartram, he was ready

167

to believe only what he saw with his own eyes. Even a maggot was wonderful. Oh, wonderful maggot! This is the voice of a lover. The use of the word "wonder" by these men is important. It was not the conventional romantic "wonder" but something deeper. Their "wonder" had an object. It was more than a rapturous exclamation.

When Collinson writes to Bartram, "there is no end to the wonders of Nature. The more I see, the more I covet to see; not to gratify a trifling curiosity but to raise my mind in contemplation on the unlimited power and wisdom of the Great Creator of all things," he was voicing the conventional side of the prevailing attitude of the Nature lovers. To refer to "the Maker" was not a pose; it was felt and believed, though it was also a convention of the day. What these men were actually interested in was *what was happening in Nature.* What engrossed them was creation.

Bartram, trusting his own vision, refused to accept Solander's verdict about his find, the Milkweed. He continued to assert it was a new variety, as yet unnamed, but he was willing to make excuses for the Doctor who could not easily judge a specimen that was already dried up before it reached him. Solander might be mistaken. Bartram is not willing to allow that his Dulcinea has been rightly seen if not judged unique.

The competent Dr. Daniel Solander had accomplished much in putting to order the ranks of the straggling plants but he himself was something of an odd species. He seems to have been looked upon a little askant by the devoted brethern of botany. For he was often addicted to laziness. Worst of all, to ingratitude. Born in Nordland, Sweden, in 1736, he was a youngster compared to Bartram and Collinson. He had been Linnaeus's favorite pupil at Upsala, and after receiving an M.D. degree, came to England at the age of twenty-three. Consigned by his patron to the care of Mr. Ellis at the British Museum, good fortune followed his beginnings. His polite manners ingratiated him in London society; his knowledge of natural history won the approval of Sir Joseph Banks who chose the young man to accompany him on his voyage around the world with Captain Cook. But the voyage and London society unhinged something in him; he was inexplicably indifferent. He even developed "unfilial traits of character rarely witnessed in a votary of the amiable science," as well as dissipated habits. He neglected his correspondence with Linnaeus, and seems to have allowed letters from his doting mother to lie around unopened. Several such letters were found still sealed after his death at the age of forty-six.

Collinson seems to have been more willing than Bartram to accept Dr. Solander's decree regarding the specimen of the milkweed family, but he tactfully refrained from pressing his opinion. For one thing, he was now beguiled by a new creation called the *Tipitiwitchet* which Bartram had described to him in a letter. If he could only be certain that Bartram had this waggish creature safe and sound in his own garden! Bartram's description of its sensitivity, how it seems to shudder when offended and how it folds itself together as the sun goes down, is almost more than Collinson can bear. If only Billy Bartram might make a drawing of this coy plant. When Bartram assures Collinson that the plant is safely planted in his own garden, Collinson implores him, "Pray take care of it. Protect its roots carefully against vile weather." Once more he suggests that Billy paint this specimen, quite forgetting that poor Billy Bartram is incarcerated in a store in Carolina, trying to make his hard way in the world. Then Collinson reminds Bartram never to let a letter pass without a sample of this plant as it progresses. He wishes to see it advance from birth to old age.

In his fever about the Sensitive Plant he almost overlooks the grand project of Bartram's journey to Pittsburgh and even after descriptions of the new explorations begin to roll in, he gnaws away at news for his new favorite, the Tipitiwichet that some call the Bashful Briar. He even threatens, "If I have not a specimen of it in thy next letter, never write me more, for it is cruel to tantalize me with relations, and not to send me a little specimen in thine of the 15th of August nor in thine of the 29th. It shows thou hast no sympathy nor compassion for a virtuoso. I wish it was in my power to mortify thee so much."

Collinson's own plants were languishing for lack of rain that season, and worst of all, a "villain" robbed him of twenty-two different species, taking all his most rare and beautiful plants. All his fine tall Marsh Martigans that Bartram had sent him the year before and which were different in color from any he had ever had, were rudely torn out of their beds and snatched away. All his yellow Lady's Slippers that he had watched for years, flowering faithfully each season, were gone. The Lady's Slippers he regretted most for he feared it would not be easy to replace them, even with Bartram's assistance, as he understood they were only come upon in the American wilds accidentally. Such disappointments did not damp his ardor for new things. The older he grew the more the frenzy for his plants' welfare and happiness seems to have gripped him. He could not bear to think that Bartram might slight some specimen sent from England. Fancying that Bartram rather depreciates the Pomegranate sent to him, he harangues him: "Don't use the Pomegranate inhospitably, a stranger that has come so far to pay his respects to thee. Don't turn him adrift in the wide world; but plant it against the south wall of thy house, nail it close to the wall. Then it will thrive. It bears fruit for me this hot year; I counted

170

twenty-four on one tree. And Dr. Fothergill has said, that of all trees, this is most salubrious to mankind."

As for the waggish Tipitiwichet, hardly a letter passes between the friends without some reference to it. Bartram was making a careful study of its behavior out of which he was to evolve his theory of volition and sensation in plants. The substance of his observations, the relation of the plant's progress and how it fared almost overshadowed the Pittsburgh journey, which is a pity, for Bartram's journal of this expedition has been lost and nothing remains but comments he made concerning the trip in letters to his friends. Even such details have to be exhumed from the tendrils of Tipitiwichet which threaten to throttle it. It is not likely that the most telling event of that trip was the almost total absence of wild animals, to which Bartram was to devote a long letter relating this fact to his friend. He saw no wild animals except two or three deer and one tame bear at Ft. Pittsburgh. Never heard or saw a wolf or a fox although he lay six nights in the woods, on the banks of the Ohio and Monongahela, and was two nights very late in the Allegheny Mountains. He claims to be much astonished in reading histories of Europe and Asia to learn that such quantities of wild beasts should abound in such old settled countries. To say nothing of the wealth of fish in the streams and the wild fowl, if one can believe their reports. Sixty years ago, in America, it might have been the same. Now, alas, in all the small creeks where once he caught trout, not one has been seen for three or four years. Nor did he see one fish caught in all this journey, nor during a sojourn in the South, except at the Wateree, a branch of the great Santee River in South Carolina. Yet only think how many great rivers he had crossed! Nor did he see any wild geese, only a few ducks and three or four small flocks of turkey.

Doubting Collinson sarcastically queries, if no animals,

from whence come all the quantities of skins he has seen in the public markets? Where did these animals hide? But he forgives Bartram all for his description of the *Pyramid of Eden*. What a glorious sight it must be in bloom! Linnaeus makes it a *Swertia*, next genus to a Gentian and differing from them by having beautiful nectariums, consisting of tiny tufts of almost invisible hairs in the hollow of each petal. Dr. Alexander Garden calls it the glory of the Blue Mountains.

Collinson's rebuttal on his account of wild animals pricks Bartram's memory. He recalls he did see a thing called an Alligator on the Ohio that he takes for a water lizard, a new genus, very good, like a catfish, and tail like a muskrat's, with a fin around it, nails like a man, with a membrane on each side, reaching from the fore to the hind foot, like a flying squirrel. The wildcat he also saw, he now recollects, and takes it to be a lynx, in every respect like a cat but with a short bob tail.

But nothing will really quiet down his London friend except a living, breathing specimen of the twittery Briar Queen, the Tipitiwichet. "Oh Botany, delightfulest of all sciences!" cries the enraptured man, echoing in spirit the earlier refrain of Sir Thomas Browne's "O Altitudo!" "There is no end to thy gratifications," Collinson thankfully declares in acknowledging a shipment of plants from the Pittsburgh area, among them the Tipitiwichet, "All botanists will join me in thanking my dear John for his unwearied pains to gratify every inquisitive genius. I have sent Linnaeus a specimen plant, and one leaf of Tipitiwichet for his pains; only to him would I spare such a jewel. Pray send more of this. I fear we can never raise it. Linnaeus will be in raptures at the sight of it."

Stirring events were on foot in the world and the loss of Pitt from the helm of government in England plunged Bartram into a fit of melancholy. Not Collinson, who mourned more deeply for a shipment of plants lost at that very time at sea. "The loss of so many fine plants affects me more than the loss of Pitt," he wrote his friend, and went on to say that he really wonders at his dear John for being so upset by this abdication of a man whose departure portends no harm that he can see. "Never fear, we shall keep Canada, and have a good peace; and Pitt is well pleased with his mercenary pension of 3000 pounds per annum, and a title in reversion; and has cleverly slipped his neck out of the collar, when it most became him to keep in, and serve his country, but he preferred serving himself before it. So now he is known by the name of the Grand Pensioner, a blast on his reputation that will last forever." Collinson implores his dear John to take heart and not to be carried away by reports, to revive his drooping spirits and to look forward and to hope for the best. Everything that Pitt did was not glorious, and everything is not lost.

Collinson refuses to blur his green horizon with the cloud of politics. Mixing exhortations to his friend to be of good heart with rapture for his magnolia, he holds up the torch of this towering pyramid with blossoms at the extremity of almost every branch. This deciduous mountain magnolia, first raised from seed twenty years before, has flowered for the first time for him, and is the first, he is convinced, ever to flower in England, and the largest and the tallest. This is the descendant of that great magnolia, sent years before to him, when Bartram returned from his first journey along the route of the Susquehanna to the Great Lakes. Such joyous news should inspire his dear John to revive. "Don't sink, and be lost in doleful dumps," and lest the magnolia fail to restore his friend he will try teasing, "I really believe my honest John is a great wag and has sent seven hard stoney seeds, something shaped like an acorn, to puzzle us; for there is no name to them." He guesses them to be a hickory and his guess is right. They were a present to Bartram from Colonel Bouquet at Ft. Pittsburgh who transported them from Illinois country.

But nothing Collinson might say was able to dispel the gloom that seems to have settled down upon Bartram who continued to grumble for the loss of Pitt and to belittle the peace. He reminded Collinson that most Americans look upon all "our boasted acquisitions" in North America as titular and that only of short duration, as the French still claimed all one side of the Mississippi and part of the English side. "They will," counselled Bartram, "draw the chief of our fur trade near them, and will always be setting the Indians against us, suppose we do keep possession of the Lakes." His recommendation was "to bang the Indians stoutly to make them fear us for they will never love us nor keep peace long with us. Nothing would do except an all out attack, to drive them back a thousand miles or to subdue them." Pitt, Bartram thinks, might have made a better peace than Bute and nothing Collinson may say, can reassure him.

Balked in his hopes to explore into the vast western territories, he sees the Indians and French as the enemies of all his plans. The fate of the seaboard even dims in his dark mood. He knows, he *knows*, what a noble discovery he might have made if he could have followed the banks of the Ohio and the Mississippi. His son William was also all afire and ready to set out as draughtsman for the expedition. The poor young fellow may well have felt life to be a hell of unrealized opportunities.

Reading in a magazine of a scheme proposed in England to search all Canada and Louisiana for natural productions, convenient situations for manufactures, and to chart different soils, minerals and vegetable growths, Bartram points to himself proudly as the man best fitted in North America to give a true account of whatever vegeta-

174

tion may be found in those localities. He knows, as well as he knows his own worth, that the variety of plants to be found is beyond expression. Oh, in Louisiana one would find the palace garden of all gardens! If he could but spend six months on the Ohio, the Mississippi, and in Florida, in health, he could find more curiosities than the English, the French or the Spaniards have done in six score years. But the Indians, instigated by the French, will not let him look at so much as a plant or a tree in this great British Empire.

The green world will melt away; it will slowly vanish and he will not be able to bear witness. He feels the blow of his frustration so keenly that he can cite only instances to prove his point; how he made a trip with his son John to Little Egg Harbour to show him the very spot where grew a pretty *Ornithogalum* (Star of Bethlehem) only three years past, but now, alas, not one was to be seen. As a rationalist, Bartram was literal in his description but his state of mind was something else. The deep gloom was not justified, not even concerning the pretty Star of Bethlehem, which continues to this day to sparkle along brooks and in meadows of Pennsylvania. But his mind was all lament. He trusts his vision and knows that on first journeys his eyes will spy every variety to be seen. In his thirty years of travel he insists he never found in the same spot, though twenty times traveled over, one single species that he did not observe on his first journey. But many times he discovered plants the first time which neither he nor anyone else could find again. Cattle, he supposes, destroyed the plant life. But once again, his gloom bounds beyond his hope; he names the *Meadia,* renamed by Linnaeus the *Dodecatheon,* from the Greek, for *twelve* gods. Crossing the Shenandoah, he saw one or two plants, stalk and seeds, and jumping from his horse gathered the seed to plant in his garden and to send to Collinson. Both sowings succeeded; had they not, this plant might have been lost to the world! For he never found it in the same spot again, nor did John Clayton who searched all that vicinity. But Bartram was wrong; this fine plant with its rose-purple and sometimes white flowers, actually grew in the vicinity of his own home. In his present state of mind, he was willing to forecast only disaster to Nature, nothing except perishing beauty.

CHAPTER X

J OHN BARTRAM's gloomy state of mind was a reflection
of the troubled climate of that day. It was not only
that he resented the fact that his life must be forcibly
twisted about events. Men of every age have rebelled
against seeming to be mere accidents of geography and
climate. The colonists were beginning to seethe against
their subservience to England. Colonial journalists of the
time were pointing out that England was thriving upon
the produce of the colony, had extended her trade to other
countries by virtue of American goods, and took advantage
of the cheapened American money. It was becoming burdensome to be patronized. The colonies felt themselves as
a hardy green shoot, thrusting up and out, and the tender
green already itched to shuffle off the hard old bark.
Within the colonies, within Pennsylvania, once united,

schisms and dissensions boiled. Quakers quarreled with Quakers. Splinter groups broke off to make condemnations of the older congregations. The country was fermenting toward an undefined future and within the ferment, men often felt fragmented, tormented with uncertainty.

Collinson's calm advice to Bartram to have patience went against the American grain. Though Bartram had often invoked Providence on his own account, it was hard now, at this juncture of his life, with age coming fast upon him, to be told that "Providence orders all things for the best." Could he wait for Providence? How long would his limbs hold out? He did not care who held the land he yearned to explore so long as he might travel safely within it. The massive dark of forest with its frail trail of human tracks was the great tormentor. He saw it in its immediacy and longed to touch. Did not want to be kept outside by Indian war whoops. He had listened to shuddering tales of settlers scalped; had felt the crawl of flesh at the immanence of terror. Certain Quakers in Philadelphia might impore their brethren to remember first causes, but Bartram would refuse to shift the blame from the Indians; he would have nothing less than their destruction and the possession of Indian lands.

History was being powdered, made worthless, lost. The emergency of the moment made fierce demands and with rapacity, thrust fiercely. Bartram knew that the country must be settled, the wilderness pushed back, opened up to homes and cultivated fields. He approved and applauded at the same time that he feared the destruction of the thing he loved. Oh, to run ahead of the pack and to gather in, *first,* and after that, to open up the pleasant land, build new waterways, make a great nation.

It was a torment to Bartram that he had to look to England for help if he was to make new explorations, assuming that the Indians would allow him to prowl in peace.

Collinson was sensitive to his situation and deplored the blindness of the rich, who were not public spirited enough to see the advantages of botanical surveys in the new wild territories. In England, he sadly summarized, court politics so engrossed the attention of all the great men that they had no room to think of anything else. He does not think Bartram should undertake such a venture at his own expense, but from whence is the wherewithal to come?

Collinson might be a modern poet balked by the general indifference, so sensitively does he outline the bedeviled situation in which his friend finds himself. And at this critical juncture, when Bartram craved encouragement and positive help, he was to suffer the humiliation of seeing honors heaped upon a head less worthy than his own. To his stunned astonishment, his neighbor Young was given sudden preferment at Court and summoned to England to become the Queen's botanist. Such distinction astonished "a great part of our inhabitants," wrote the outraged Bartram. "They are daily talking to me about him, that he has got more honor by a few miles walking to pick up a few common plants, than I have by near thirty years travel, with great danger and peril." He suffered from the deep rebuff; that a novice should be rewarded for obscure reasons divorced from accomplishments! The plants sent by Young and now so unexpectedly elevated beyond their merits, were not new to England, for Bartram had been sending the same for thirty years, and many of those sent by Young had even been known in England for a hundred years.

But Bartram had loyal friends and their indignation upheld him. They put him up to making a new attempt of his own to win the Royal favor, and it is touching to see his readiness to swallow personal pride for the sake of the greater pride of his dedication. Yes, he will make up a box of *newly discovered* items to dazzle the King, and such as he is certain, the King's eyes have never looked upon before. Confident of the loyal Collinson, he sent a box to the King in his care, with a letter enumerating his own treasures. Franklin was as incensed as Bartram and advised Collinson if he did not "feel free to undertake the mission, to turn it over to Dr. Pringle, who would."

Bartram refused to be downed by this display of irresponsibility on the King's part and hoping he may yet win favor, set about making plans for such an outcome. "I am too old," he writes Collinson, "to make the trip alone but I think my son William will be a fit person to accompany me, and by this time, can draw well."

This is the first hopeful reference made to Billy for several years. Now, at last, it appears there may be a chance to rescue him from the doldrums at Cape Fear. In earlier letters between the friends Billy's name was seldom mentioned without some kind of sad, though kindly meant, disparagement. Bartram's fifth son, John, had now become his father's support and helper, and the father praised him for the very virtues poor Billy seemed to lack in his struggle with the world. Young John was "worthy, sober, industrious." He also delighted in plants. William, on the other hand, draws the fearful prophecy: "I doubt Will will be ruined in Carolina." The father no longer called this son "Billy" but gave the more adult name as if in expectation that the young man might reach up to it. Collinson's rejoinder might have been for someone who had already died: "William was a very ingenious lad, but I am afraid made some mistakes. Johnny seems now to be our sheet anchor. I hope he will inherit his father's virtues and at leisure and suitable opportunity make Nature his study."

To make William's defeat the more conspicuous, other men's sons began to show up handsomely. The son of Lord Petrie, Bartram's first patron, had now reached manhood and had put in his first order for a ten guinea box of American plants. "It may truly be said, the spirit of Elijah rests on Elisha," wrote the delighted Collinson of the son of the patron he had adored. And as if reminded by this circumstance of Bartram's situation, as a father, Collinson praised John who, he is glad to see, also inherits the spirit of *his* father. But it is impossible to forget Billy, that once grand hope, and even in praise of John, he slips in a regret, "Poor Billy, who was so ingenious, now lost in indolence and obscurity."

But in spite of the negation concerning Billy, John Bartram unquestionably nourished secret hopes for this son. No one could draw as he did. Not one of his children adored plants as William did. Perhaps if he is taken on the Florida trip—although, as yet, it is only a dream—he may emerge from the curious swamp of defeat and assert himself in his former promise and glory. William has disappointed him sorely. And deeply puzzled him. If his son, Moses, could resurrect himself from a ten years tomb at sea, why could Billy not have fulfilled his mission at the posts assigned him? What troubled Bartram most, was a certain unreliability, a kind of whimsicality in William that baffled the downright father whose approach to anything he did or proposed to tackle was direct and firm. To the father's eyes, this son was indirect and wavering, twining as a grapevine that grabs now this, now that, and often seems to be entangled and borne down by the very branch it would mount. When he would put William on the spot and command a duty to be performed, William slipped out from the noose and was nowhere. There's the time he was expected to send seeds from Carolina and none came. Bartram felt the disappointment keenly and did not hesitate to say so. Why, the seeds he might have sent were within a mile or two of his common walks! "I have not received one seed from my son who glories so much in the knowledge of plants, and whom I have been at so much charge to instruct therein. I don't want thee to hinder thy own affairs to oblige me; but thee might easily gather a few seeds, when thee need not hinder half an hour's time to gather them, or turn twenty yards out of thy way to pluck them." Yet with all the reproof, he remains, "thy loving father."

No doubt about it, he was a loving father and a tenacious one. But the two men, beneath their apparent similarity, are so very unlike. One has only to compare the father's concise accounts of the wilderness with William's rapturous prolixity when he was finally to encounter the southern savannas and fountains to see the temperamental difference. The older man could not understand the hesitations of the younger; such behavior seemed weakness, a matter to be overcome by an energetic will. John Bartram had so few doubts concerning his own being. He was almost like a plant, animal or star who never has to decide what it will do the next instant. He seemed to know what had to be done and to drive straight for his goal. But his son was the more modern man, caught in indecision, trapped by events.

To make matters harder for the father, he felt himself growing old. Now when he traveled, he was inclined to emphasize the mileage covered, the bad roads undertaken, the icy rivers crossed. In a letter to his brother, written when Bartram was sixty-three, he even complains of his supperless nights on the open ground during a trip through the Carolinas. Perhaps he felt it the more keenly that younger, less expert men were being rewarded beyond their deserts. In another sense, he appears to want to prove that he is as hardy as ever, and could stoutly risk what younger men would not endure. At times he even seems to vaunt his powers as a flag to William whose spirits wilted at what the father conceived as no more than simple duty. He could not understand his son's brand of responsibility, so committed to one thing only, that other occupations whittled down his very power to exist in life at all.

This was a battle between the scientific mind and the artist's approach to his material and his life. For William could not function half dull trader and half inspired explorer of the wild. Nor would he ever be able to become, at one and the same time, solid practical farmer and conscientious botanist. John Bartram might tread two paths, conjunctive and sustained each to each, but not William. His way was complete committal or defeat. Like most fathers, Bartram expected this son, who favored him in his passionate interests, to be like him in other ways, a true stamp of the old coin. But he was also determined that this good seed should not fall upon barren ground, and, if he could, he would prepare more favorable soil.

He would not let petty, personal pride stand in the way of his grand plans that might also mean a new life for William. In October, 1764, a month after he had received the news of Young's appointment, he sent a new shipment of plants to Collinson, for his own use, and reminded him of the box, sent a few weeks earlier for the King. He had a shrewd intention in his mind in challenging the attention of the King. In his box were rarities to spread before the King for comparison with the paltry selection that had won, for Young, honors. He does not depend on such preferment as Young received, and yet, in justice to himself, it is only fair that his own specimens be laid before the King.

Actually, he did not want an appointment in England. What he craves is solid backing for an expedition to Florida, and in the midst of his maneuvering for the King's attention he cannot help but wonder what success the more fortunate Young is having in England. Most of Bartram's neighbors seem to think, he confides to Collinson, that he will make such an awkward appearance at Court he will soon return home. Others believe that the Queen will take care of the "German gentleman." But Bartram himself is magnanimous to the victor and fancies he may make a botanist, if he is put under Dr. Hill's care, as "Young is very industrious and has a good share of ingenuity."

Bartram will not confide all his hopes in the King. Once more he implores the faithful Collinson to search about among the nobility, with whom he is well acquainted, for men of curiosity who may be prevailed upon to back a venture into the King's new southern acquisitions. So convinced is he of eventual success that he can even state his own conditions; he must have someone accompany him; there must be an allowance sufficient to make full discovery and not to be hurried for time; there must be carriage to transport specimens he may discover. He ends his plea with the reminder that he is now sixty-six years old and cannot expect to perform such tasks many years hence. He must yield eventually to the infirmities of age or death.

His appeal struck home in Collinson and with his customary zeal he bustled about to win favors for Bartram. Franklin also put his back to the wheel. In November of that year he sailed for England with a consignment of twenty-two boxes of plants, a little package of one hundred different seeds, a parcel of Chinquapins and willow-oak specimens for the correspondents. Arriving in England, he joined forces with Collinson in behalf of Bartram, and by April, 1765, Collinson could write the triumphant news that Bartram had been appointed botanist to his Most Gracious Majesty at fifty pounds a year.

The good fellow was all of a twitter at the glorious opportunity opening up for Bartram and as full of advice as any old Granny sending off some tender sprig of a child into the unknown. Bartram is to collect specimens of plants, fossils and ores and make observations on the soil and the lay of the land. He must provide paper for specimens and get a leather cover of the same size as the paper to protect it from the weather. He should have leather bags for seeds to secure them from rain. Also he must take flat boxes and pins to catch insects, bees, beetles, wasps and locusts. Moths and butterflies will be too difficult. Pray look out for land snails and river shells. And, oh most important, at the same time that he is collecting seeds for the King, do not forget Collinson and all the eager correspondents.

In a follow-up letter he admonished Bartram not to overdo himself. "As thou grows in years, thou will do well to consider if thy present constitution and habit of body can undergo the fatigue of such an expedition." Collinson seems to have had sudden qualms about sending this old friend out upon another arduous expedition in an unknown wilderness; he bids caution. And he drops a hint at what this favor to his friend has cost him; "John, thou knows nothing of what it is to solicit at Court any favor; they are so taken up with public affairs, little things slip through their fingers. For all I can do, I cannot get thee letters of recommendations to any of the Governors." Mr. Ellis, of the British Museum, was more obliging; he had recently received some appointment in the Floridas and had written on his own authority to the Governors of the southern territories to look out for Bartram. Perhaps, worries Collinson, Bartram will not think the sum allotted enough. He admits that he did not expect anything. "So thou may use it, or refuse it, as thou likes best, or search as far as the salary will go to support it. In this case I cannot advise thee."

But Bartram was only waiting for the word *go*. Nothing except accident or death could have restrained him. During the winter months his spirits had been enlivened by other hopes. Before he had confirmation of the King's appointment, he had learned that Lord Bute and the Earl of Northumberland had declared it was necessary to search the Floridas and that he was the proper person to do it. Then, his friend, Colonel Bouquet, with whom he had continued to correspond since they met at Pittsburgh, appeared at Bartram's house with Lord Gordon, and the Governor of Pennsylvania. Lord Gordon had proposed that Bartram accompany him to Quebec, taking in all the seaports on the way; he promised to bring him back again, at his own expense. Nor was Colonel Bouquet behind in his proposals. He urged Bartram to go with him in his ship to Pensacola, where he would find a man to wait upon him and an escort through the dangerous passes—and, it would not cost him a farthing. While Bartram was considering these glittering offers, the news came that the King had unbent in his favor.

Now he was all set, in wherewithal and esteem. He wrote William to get ready to go with him. He will sail with Colonel Bouquet in two or three weeks for Augustine; if they stop at Charleston, he will disembark there. William is advised to sell off all his goods at public auction and to give his accounts into the hands of an attorney who will recover his debts better than he can do. He should also write his creditors to let them know how matters stand. But he must have sat for a few moments, brooding about this unpredictable son. Splendid as the opportunity is, will he take it up? Returning to his letter, he added the brisk advice that if William does not intend to come along, to let him know at once. He will seek another companion. As if to drive him to this bargain, he adds what must have seemed to William a threat; William's brother-in-law, George, who had married his sister, Ann, wants him to come home and go into partnership with him, in his business.

Delay, halt, hesitation; these had been the sum of William's efforts to reach out, to touch and to hold the only possessions he valued. Accumulations meant little to him; he wanted to be as disembodied as his birds and flowers that he might more closely mingle with them and come to understanding. He is a little crippled by misfortune, by this time; his experience has made him hesitant, and once more, he is to progress under the weighty authority of a most weighty father. But he takes the leap, gladly, from Cape Fear.

The next we hear of the pair, they are safe in the southern sun. But Bartram had hardly landed before he committed indiscretions. He had wandered in a Charleston garden in noonday heat almost to the point of sunstroke. Some distemper had likewise seized upon him. When Collinson hears the news, he scolds his friend; "I wish thou might temper thy zeal with prudence but do not think it an instance of it, when thou and Mrs. Lamboll rambled in the intense heat of a noonday sun. Perhaps it was to procure thee a seasoning." Bartram's rash exposure called for more advice, tinged with some envy of the man who could sport so gaily with other men's wives in tropical gardens: "To think a wise man should have so little prudence! What cannot be cured, must be endured, for I see no remedy." He was a little fretful with Bartram, who, though he now had his heart's desire, was beginning to pepper his correspondence with complaints. Besides, the English summer was stifling. It had gone up to 95 degrees in Collinson's own parlor. He was in no mood to sympathize with a gallivanting friend.

Still, he cannot refrain from perpetual advice. Now it is a horse that Bartram must certainly have. It is a necessary adjunct to a King's botanist. Though the King only allows fifty pounds, and a horse may come to forty pounds, still, in American money, a horse may not be that dear.

Perhaps they are even cheap where they may be found wild and to be caught for the trouble. Then Bartram could sell the horse after the trip and recover something. Sitting in his stuffy parlor in a hot dry summer with all his precious plants wilting away in his garden, Collinson bent his mind toward his friend, cajoling, explaining, informing, and being a busy-body to all Nature.

As late as September he had not yet delivered to the King Bartram's box of specimens intended to inform that Monarch of the imposition of Young's claims. Young, too, has been lost sight of. Collinson believes he is "studying." The Queen has paid no attention to a splendid seed vessel of *Faba Egyptiaca* presented to her by Collinson. There have been so many revolutions at Court that Collinson is of the opinion that this is no time to bring forward Bartram's box of specimens; it would get little attention from the Crown. By November he was thoroughly provoked. Bartram's brother, William, of Cape Fear, had decided to sidle up to the King on his own account, and without asking leave of anyone, shipped a box of ores to the King in care of Collinson. "Thy brother making so free with the King is ridiculous," fumed Collinson, and, moreover, had given him trouble at the custom house, to say nothing of a charge of six shillings, six pence which he would be obliged to add to Bartram's account or else sell the ores to pay the sum. It was really impossible to know the trouble, difficulty and attendance necessary to get anything to the King. "Though I undertook it for thee, I shall not for anybody else."

England was again in a change of ministry. Though Bartram had hinted that his meager fifty pounds should be boosted to a hundred in all fairness to his efforts, Collinson was obliged to remind him that nothing could be expected with the members of the helm joggling and shifting. Moreover, he was getting worn down with complaints. Unable to roam himself, he seems to have suddenly become weary of any more talk about the salary. "Thou knows the length of a chain of fifty links," he admonished. "Go as far as that goes, and when that's at an end, cease to go farther." He pointed out that Bartram had received fifty pounds and if they all lived until Michaelmas he will have added another fifty. It was even possible that if both Bartram and the King live, his friend may, in time, be the gainer. It's true that the premium is not worth the risk, but in such unsettled times there is no hope for more. Collinson thinks that Bartram should watch his health and not expose himself or wear himself out to serve others on so slender an encouragement. Go home, he continued to reiterate in every letter. Sit under your own vine and fig tree. Contemplate the wonders you have seen and "give thy old friend a taste of these dainties, who, thou knowest, will relish them as they deserve, and treasure them up with the rest of thy curious and ingenious observations."

They are two old men whose strength is failing, and, from across the ocean, the one looks out for the other, as tenderly as he cares for his plants. But Collinson's rare collection was not secure in this world. Once more his garden was robbed of prized wonders; his deepest regret was for his Loblolly Bays, which had been so thriving; then Bartram's sod of Orchis in full flower; also the long leafed Pitcher plant. There is a list too long to mention and Time is running out for Collinson. Still, he will not give up the fight and implores Bartram to look about him, while he is still in the South, for four or five Pitcher plants and don't forget to pack each in moss, tied up well. With this robbery he feels he is ruined and can no longer stand in any competition. "Once I bore the bell," he remarks plaintively, "but now I very humbly condescend to be on an equal footing with my neighbors."

Bartram was struggling with his own difficulties in

Florida. Back at his own house in June, 1766, he is able to write the first intimate account of his sufferings. His journal has been faithfully kept and is to be sent to the King, as well as many fine Florida and Georgia specimens. It will take time to satisfy Collinson's curiosity, but for a start, he will tell him that the collection being sent cost him many score pounds, pain and sickness, which held him constantly for nearly two months in Florida with fever, jaundice and a looseness that stayed by him all through North and South Carolina. Yet, somehow or other, he did not lose an hour's time traveling through those provinces. In St. Augustine, though he had fever and jaundice, he traveled by water and land all around the town for many miles and got to Picolata, to the Congress with the Indians, although he was so weak it was hard to get up from his bed. During the meeting between the Governor and the Indians, he was forced to sit or lie down on the ground, but kept close, so he could observe all that passed.

All sorts of specimens are on the way to England including drawings from Billy. When the drawings arrive, Collinson took pains to show Billy's work to Mr. Ehret, the English flower painter, who admired them as fully as he did. Especially the fine red *Centaury*, a most elegant plant, which Collinson hopes may land in English gardens. Billy's butterflies "are nature itself." And he is especially pleased to see that Billy has found so "pretty a way" of drying fish.

There is so much of interest passing back and forth between the friends, so many fabulous boxes to pack and unpack, that Collinson really wonders at Bartram, now home again, and safe, at last, for troubling himself to inquire about the Queen's favorite, Young. There is no use in inquiring about the Queen, either, for she has Young, and every favor will be shown him. Nor can it be expected that Young will go out of his way and put in a word with the Queen for Bartram. Young is now so new modelled, and grown so fine and fashionable, with his hair curled and tied in a black bag, that he was not recognized by the people at Collinson's office when he called to pay his respects. As Collinson was out at the time, he could not inquire what scheme the transformed gentleman might be pursuing.

What Collinson advises, is less talk about Young, a hopeless business, and more information about the great trip. When is his Journal arriving? What new plants may he expect? As usual, he is in a fever of impatience.

CHAPTER XI

Bartram was very much shaken by his Florida trip. He was dreadfully seasick on the return voyage which seemed to weaken his tough frame. But money difficulties also harassed him; his inquiries concerning Young by no means sprang from idle curiosity. He had heard rumors of the rich awards accruing to that upstart and his own miserable pittance, for so perilous a journey, rankled. The sum at his disposal had not sufficed; during his southern trip he had been forced to draw bills upon Collinson, once at St. Augustine and twice at Charleston. It was not only that the maintenance of himself and Billy could not be covered by the allowance, but upon leaving the south, he was put to an additional expense by an unexpected "whim" on Billy's part to remain. As Billy could only hope to remain on the reasonable assurance that he would engage in some enterprise thought practical by his father, he had elected to become a planter on the St. Johns River. Bartram was not entirely impressed by his son's belated ambition. In a letter to Collinson he not only apologized for drawing upon him for expenses in Florida but for funds to indulge Billy's "frolic." Nothing will do for Billy, he writes, except he must be a planter on St. Johns River, about twenty-four miles from St. Augustine and six miles from Picolata.

Collinson was inclined to take a more favorable view of Billy's new situation. Now he will have someone right on the ground to send seeds from that quarter to England. There is no question about it, people are beginning to tire of the old seeds. Billy will find new varieties to please them. Then, once he is settled, he might look out for insects. In such a climate, these creatures are certain to increase in size and beauty, with many new species to be found only in that quarter.

Collinson sees only the favorable aspects to Billy's new situation, but he cannot resist offering advice. Billy is an ingenious young man, and he only hopes his ingenuity will prompt him to industry, and to improve the opportunity which Bartram, in his paternal goodness, has given him. But one thing must be taken care of; Billy must get a virtuous, industrious wife, "such as knows how to share the toils as well as the comforts of a married state. He will not settle rightly to business until this is done; for then home will always be agreeable to him. If this is not done, he'll fall into the snares of a loose, unlawful way of life, from whence no good can come, but much evil and inconvenience."

They meant well, these two friends, and they loved Billy Bartram. But they had no inkling of the young man's true nature or its complexities. They did not recognize the worth of his dreaminess as a step toward an imaginative reach they could not fathom. He was in a world where, to use Franklin's words, "industry and constant employment are great preservatives of the morals and virtue of a nation." Children were apprenticed to trades and there were trades for all; there was land for all who were willing and able to tackle it in the raw. What to do with someone like Billy, who, placed in a situation that called for a grappling-iron of endurance and sustained energy, simply wilted down? The young man behaved as if he were under enchantment. And he was. But to be enchanted was not in fashion. He must be industrious and frugal, save and make headway in a practical way. He had been given a chance as a trader and he had failed. His heart was not in it. If his heart had not been elsewhere, that might not have mattered, but he knew where his heart's interest lay and he held on, in his own fashion. In a sense, he was a passive-resister. He did not know it, probably, but he was. He simply passively resisted the life of a trader. He didn't want to keep a store; to barter, buy and sell. He didn't have it in him. Not having that quality, he was almost obliged to give up the ghost in a world that valued getting ahead.

But he knew when to stick to his ground, once he had found it. What was the alternative to staying in Florida? He might have gone back to Cape Fear, where his uncle and his brother had succeeded. But his business there had folded; it was doubtless more than his nature could bear to place himself once more in odious comparison to those who knew the ropes. He might have gone back to Pennsylvania; his brother-in-law had made him a generous offer to go into business with him. Another jail. He was too alert to his own nature to succumb. He did not want to fasten himself upon the neck of someone determined to get ahead. Getting ahead was not his line. Perhaps he thought he might make something of the venture in Florida, but more probably, it was a desperate straw, to keep him in the place that had enthralled him at first sight, and to allow him to be free. Everything grew so lushly that he no doubt underestimated the labor it would require to make something grow. But his first consideration must have been simply a pretext to stay, and to be let alone. He would have had to make it practical to win the consent and help of his father; and his project to raise indigo seemed entirely practical.

So the two old men fussed about the boy who was no longer a boy. He was twenty-eight years old. High time to get him married and settled! As they could not understand Billy, they tried to palm off his intents as "trivial." Doubtless he did seem whimsical to these hardy old men; he bothered and tormented them with a sense of waste. They knew so well what he needed and should do; marriage was good medicine. He should swallow his medicine and become a responsible citizen. To be responsible, in his own way, was exactly his virtue, and his salvation. But that would continue to take time.

The South had cast its spell over Bartram, the father, as well as over Bartram, the son. Almost anything new, that had not yet been explored, would have delighted Bartram. St. Augustine had a kind of hazy glamor, then as now. The English settlers had chopped around in it and had destroyed a good deal but they couldn't hack down all of the trees. Collinson, who could not imagine English settlers as anything but superior to the earlier Spanish inhabitants, inquired particularly about the improvements the English were certain to have made. He could not visualize the Spaniards as anything but slothful and content to laze around in the sun, doing nothing.

But John Bartram was an extremely careful man; he was a fine reporter and did not mince the truth. It is the English who have been ruinous. They have pulled half the town down, since the Spaniards left, for the sake of timber to burn. Several of the best houses still stand, but altered to British taste, which required that a chimney be driven through the tops of the house roofs. Sun now begins to shine through glass instead of wooden spindles. But where once there were well cultivated gardens, all is now overgrown with weeds and is common pasture for roving cattle. Many orange and fig trees, a foot in diameter, were cut down and grubbed up for firewood, for which the English seem to have been as ravenous as the Spaniards for gold. Nor do the English make any use of the fine sour oranges as the Spaniards did. They take care of the limes, lemons and guavas, but most of the limes and guavas were killed by a heavy frost during the last winter, as were the bananas. As for figs and pomegranates, the English are not very fond of them, in spite of Dr. Fothergill's recommendation of the latter as the most healthful of fruits. Even Spanish improvements beyond the town have gone to seed. Formerly they had large roads to distant parts of the St. John's River but after the Creek Indians, with the help of the British, turned against the Spaniards, they were cooped up in their fortifications and could not till any ground beyond the protection afforded them by their own cannonballs. Nor could the Spaniards keep any cattle or cut a stick without a guard. Bartram seems to have melted a little in his estimation of the Indians during his Florida sojourn. He now estimates them as friendly, and surmises they may remain so "if the British don't give them just occasion to break out."

By August Florida seeds and fossils came safely to England and were delivered to the King. Collinson reported that the Monarch "was pleased" with them. Fossils for Collinson had been sent by Billy as early as May and the enthusiastic Londoner had pored over the specimens, marveling how the "lapidescent juices" had entered into the grain of the wood. The busy man sat down, at once, to tell Billy of his satisfaction with the fossils and his drawings; he was "glad to see thee has not lost that curious art, which so few attain. I wish it could any way be turned to thy profit." But whether his drawings gained credit or not, Billy was not to be budged from Florida, as yet. While his father busied himself in the north with boxes and accounts to England, in the expectation that a rather lethargic King might rub his eyes and exclaim at the wonders, and perhaps loosen up the royal purse, Billy dug in on his "plantation" on the St. John's River.

Collinson soon had a chance to exclaim with delight as he read Bartram's Journal, which he "valued more than all the rest." It was a precise account written with an eye to what might interest a mercantile King. Bartram knew he was sent to Florida with an eye to development of natural resources, not to enthuse over Nature and its blessings. It is a pedestrian description in comparison to what William was to produce when his great chance came, but, as it would have been impossible for Bartram not to be interesting as well as precise, even his reduction of trees to useful timber, land to productive or nonproductive soil, cannot limit what he sees to future merchandise.

Doubtless he took the criticism of his earlier journal to the Great Lakes to heart, for his Florida journey is more carefully written and goes into greater detail. But he was never to have a journal published in England without an additional comment by someone else. When the Florida account was published it was under the name of William Stork and was entitled: "An Account of East Florida with a Journal kept by John Bartram upon a Journey from St. Augustine up the river St. John's." Stork tactfully dedicated the little volume "to the most Honorable Charles, Marquis of Rockingham, First Lord of the Treasury, etc. etc. etc." with an eye doubtless to future patronage. It is a little brochure which might do credit to any Chamber of Commerce for its purpose was to display the advantages of Florida and to tantalize possible settlers with a dazzling array of riches if they would only summon up nerve to pay the price of a little industry. There were ugly rumors afloat in England regarding the new Florida possessions, ceded to England in 1763, and Stork set about to crush them at once. Florida was *not* a sandy desert, as most people in Great Britain had been led to believe; it was *not* unhealthful. White people as well as Negroes worked in the fields without prejudice to their health. If anything the climate was superior to that of the West Indies and the potential for productive enterprises fully as great. As much as any modern realtor Stork is inclined to vaunt the advantages, even to gamble on futures, and to laud the harbor of St. Augustine as the finest in the world *if*—oh that *if*—the sand bars could be cleared out of it to allow ships of tonnage to pass.

Stork's picture is honorable and workmanlike. He includes a proclamation of the Governor's offering a hundred acres to every person, and fifty acres for every white or black man, woman or child attached to the family of the grantee, with a further offer of a thousand acres to be obtained by anyone willing to pay five shillings sterling for every fifty acres of such an additional grant. The quit rents for all lands are a mere halfpenny per acre, to be paid from two years after the date of the grant to his Majesty, his heirs or successors. In return, the settler must obligate himself to clear and work three acres of every fifty acres of plantable soil allotted to him within three years from the date of the grant.

Stork did not allow his case to rest upon the succulent offer of free land. Free land was to be had to the north, also, and to make Florida tempting he had to present some facts. He dangles before the eyes of his British readers the opportunities which lie in wait if they will only snatch them. Clover, turnips and potatoes are now commonplace in England but once were exotics. Why should not new products be added to the delicacies for British tables? He is certain rice would thrive in Florida. Only look how it flourished in Carolina where by chance a mere handful left on board ship was sowed, almost accidentally, and succeeded beyond anyone's dreams. He has called upon Mr. John Ellis, of the British Museum, to state the case. Ellis whose great speciality was the transportation of seeds from all over the world and who discovered the method for best preserving seeds during long voyages, has ready a neat table of plants that he believes should do well in Florida.

Turkey madder, Ellis suggests, would certainly grow in Florida soil. The same plant is now cultivated in Smyrna for crimson dye. Buckthorns that produce yellow berries of Avignon are in demand by painters and dyers. Olives now grown in France, Italy and Spain should thrive. Two sorts of annual cotton such as are yearly grown in Turkey are recommended. The locust tree or St. John's Bread would produce pods now used as fodder for hard working cattle on the coast of Spain. The pistachio tree from Aleppo, the tallow tree growing on the moist plains of China, the Daidfus, a kind of kidney bean used for making Indian ketchup, the cinnamon tree from Ceylon and the camphor tree from Japan are all possible for Florida. What about the true bamboo from China? Tea from China and Japan? Sarsaparilla root from the bay of Campeachy and the gulf of Honduras? It is an Arabian Nights list; one has only to touch the magic Aladdin lamp of Florida soil to make treasure. Then there are Turkey Figs, currants or Corinthian grapes to be procured from Zant, Jordan or bitter almonds, and how about the caper tree now flourishing in rocky soil around Marseilles and Toulon? Tumerick could be fetched from the East Indies and gum myrrh from Abyssinia; pepper from Sumatra and cloves from the Moluccas. Sir Hans Sloane contributes his bit, suggesting the True Balm of Gilead tree, lately discovered in Arabia, and identical, in his opinion, with a species found in Jamaica. In his book on Jamaica, Sir Hans identified the *Amyris balsamifera* as the same tree that sent a pungent fragrant scent out to sea as Columbus was cruising along the south side of Cuba. In Jamaica it is called White Candlewood and Sir Hans believes it would be profitable to rear this tree in Florida and to extract its balsam which he thinks would yield a valuable drug, the same as that derived from a tree known as *Balsam of Mecca*.

The words have a kind of magic; they touch off wonder. The magicians are all friends in a huddle to conjure bountiful prospects. Their ardor is mixed with many diverse elements, with expanding trade, a colonial status in the New World, an imperialistic reach for the control of empire for Britain; rivalry with Spain and France. If the botanists are being used for ulterior purposes they are singularly innocent; they are only doing their duty. As for John Bartram, he is King's Botanist at last, and his obligation to himself demands that he give everything he is capable of.

His Journal once more reads like a captain's log of a ship at sea. Each day he sets down the date and the thermometer reading until the time when he breaks the instrument trying to pry some honey from an old tree. The journey southward is to follow the meandering of the St. John's river to its source, if that is possible. They will go in a "battoe" with Robert Davis, appointed by the Governor as a guide and to hunt game. Davis's Negro will row the battoe and do the cooking. A handsome map of Florida accompanies the account and compared to a modern map is stripped down to essentials. The rivers run in their main streams parallel to the coast and the St. John's is the most impressive with its elusive shifts into lakes and swamps. Bright fountains play into it, cypress swamps turn to magnolia green; orange groves break off into pine forests along its banks. This is no longer the Bunyan's *Pilgrim's Progress* map of the earlier journey to the Great Lakes. English and Spaniards have pinned the names down prosaically; Indian nomenclature survives unwillingly. Forts mark the journey: Ft. George; Ft. Picolata; Ft. Poppa. Rollstown marks the advance of progress. Mr. Rolls has set himself as the high mark of what a settler can do; he has gorged some twenty thousand acres for himself, mostly rich swamp land.

Bartram's account begins with the party leaving the Governor's house on roads that are soppy with a recent heavy rain. It is December 19, 1765. The road passes through large oak groves sprinkled with *Magnolia Grandiflora* and a fabulous American gum tree known as Liquid Amber which wears a thick spongy bark capable of exuding a sweet balsam when it is wounded. These trees shoot up a hundred feet and stand on a high bluff above the river which "runs 18 inches at high water; in dry weather the water is brackish." It takes two days to launch the battoe on the river and when they finally succeed, they can make no headway as the wind from the south blew strong. Disembarking, they decide to spend the night with Mr. Davis in the midst of his magnolias, evergreens and water oaks, all mixed with some curious new shrubs Bartram had never seen before. Orange trees are spotted among the other masses of green like cloves in a crusty ham, with their ripe fruit coloring the moist ground.

The next day they try once more to row but after going a stiff four miles, they land for a reconnoiter among the trees where Bartram finds a new kind of evergreen with nuts as big as acorns and sweet to eat. The shores of this river are very shoal for more than a hundred miles, he notes, and the banks begin at a distance of about fifty yards from the running water and then rise to lowish ground leading to pinelands. He stoops to finger the soil; it is sand mixed with a black mould.

When they leave Ft. Picolata it is chilly with the reading at 50 degrees. Davis shot a deer and his Negro brought down a turkey. William and his father stroll in the woods with a man on the hunt for wild honey. The first tree hacked down exposed nothing but a wasp's nest; the next brought out a swarm of bees and honey. Some trees yield as much as ten gallons in wax and honey, and Bartram adds a tasty recipe used by the Indians who liked to eat oranges and honey with venison. Take an orange, cut off one end, pour in honey and then scoop it out. Just below Ft. Picolata Bartram comes upon his first exhibit of rocks embedded with congealed snails and mussel shells; this is something Collinson will appreciate.

Now the landscape begins to unroll in a pattern of swamps near the river with an occasional abrupt tongue of land thrust sharply into the limpid water; then a rise of land, sometimes with a perch of palmetto thrust against the sky in a prickly dome of swords. The swamps are "good" or "excellent." Ground rises from them to clumps of oaks, hickory, chinquapin, magnolia rearing sixty feet high, a red maple, three feet in diameter, ash and bays. Rolls' place is on a bluff seventeen feet high and five feet of this bank is composed of snail and mussel shells mixed with black mould and rotten vegetation, some sand, diminishing to yellow soil where large evergreen oak and pines begin to make a bolt toward the savannas. Now and then they find fragments of Indian pots as they near Latchaway, an Indian town, where the Indians instinctively chose a superior location for good corn and pasture.

By Johnson's Springs there is a run of clear sweet water and the ground is thick, woody, loamy, rich with leaves

202

ever falling. Here "the sun never shines strong enough to exale the virtue of the soil" and the ground is lavish for anything that grows. The grape vines are monster pythons, eight inches in diameter, strangling oaks six feet in diameter. A swamp magnolia shoots upward seventy feet and mixed among Liquid Amber are oranges in bloom and in fruit and something called "Cluster Cherry," the wood of which is much esteemed by cabinet makers.

It is all dim and shadowy but Bartram has his keen eyes and his sense of measurement. If birds are about he does not name them. This account is for the King who is more interested in hard cash products than songsters. Though all is leafy cavernous dimness, this is not the terrifying pit of darkness that Bartram found in the northern wilderness. The foliage is milder; the sun filters an occasional silver star downward where on Christmas day all is shiny green growing in a mass of white or yellow soil, "sixteen feet or so above the surface of the river." Now the party is beginning to tread the ground of fable; this is the beginning of country that bursts into fountains. But Bartram is no Ponce de Leon hoping for the miracle of perpetual youth but a sober Quaker who is less curious about an Indian pot, broken and cracked symbol of a tribe's destruction, than he is for Nature's mixture of sand and rotted leaves. He tastes the water, judiciously, making a wry face. It is clear and warm and looks delicious. But it smells of "bilge water or the washings out of a gun barrell." The gush of water appears to issue out of the very earth from a rock above a steep declivity and then to boil hard in its fall, spreading outward into a pool where dead trees lie fallen in a spectral pallor of pale ashy white with a bluish cast, covered with some sediment secreted by the fountain.

The myth-like water begins to cast its spell over the sober journey. History has been ground into the earth with the remnants of Indian pots. This was a battleground, for here the original Indian tribes were driven out by the Creek Indians. If there is blood in this soil it has long seeped into the roots of trees and mosses. The fountains that Ponce de Leon hoped to drink are bitter to taste. The swamps and little hills rising with stiff palmetto leaves or bluish pine are more to Bartram's liking, but he pins a badge of honor on every fall of water that is "big enough to turn a mill."

This is a man who does not look backward but forward to a new age; he does not seek gold, but hopes for the wealth that comes from good soil. For him the myth lies in the land itself and in growth; he would uncover such mysteries and find what kind of mud lies at the bottom of the swamps. The fountains are secretive, mysterious, springing from an underground that smells of brimstone. But Bartram is not superstitious; he will not be reminded of Hell or Satan. The fountains are Wonders and his son, William, will be haunted by them. He will return, alone, to try to track them down to some source, to count the fish and alligators that sport in their deep basins. Now it is Bartram, the father, who stands before each fall of water, to speculate, to taste and even to hold his nose from an overpowering smell. The stench of sulphur is in the air.

Night finds them on a low bluff of snailshells in a shelter of bittersweet orange trees. They have only to reach out a hand to eat. Below them is a dry kind of rich swamp full of shells mixed with a black tenacious mud, under which Bartram finds a sticky clay or marl. The banks of this river, he summarizes, seem to be a continuous alternate change of pine land, bluffs, cypress, swamps, marshes and rich ash and maple swamps; the hummocks of live oaks and palmettos are generally encircled by swamp; sometimes the rich swamps are two or three miles deep from the river to the pines and stretch along the river side from one to six miles. The swamps are his treasure; he

204

enthuses at every step and endows them with rich epithets of praise. Oh excellent, oh good!

His descriptions derive straight from his homely experience. A little island in the river is "hard enough for a horse to walk upon." The entrance to the Great Lake, renamed by the British, Lake George, is choked with something "like a houseleek." The current from the river drives this stuff in jellied masses along the shores of the river and all about the fringes of the islands, where it mixes with a larger species of water grass and saxifrage, sending down long fibrous roots to such effect that the mouths of small creeks emptying into the river or into the lake, that is really part of the river, are stopped up and the boat can hardly be pulled through them though there may be a good four feet of water. Storms break these plants from their natural beds and the current takes them down the river in huge patches, where their long roots strike the muddy bottom and often anchor fast, forming a stiff barrier to other floating patches tangling with them, thus forming new little waving islands of green.

By the first of January they have come to Spalding's Upper Store, the first settlement since they left Rolls'. The river is two hundred yards broad and nine feet deep in the channel. It's hazy and the temperature is down to 52. They land on a high shelly bluff and find themselves among thousands of orange trees, mixed with red cedars and live oaks. Beyond this sweet smelling grove the rich swamp and marshlands stretch to pineland. The next day brings a sharp drop in temperature; it is down to 35 degrees and "there is white frost on the boat." It is even colder the following day with wind from the northwest. The ground is frozen an inch thick along the river banks. Bartram adds a comment that could only have been made after he returned to St. Augustine: "this is the fatal night that destroyed the lime, citron and banana trees in St. Augustine, and the young green shoots of maple, elm and flowering plants and shrubs that were never before hurt." From Clements Bluff they row past rich swamps and marsh filled with alligators but the cold had frozen all the great convolvulus and coreopsis. Where are the birds? Still not a mention of a single song. Bartram is preoccupied with water reeds, the depth of the river and the richness of the swamps.

It takes him two weeks to speak a word for any fish. The party row up a creek and Bartram takes its measurements; it is thirty yards broad and four to six feet deep. But taking measurements does not prevent him from noting the color of the water; it is like the sea but smells quite different. This is the old "bilge water" again and the taste is sweet and loathsome. At the bottom of the clear depths lie trunks of trees, sprawling in a network of skeleton twigs and trunks, whitish and sickly with a curious sediment. The head of this spring is broad, at least thirty yards, and boils up briskly from the bottom "like a pot." Plumbing it, Bartram found it five fathom to the bottom and at last he gets around to the fish. Multitudes of finny creatures throng this vast boiling bowl of water; he notes large gar and catfish. Alligators sun themselves upon the surface of the stream; some lift big indolent heads to a vast yawn, so "tame or so bold as to make no move when the boat rowed near them."

Water oozes into land, land is saturated with water. Where does the one begin, the other end? Bartram speculates about the vast amount of space; distant pinelands, ponds, savannas and swamps, continually tapped through underground sources to feed this vast boiling fountain, gushing out from what appears to be a mass of deep rock. The eye cannot follow so secret a track nor can it even pursue the flight of the cypress swamps which run away endlessly into a blue distance. This is a world of moist beginnings; here, out of water and oozing soil emerge myrtle, oak, cypress and pine, springing out effortlessly from spongy tussocks. There are two sides to the river; the "Indian side," to the west, and "our side" to the east. "Our side" is the one most examined by Bartram. But the blackness of the soil on the Indian side appears to him to be even richer and often "so stiff that cattle may walk upon it very safe." It bears choice grass under a heavy curtain of green foliage.

By the 7th of January they are as far as Cabbage Bluff, so called for the palm or cabbage trees, and that day "they rowed several points of the compass." There is no other reckoning in this swirl of water and green growth. Now the river bends and twists its snakelike way through "pretty groves." A "pretty stream of water small enough to run through the bung-hole of a barrel" trickles into the river and two hundred yards beyond, a large stream pours forth its warm contents. Bartram sticks his thermometer in and announces it to register 71. It feels warm "to a coolish hand and tastes more loathesome than any before; it may be smelt some rods distant." But the shore surrounding this stinking flood is formed of the "most delicate crystalline sand" Bartram ever saw anywhere.

The fountains are taking over; the land dissolving back to some primate state. Another loathsome fountain disgorges into the river in a stream thirty yards broad. This boiling dragon has three heads and the water is warm "but not so hot as one's blood." Its banks are scaly with shelly stone. The river widens to accommodate the fountains, then abruptly cramps to the pressure of ridges of snail and mussel shells hardened into rock. Bartram, the practical, eyes them wondering if they might not be useful for building purposes if split and burnt into lime.

The massy banks of shelly rock where sea shells, periwinkles, cockles and clams lie entombed leads Bartram to his most daring conjecture concerning the formation of this soil. He stakes his bold claim, saying, "This I believe, that this shelly structure reaches under all this low country to uncertain depths and supports the superior soil under which the prodigious sulphurous and saline fountains run, which are continually fed by the slow settling of rain water." He is imagining Creation now, visualizing the union of water with land and animals rising from the marshes. It is written more evidently the further they move southward. The ground is all reedy and wet, with the banks raised a foot or more by the trash floating down the river which "being drove on shore by the wind, there rots and is converted into stiff soil upon which alligators love to bask in the sunshine; every 20, 50 or 100 yards distance they are found."

There is an Indian side but no mention of an Indian. Once they spy an Indian hunting cabin covered with palmetto leaves. On the twenty-first day of their journey wolves howled for the first time in Florida and they come upon a great nest of a wood rat, built of long pieces of dry sticks, near four feet high and five inches in diameter, all laid confusedly together; "on stirring the sticks to observe the structure, out ran a large rat and up a very high sapling with a young one hanging to its tail."

Now the river masquerades once more as a lake. Thus it has progressed, lakes in a chain of beads, all strung to a thinner string of river. Marshes ooze away from the shore to stiffen to cypress swamps; sometimes the shore is sandy beach from which a ridge rises bristling with oaks, only to fan out again at a distance to a marsh abyss beyond. Branches of water seep into the lake, or flow from the lake —they hardly know which is which—vegetation appears to float with only an occasional hummock of oak brazening out the general liquidation. When a savanna finally emerges, it brings a shout of joy—at last, here is soil that is black and "stiff enough to ride upon." But even this solid ground leaks a small pond where ducks sport.

This river is an animal or a snake. It slithers and slides, emerges stout as a bear bristling with vigor against the sky. It is land, it is water, it is a conglomeration of elements. It is a magic maze, now island, now swamp, now sour tasting spring, now clear bubbling water, now limpid stream. A magician in its aspects, it misleads the travelers deceived by small particles of islands, by rivulets, by broad stream dissolving into a chain of lakes. So much wet, so much mystery, resolved only by the thread of a strong current that winds and turns, leading them back to the main stream! With joy they welcome a momentary end to endless bog and water where they can plant their feet on solid ground. It is not an enormous plot, not more than six acres, but it is rich with a foundation of substantial light black shelly soil producing red cedar, Celtis or the Nettle tree (a specimen growing very large with wood much esteemed as "it is tough and pliable, the best wood for shafts of all kinds of carriages"), zanthoxylium, and several new varieties never seen by Bartram before. Of course there were some orange trees, including a brood of young ones.

This is a party endlessly rowing, impeded by the chameleon nature of the river; now brusquely stopped in midstream by clumps of thick grass. But they skillfully circumnavigate the impediments, pursue the current, evade the lagoons and skip forward through long low marshlands searching through turnings and twisting for the delicate tongue of the current. Sometimes the water reeds grow "dense as hemp;" again these reeds are so mixed up and matted with other water plants as to clog the flow for what Bartram estimates must be thousands of acres of the watery St. John's.

When a fish at last makes its entrance into Bartram's

narrative it is no more than a humble mullet but it jumps "three times a minute." When they kill a bear it is a big event. The creature is seven feet long and their hunter calculates its weight as at least 400 pounds. His carcass is so embedded in four inches of fat that it revolts the sensitive Bartram who admits that he "loathed the sight of this thick blubbery fat." Here is Bartram, the paradoxical; the tough oak who is also squeamish about touching insects, hates the smell of the opossum, kills a snake with horror in his heart. But how handsomely he admits his own nature; how little he is given to putting up a front against such delicacy! His son William, so much the introvert, is not as unwilling to touch, to handle the obnoxious, or even to shoot birds if by doing so he can minutely examine the structure and thus resurrect the living aspect in his drawings or paintings. There was a delicate fibre in Bartram, the father, that he never attempted to deal with except by pure admission. But though he was revolted at the sight of the fat, his rugged appetite braces itself to the taste of the oil rendered from it. He says it is as delicious to eat as the oil of olives and incomparably milder than hog's lard. The meat was even preferable to venison or turkey; for they had a choice of the three, having shot a fat young buck that day and three turkeys. The flesh of turkey, venison and bear were all stewed together and everyone in the party pronounced the bear meat superior.

Now the heat begins to bear down and the mosquitoes tune up for torture. Ticks crept over their bodies and lizards ran in and out of their tent. Worst of all, "flies blowed our meat before ten o'clock in the morning," and they had to stay on the spot all that day to barbecue the meat which otherwise would have been unfit to transport down the river. Salt it they could not do as they carried only enough to flavor their food. Rains added to their discomfort and to shake off the soggy damp penetrating to their skins, they saunter off on a reconnoiter only to discover more springs with a greenish cast and a loathsome taste. But great gar fish found the water most compatible. Another spring got Bartram's hackneyed stamp of approval; "it was big enough to turn a mill." This fountain had five heads and three of the heads boiled up merrily "like a pot" on a stove, in pure white sand. As the pot boils up, the surrounding white sand slips down pressing upon the spring until the water below collects in sufficient force to toss sand and water above the surface once more. This steady rhythmic motion fascinated Bartram suggesting some deep-seated mesh of causation and effect. Though he was "all of a sweat" on a hot day, "the spring seemed warm to his warm hand." Its odor was loathsome and could be detected many yards away.

On a cold rough day there is nothing to do but idle time away. The hunters rendered the bear's oil and stretched its skin. The fat yielded fifteen or sixteen gallons of clear fine oil. The next day allows them to take to the boat again and to inspect the Indian side where Bartram confesses to seeing the "finest piece of rich dry ground" he has had a chance to comment upon. It produced palms and live oaks and they cut down three tall palm or cabbage trees to lift out the delicate top bud, the white, tender part or the rudiments of the great leaves which when grown would be six or seven feet long. This tender bud section, some three or four inches in diameter, was then sliced into a pot and gently stewed with a little water until almost tender. Bear's oil was then added. Bartram says "it cuts as white and fine as a turnip" and "eats pleasant and much more mild than cabbage." Hunters generally eat it raw, he's been told, and may live upon it for several days. The small palmetto yields a white bud no bigger than one's finger which is commonly eaten by men, bears and horses. This situation of rich land, palms and pleasing view enthused Bartram so much that the party gave the name of "Bartram's Bluff" to it, though it was on the "Indian side."

Will they ever find the fountain head of this evasive river? It seems to dissolve in a mesh of lakes, swamps and inlets and they begin to retrace their way back when the going leads to a blind maze. On the retreat they steer near the Indian side, but the mosquitoes torture them. Twice during the night they smoked the tent to try to get rid of the pests. It is becoming warmer with each day; a heavy sleepy haze falls upon the steamy land. At last Bartram has leisure to report the birds; they are tuning up at dawn in a great chorus. The wild turkeys, which William was to describe so minutely, set up their rich gobbling calls, one to another, halloo after halloo spreading in a wild echo for miles. The fish leap from the bright water in a splatter of rainbows. In their daily trudges over what land can be found above the seeping stream they discover a big pond where geese feed. At one point they mount a shelly bluff to find orange trees growing so thickly it was impossible to pass between them.

Bartram takes a crack at his old enemies, the Indians, commenting drily that though they seem wise in knowing instinctively good land for corn they neglected the marshes, the most fertile spots of all, where they might have raised rice only they "never took the pains to raise or shell it." Here he goes off the track considerably; where would they have got the rice when it had only been imported into Carolina on a British ship in fairly recent times?

Near another enormous spring, on a bank of tenacious earth, William found a "lovely sweet tree" with leaves "like sweet bay which smelled like sassafras and produces a strange kind of seed pod but the seed was all shed; some grew twenty feet high, a charming bright evergreen aro-

212

matic." In a nearby pool great families of large gar, catfish, mullets, trout and unknown varieties of fish thronged in a jumble of flashing pursuit; fish chased fish, with the smaller ones racing into clumps of grass to hide from their enemies, leaping from the water and falling with a continual plopping splash that kept the air iridescent with fine spray.

On the 25th of January they come to the pine lands with a little frost on the ground in early morning. Flocks of pigeons are soaring above Mount Royal as they landed to examine an Indian tumulus. Bartram took the measurements; about one hundred yards in diameter, nearly round, and about twenty feet high. Bleached fragments of bones littered the grass upon the mound; live oaks thrust upward among the bones and sandy deposit. Some of the oaks had grown three feet in diameter. Bartram thinks "a prodigious multitude" of Indians must have labored to raise it, to what original height, he can't say, as time must have settled it in such a number of years that allowed the oaks to grow so big. Where did the Indians get the sand for this tumulus, he ponders, and how was it brought? The Indians had nothing except baskets and bowls with which to transport such a quantity of sand and must have toiled away for a long period to have achieved this mound. Sand was not common in the vicinity and might even have come from a distance. Trees had locked their roots around the sacred remains where once all had been smooth and doubtless as symmetrical as an inverted bowl. The Indians had honored their dead with a fine straight avenue some sixty yards broad and extending some three-quarters of a mile to a little lake. The surface of the avenue had been scraped down to a hard shelly structure and was as level as a floor. The soil scraped off had been thrown in banks on each side of the road which was sheltered from the sun by trees planted in such a way that their branches intermingled above the avenue in a leafy archway. Even the pond seemed to have been worked on by the ingenious Indians who had shaped it to an oblong with banks gently sloping toward the water. The mound thus faced the water through a vista of avenue.

On the far side of the great mound lay an enormous rattlesnake sunning himself. In the vicinity of the tumulus had been a large Indian town. Fifty acres or more of planting ground had been cleared; it was middling soil and a good deal mixed with multitudes of tiny shells. Bartram speculates about the dead Indians lying within the sepulchre. He is not certain if the Florida Indians buried the bones after the flesh rotted off as the present tribes of southern Indians do, nor does he have any inkling as to what fate, other than defeat by the Creek Indians, befell this lost town, now overgrown, with a rattler as keeper.

This journey, the last long trip Bartram was to make, was ending in glorious weather, as good as "the first of May." All the territory toward St. Augustine was now being claimed by someone or other, in huge hunks of land. Mr. Rolls had a vast claim; a Colonel Middleton had laid hold of a rich marsh. Barons of a wilderness, they cleared land and planted slowly, waiting for time to catch up with them. Now Bartram finds leisure to report one more tasty dish; they breakfast on "a mess of tanniers," a species of Wake Robin. The leaves are called "Indian kale" and Bartram insists they make a delicious feast when boiled with the roots and meat. Good managers on vast estates beguiled Bartram into hopefulness. On Oglethorpe's island he notes with approval the many ingenious devices used by Mr. Hazard, one of the best planters in Florida. Then he eyes another relic of the lost Indians; vast heaps of oyster shells which Bartram concludes must have taken hundreds of years for thousands of Indians to collect. Broken fragments of Indian pots lie among them.

He sums up his trip in sober reckonings; marshes could be "drained dry" for corn and indigo; without much draining they would produce rice. Cypress trees would make choice shingles, pales and boards of long duration; live oak timbers could be used for shipping, long leafed pine for masts and yards, and from other varieties of pine, turpentine, tar and pitch could be procured; also planks and scantlings. In the St. John's River he reports bass, sea trout, sheepshead, mullets, cats, gar, sturgeon, stingrays; near the mouth are oysters, crabs, shrimps, sharks and porpoises.

If Bartram had missed seeing much that was to intrigue William when he came to dive alone into the Florida marshes and glades, he had a serious aim in mind; he had an official position. He was the King's botanist and his report must include the practical. Both father and son must have been lured by the rich luxuriance of the vegetation; the ease with which one reached out a hand to eat an orange. If William handled the fragments of Indian pots with more curiosity and care, he doubtless did not argue with the older man, knowing all too well his violent feelings. But he did keep some secret, and the bits of broken pottery were to be clues to lead him straight to a study of Indian life.

Once Bartram was safely home he naturally longed for some reaction from the King. He got off his box of richly assorted items for the King in charge of Collinson and followed it by persistent inquiries: how had the King received it? Collinson's answer must have been cold comfort. The box of plants and seeds had been delivered and no doubt were acceptable; "the honor of giving is sufficient." No notice had been taken of the freight and charges by the Crown so Collinson will be forced to charge this to Bartram's account. However, so long as his salary is paid, he should take heart. It would also be a good idea always to keep a Journal of any trips he might make and to see that the King received a fair copy. One such Journal a year ought to be enough to keep Bartram in the King's memory. If he sent more the Monarch might be cloyed by too much.

Bartram must have read this advice concerning the attentions he must give the King and the probable condescension he might expect with some chagrin. It came at about the time that he chanced to encounter his rival, Young, just back from England. This upstart in the botanical field astounded everyone in town by the figure he cut upon his return, strutting along the street, whistling and wearing a sword and gold lace. He called three times upon Bartram professing great respect. And he announced, nonchalantly, that he was on his way to winter in the Carolinas, there being three hundred pounds sterling annually settled upon him.

In spite of Young's bravado, odd stories were in circulation about him. Captain Chancelor who ferried some of the American plants to Europe told Bartram that Young had been put in prison in London from whence he had been escorted by two officers and placed on board ship. Young's friends in America utterly denied the rumor and in relating the report to Collinson Bartram charitably declared that it was a pity the truth was not known and the lying party snubbed. Collinson replied that the rumor about Young was all too true. The Englishman protested that he hoped the foolish man would live to repent his extravagance and folly. He had advised Young not to sacrifice everything to pleasure, to be economical and industrious, but it soon became apparent from the way he was going, how it would end. His salary could not possibly support his expensive way of living.

However Bartram may have received this news, he was not the man to glory in anyone's downfall, and, by the time the letter from Collinson arrived, he had deeper troubles to agitate him. Billy Bartram had foundered in his project on the St. John's River.

CHAPTER XII

FREEDOM? FREEDOM is not so easy. Billy Bartram had remained in Florida of his own choice but why he had selected that particular spot is puzzling. His location was on the banks of the St. John's River, some twenty-four miles from St. Augustine and about six from the fort of Picolata. His situation, as described by Henry Laurens of Charleston, who twice encountered the young man during his journeys to that part of the country, was the least agreeable of any place Laurens had seen. He had settled down on a low sheet of piney but barren ground, verging on a swamp. Before the door of his hut, ran a thin finger of sandy soil separating him from an inlet of the St. John's River, which was so shallow that it was covered with umbrella-like fungi and so stagnant that it sent up a stench when stirred with the oars on the two different days Laurens landed. The river was not low on those days, but was said to be running rather high, and what the situation must be like in the dry season, would be hard to imagine. Certainly, in Laurens' opinion, most unhealthy and hard to reach.

The swamp adjacent to Billy's hovel might, without doubt, produce good rice when properly cleared and cultivated. But where was the strength to come from to put such a scheme into tolerable working order? So far as Laurens could see, Billy had hardly enough of that commodity to make any progress above daily bread and that of a coarse kind. Everything that might be done, required more strength than Billy Bartram appeared to have. As soon as the sympathetic Laurens had taken in the grave plight of the forlorn young man, he set about, on his own responsibility, to communicate the facts to the father.

He begs to differ from Bartram's opinion on the question of the pine land; he thinks it is very ordinary, and, in fact, considers there is no good pine in the whole territory. However that may be, Billy's pine is definitely inferior. There is some cypress, which might be converted into shingles and ready money. If Billy had the strength for it.

The young man had not been idle. On Laurens' first visit, he showed him a growth of peas, beans, corn and yams, planted only four days before in sand at the swamp's edge. It appeared to be flourishing. But luck was against Billy. For the next three weeks there were heavy rains and by the time Laurens showed up again, the shoots had made little headway. They appeared to have been drowned out. Billy had taken Laurens' advice and had begun to clear the swamp. In the three weeks interval, he had cut down part of an acre of trees. But that sort of work goes heavily for want of strong hands. Bartram had left his son with six Negroes as helpers on his new planta-

219

tion, but among those six, only two knew how to handle an ax, and one of these had been insolent to him.

In spite of this discouragement, Billy had put some rice in the ground after Laurens' first visit. But there was little he could do to improve his hut. It was not only extremely confined as a place to live in, but it was not proof against weather. Heaven help him when a heavy rain fell! Even its location was deplorable for it was bound to be insufferably hot. Laurens even makes the claim that to his knowledge, Billy's place is the only disagreeably hot place in East Florida.

What's more, all his provisions are scanty. What he had on hand of grain, flesh and spirits brought him to the status of downright penury. His health was very imperfect. The first time Laurens saw him, he had a fever. The second time, he was very poorly.

The man who has taken upon himself the task of writing to John Bartram about his son, was at that time forty-three years old. Henry Laurens was later to become President of the Continental Congress, succeeding John Hancock. Doubtless he had some qualms about confronting the formidable, independently minded father with what amounted to a reproach for the predicament of his son. But he stuck to his guns, and fired away. Probably he sensed that this proud, shy young man would never admit another failure to his father, and that it would take a determined stranger to rescue him. He was not going to leave Billy Bartram to perish without making a downright effort to save him. The first thing he did was to send him a little rum, wine, sugar, tea, cheese and biscuit, with other trifles. This he intends to charge to John Bartram's account, although he would most freely give Billy the whole of it, if he did not fear the father might take it amiss.

All this he recounts to John Bartram. Then he digs into the problem as he sees it. "Possibly, sir, your son, though a worthy, ingenious man, may not have the resolution, or not that sort of resolution, that is necessary to encounter the difficulties incident to, and unavoidable, in his present state of life. You and I, probably, could surmount all these hardships without much chagrin. I verily believe that I could. But at the same time, I protest that I should think it less grievous to disinherit my own son, and turn him into the wide world, if he was of a tender and delicate frame of body and mind, as yours seems to be, than to restrict him, in my favor, just in that state to which your son has been reduced. This is no doubt more than you ever apprehended; and admitting that my account is in part erroneous (which I do not admit, meaning to speak nothing but the truth) yet the general outlines of my description must affect and grieve you. It is by no means part of my design to color too strongly. In fact, according to my ideas, no coloring can do justice to the forlorn state of poor Billy Bartram."

Poor Billy Bartram! There seems no way for him to escape becoming an object of compassion. How had he planned to survive in that impossible situation? To the kindly, imaginative Laurens he appears as a gentle, mild young man, without a wife, or a friend, a companion or a neighbor. To be precise, there isn't a human inhabitant within nine miles. The nearest neighbor must be reached by water and Billy has no boat. Even such neighbors as he might come to by that route are rough soldiers at the Fort, not exactly enlivening companions for him.

Laurens sees the young man stranded in life on a beggarly strip of land, scant of bare necessities, and totally void of all the comforts of life, except an inimitable degree of patience, for which—in Laurens' opinion—he deserves a thousand times better fate. His location is unpleasant and unhealthy. His Negroes, rather plagues than helpers. One Negro was so insolent as to threaten his life. A second

Negro was a useless expense; a third, a child in arms. Billy was thirty miles from the metropolis, St. Augustine, without any money to pay the expense of a journey there, even on an important occasion; if he were to attempt it, the road would be certain to be bad, and in wet weather, impassable.

"These circumstances," wrote the intrepid man, who, during the Revolution, was to be captured by the British and taken as a prisoner to the Tower of London, "are, I say, discouragements enough to break the spirits of any modest young man; and more than any man should be exposed to, without his own free acceptance, unless his crimes had been so great as to merit a state of exile."

Exile it certainly was, but from the father's point of view, it must have appeared self-chosen. Billy had asked for it, but what desperate impasse the young man must have felt himself to be in, to take so forlorn a risk, the father had no way of knowing. It must have cut him to the heart to read of the dire necessity that brought the proud Billy, upon parting with Laurens, to request the kind stranger to communicate the facts to his father. The strings he had wished to cut must still be guide ropes to his existence, and another galling defeat added to the sum of his humiliations.

That his situation had brought Billy to the brink of hopeless despondency, Laurens ventured to indicate. Billy did not open his mind to this friend; doubtless he opened his mind to no one during the difficult years in which he was storing up all his impressions, all his vital feelings for that moment of release when freed from his peculiar and in some ways, self-inflicted prison, he might pour out his mind and his heart. Laurens was so aware of Billy's modesty, shyness and unwillingness to impose his troubles upon anyone, even upon his kind father—perhaps *especially* upon this kind father, for there his pride was peculiarly at stake—that he warns Bartram not to expect too literal an account of his sufferings from his son. "But if you pay any regard to what I have been so bold to write, *quickly* give orders to supply him with those things which will make his banishment less galling, and present him with some prospect of reaping the fruit of his labors."

John Bartram acted promptly. Billy Bartram was recalled at once from his Florida banishment, and from any immediate hope of independence. What his dejection must have been, we can only surmise. Collinson, as sensitive to the feelings of persons whom he loved as he was to plants, tried at once to think up some plan to revive the young man.

Wouldn't he like to draw the *Colocasia* with its pale, arrow-shaped leaves? Collinson would like nothing better than a drawing of this specimen, so difficult to rear, together with a description from Billy of its habits. Momentarily he even forgets his irritation over the question of the *Agave* which he claims to have yearned for some thirty years. An account of it has driven him to a passion of longing for this succulent American Aloe, with its thick spiny-toothed leaves. But, he remarks somewhat petulantly in a letter to Bartram, he can see that the heart must not be set on anything. He believes the *Agave* never was in England and even a drawing would be acceptable and quite new. Here is another opportunity for Billy's pencil, he argues, forgetting his own disappointment in generous concern for Billy. He has often conjured how he could best serve Billy so that his ingenuity would be of use to him. Bringing him to London would not solve the problem. While he was trying to make himself known, he would starve. Such a fate seems to have been the hard lot of several ingenious foreigners who had attempted to establish themselves in England. Once more Collinson proposes his sovereign remedy: let Billy get himself a good notable wife, a farmer's

223

daughter. With such an asset, he might then return to his "estate" on the St. John's, and put his shoulder to the wheel. In Collinson's opinion, a moderate industry goes a long way, in so fine a climate, to supply the belly as little is wanting for the back.

Nor will he depend too much on advice to the father; he writes directly to Billy in praise of his wonderful drawings which have accompanied his father's Journal from Florida. "When art is arrived to such perfection to copy close after Nature, only see how the moving pencil displays a sort of paper creation, which may endure for ages, and transfer a name with applause to posterity!" This good friend pours the balm of affection and esteem over the afflicted Billy, and upbraids him for using such vile paper for masterpieces that deserve finest vellum. He is fixing on the best paper to be had so that these delicate strokes may not be exposed to accidents.

Good paper and kindness; they go far. But it will take another five years for William to uproot himself from stagnation. What he does in the interval, it is hard to say. His brother John was managing the farm; his father was in such poor health that Collinson sought medical advice for him from Dr. Fothergill. He warned his friend not to trouble himself about sending anything, for the time being and until he recovered, unless some new and startling rarity popped up. Though Collinson is old, and troubles have been thickening for him, too, as his son was to discover when he came to examine his affairs after his death, he refuses to parade either ailments or worries before his American friends.

William continued foremost in his thoughts. It is evident that the young man will not take Collinson's prescription and get a hearty wife. Collinson fears for Billy in his adversity. "Amongst thy numerous acquaintance, it will be very hard if he cannot be got into some business above the servile drudgery of a day laborer," he wrote Bartram, in indignation at the news that Billy was toiling away as a farm hand on a neighboring farm. But he was such an optimist that he manages to see a bright ray even in such a reduction, which "should operate in his favor; as an instance of his industry and humility, which I hope will be rewarded, at last, with something more suitable to his abilities." And to keep Billy geared to those remote opportunities, he tactfully requested a plan of the town of St. Augustine, with the situation of forts, churches and Governor's house indicated. Probably Collinson was not so interested in a plan of this town as he appeared to be. More likely, he was trying to arouse and hold Billy's interest in life, and, during this period thought up many a fanciful pretext to keep Billy busy.

Collinson was in raptures over Billy's drawing of the *Colocasia.* He and his son first looked at the drawing by candlelight and argued as to whether it was a drawing or an engraving. "It is really a noble piece of work," praised this noble friend of Billy. Oh, if the King only had some taste in flowers or plants! But there is nothing to look for from that quarter. Collinson intends to try his luck with Lord Bute, who is the only great man who encourages ingenious men in painting botanic rarities. Then there is Billy's drawing of the crimson Hibiscus; without it, he would be in ignorance concerning this specimen. Whatever Billy's disappointments, he continued to study and to make progress in Linnaeus' system, to the joy of his London friend. Paper was always sent him and once, as a token of appreciation, Collinson sent him a guinea with the apologetic explanation that it could not begin to represent the worth of Billy's drawings.

Collinson's business was not prospering as in the early days, but he was never so low in mind as not to rejoice at a new arrival from America. Bartram had taken his reproaches about the *Agave* to heart, and a living specimen finally reached London safely. During this twilight period of Collinson's long life, he did not once forget Billy Bartram. A year later, in 1768, he was agitating among the great in Billy's behalf and had managed to stir up the Duchess of Portland to such a pitch that she was willing to gamble twenty guineas for a trial performance. Collinson wrote a fussy letter to Billy, in a fever of excitement over this long-awaited opportunity. Billy is to make a drawing of the *Faba Egyptica*, for the Duchess, same size as the one he made for him. Then he is to start drawing all the Land, River and Sea Shells, from the very least to the greatest. The drawings "should not be crowded and most carefully done." When finished, they should be rolled on a roll and put in a box for fear of getting wet. There is no knowing where all this may lead. Collinson is as jubilant as if it were Billy's true path to fame and fortune.

His mind races with new schemes for Billy. He wrote Bartram that he has other views for Billy which he will divulge if he can only bring them to bear. He is seething with his old sense of glory; he wishes they had known from the start how best to nourish American plants. Many were lost that might have been saved, for since they have planted the specimens in bog earth, not one has refused to take a liking to England. His thoughts whirl upon the future of America; its luxury will increase and then artists will be encouraged! Doubtless he was thinking of poor Billy who cannot wait that long, it is certain. Nor will Collinson allow him to wait, if he can help it. A short time later he was able to trumpet the news that Dr. John Fothergill had pronounced himself enthusiastic about Billy's drawings and intends to become his patron. The Quaker physician was a patron worth having; his generosity had extended itself to more than one experimenter in the botanical field. Fothergill, like the Duchess of Portland, wants drawings of all kinds of shells, including those of turtles Billy saw in Florida; he wants particularly that Soft Shell Turtle and the Shovel Nose. Billy's brothers, Moses and John, should be alerted to keep their eyes open when they are out walking or gathering flower seeds. Let them watch sharp for any kind of land shells or snails.

Shells—snails—turtles—Collinson tosses them out to the stranded Billy with the grand, splendid gesture of one plucking jewels from a crown. The ardent fellow, fussy, precise, and loving, had opened the way for Billy Bartram. It was his last letter ever to reach the Bartrams. Twenty-four days later, he was dead.

CHAPTER XIII

C OLLINSON WAS DEAD but the projects dear to his heart continued to flourish. Plants made their journeys and his last effort to rescue Billy Bartram bore fruit. Not at once; time moved slowly as a sailing ship. Disturbing events distracted the botanists and for a while Billy was almost lost sight of. In the American colony the citizens seethed with a sense of the injustices they felt were heaped upon them by England. Nothing the mother country could do any longer pleased them. When import duties were levied to help lift the enormous burden of England's war debts, the colonists cried out. When they were lifted upon every item except tea they complained that this was a shrewd attempt to flood American markets with cheap British goods and thus drown out the infant manufactures of the new world. William Bartram almost vanished in the obscurity lamented by Collinson; he continued as a day laborer on a neighboring farm and in his free time attempted to draw as many shells and turtles as he could find for the gratification of the Duchess of Portland and Dr. Fothergill.

Collinson's last letter to the Bartrams had been filled with loving concern for William; that brave effort to lift him up rested like a beam of light upon the stranded young man. But everything moved so slowly. John Bartram recovered slowly from the effects of his Florida venture. He had lost his great friend and he was seventy years old. But so long as he lived he would never be able to sit down, idly, to contemplate the passing scene with complacence. He would expect new achievement from himself to the end; he would die learning. He would continue to sit at meals with his food in one hand, a book in the other. If war was to come he would expect men of sense to keep the line of communications open, on both sides of the ocean. It had happened before. During the wars between England and France, he had often been uneasy for the fate of his prized specimens. If the French seized the ship, he hoped that his cargo might fall into the hands of Buffon and not be destroyed by ignorant hands. "If I could know that the goods fell into the hands of men of learning and curiosity I should be more easy," he wrote Collinson. "Though they are what is commonly called our enemies, yet, if they make proper use of what I have labored for, let them enjoy it with the blessings of God."

He trusted in a universal tongue and accepted as a fact that the pursuit of knowledge held men together in a tie beyond all other considerations. With Collinson dead, other hands must now become responsible for the shipment of plants to England, and Dr. Fothergill at once stepped into the breach. He had been in correspondence with Bartram on his own account for some years, but his earlier interest had seemed to center in medicinal herbs, fossils and stones. Once he had requested some bolar earth; another time, he wanted to know what mineral waters prevailed in the new world. Bartram had to tell the doctor that he had little time for the pursuit of mineral waters but knew there were reports of many curious kinds. One sulphur springs on the Mohawk River was used by the Indians to cure their sick. Another had been located on the highlands by the North River in New York. Several passengers going up the river had ventured to imbibe freely from this spring and had been purged stoutly. A Dr. Shaw, a brewer in Burlington, New Jersey, had affirmed that a Spa water had broken into his well from which he brewed beer and had so purged the customers that they fancied a trick had been put upon them. From another doctor he had the report of a spring that was a certain cure for the ague. But Bartram seems to have had no leisure to chase this interesting side-line. He continued, however, to correspond with Fothergill and to send specimens of American plants. One such box, including ginseng, was sent shortly after Collinson's death.

Dr. Fothergill wanted to be helpful. He had several suggestions about the future shipments to England. And he was anxious to pay Bartram for the box of specimens sent him; he did not want his friends "to make bricks for him without straw." Michael Collinson, Peter Collinson's son, would be the ideal person to receive the shipments if he would consent to do so. Lacking him, perhaps his own nephew who had rented Collinson's country place at Mill Hill, might be persuaded.

Plants certainly continued to flow to England, whatever arrangements were made, and were still on their way up to the outbreak of the Revolutionary War. As late as 1777, the year of Bartram's death, Franklin was negotiating from Paris for a shipment of seeds to be sent to

France. Bartram was advised to send the same number of boxes that had formerly gone to England to France and he enclosed a list of specified items. The shipment was to be consigned to him and he promised to take care of the sale of the boxes and to make the returns to Bartram.

Collinson had managed to interest fifty-seven subscribers in American plants before his death, and these continued to receive shipments until the war stopped the flow of goods. There is no precise reckoning of the number of plants that Bartram sent to England during the many years that he served his British patrons. In his study of Bartram's services to horticulture, John Hendley Barnhardt established that, though he was not the first to send plants to England, the migration accelerated at an enormous rate during the period beginning in 1735, when he was making shipments to England.

Even in the early days of discovery and exploration some new plants had found their way to the old world. Most were tropical species that did not survive. Before 1620 only a few plants were sent from the temperate zone, such as the sunflower, the potato and tobacco. In a brief history of the introduction of plants into European gardens, Gregor Kraus has claimed that until 1560 all plants in European gardens were natives of Central Europe. The interest in botanical gardens was widespread in Italy in the Fifteenth Century and men of wealth aimed at collecting the greatest possible number of plants in all their species and varieties. Paintings of the time, as Jacob Burckhardt indicates, reveal the record of the prevailing passion for fruit and flowers, for the minute particulars of each species, for that richness of color which seems to convey the very odor of a garden. Until the influx of American plants, English gardens tended toward the stiff and the formal but after 1700 plants from many parts of the world, as well as from America, changed the landscape of rural England.

From 1560 to 1620 there seems to have been a flow of plants from east of the Mediterranean to Europe but few from America. From 1620 to the American Revolution in 1775 a steady migration of plants, especially woody ones, poured in from Eastern North America. Seeds and plants sent to England later traveled to the continent. Barely half a dozen American varieties were in cultivation in England before 1600. In the next fifty years, the number increased to about fifty; by the end of the century to about one hundred and fifty, according to Barnhardt. From the beginning of 1700 until the time Bartram began to ship plants, in 1735, the number had doubled to about three hundred; but during Bartram's active service the number of varieties sent to England more than doubled. Some three hundred and twenty species of plants went to England from America during this time and it is safe to say that the majority of these originated with Bartram.

Besides new varieties, Bartram also shipped supplies of plants already in cultivation but only in scanty quantities, and British growers thus got shrubs and trees that up to that time were considered rare. Though he increased the abundance of plants already known, his greatest contribution was in the introduction of rarities. Most of Bartram's time was spent in gathering seeds of flowering plants and lifting specimens of flowering perennials for transport to England. Such plants were little understood at that time, not for lack of interest, but for lack of facilities. Botanists were discovering a new world; a new plant was a fresh continent for their exploration. No wonder Linnaeus, Gronovius, Catesby, John Ellis, George Edwards, Philip Miller and even Queen Ulrica of Sweden pined to communicate, and did, with Bartram, whose garden contained more rare species from the wilderness than any other garden in the new world. Benjamin S. Barton considered that "there have been but two or three native Americans whose correspondence with the learned men of Europe was so extensive as that of Mr. Bartram." After his death when the garden was carried on by his sons, and when William had added to the fame of American discoveries his explorations of Florida, visitors continued to come to see the spot that had become unique. Hamilton, Washington and Jefferson viewed the scene which Alexander Wilson called a "little Paradise."

Until Bartram began shipping specimens of living plants to Europe, botanists had to rely upon dried specimens in a herbarium. But, as Bartram more than once pointed out, a dried specimen could deceive. In the beginning he prepared some rough samples to send to England, merely to show what kind of plants he would be able to send, but under Collinson's tutelage he improved his methods and continued to send botanists dried specimens as well as fresh plants. The Natural History Museum of London now has an exhibit of the dried varieties that Bartram sent for the botanists' inspection.

In 1735 Bartram sent Collinson a specimen of the skunk cabbage which the Londoner found "very beautiful." Early shipments included the sugar maple, witch hazel, climbing bittersweet, southern white cedar, the mayflower, the rose bay, wild honeysuckle and the cucumber tree. Collinson introduced to England from shipments made by Bartram the mountain laurel, button bush, three species of arrowwood, the steeple bush, sand myrtle, the stagger bush, river birch, the false alder and hemlock. Bartram introduced the shooting star to England by sending seeds to Collinson after the only living specimen in England, growing in Bishop Compton's garden as early as 1709, had died out long before Bartram's seeds succeeded in English soil after 1740. He sent as well the dog-tooth violet, wild asters, gentians (Collinson's favorite) and fiery lilies.

On the banks of the Altamaha during his journey to Florida in 1765 he came upon the beautiful plant now known as *Franklinia Altamaha*. It was in flower with no ripe seeds. Ten or twelve years later, William rescued this flowering shrub from oblivion. He described it as a shrub "of the first order," and at first believed it was a species of *Gordonia lasianthus*. He soon discovered it belonged to a new tribe and named it for his father's friend, Benjamin Franklin. Seeds were carried back to Pennsylvania and it has never been lost to cultivation since, although no wild specimen has been found for more than a century. William claimed that they had never found this rare plant growing in any other place.

A horse balm raised by Collinson from seed sent by Bartram was designated by Linnaeus *Collonsonia* somewhat to Collinson's chagrin. He thought the plant should have been named for Bartram. Bartram's name in science is memorialized by two types of *Bartramia*, one—named by Gronovius—"a tropical plant with burr-like fruits, section of the genus *triumfetta* (*Tiliaceau*)"; the other, named by Hedwig, a "genus of acro-carpous mosses." But neither Bartram nor Collinson craved this kind of fame. To get the plants in circulation, to discover their true nature and to extend the horizon of knowledge was their aim. It was not all one way; English lilacs, tulips, roses, crocuses, gladioli, iris, snapdragons and poppies, in addition to many species of fruit and shade trees, found their way to American shores. One pear tree, known as Lady Petrie's pear, grown from seed sent by the wife of Bartram's first patron, Lord Petrie, was in existence in the garden many years after Bartram and his children, too, were dead.

By the time Bartram reached the latter part of his life his name was universally revered among men who adored what was then largely referred to as "natural science." Linnaeus called him "the greatest natural scientist in the world." Franklin proclaimed that John Bartram was "at least twenty folio pages, large paper, well filled, on the subjects of botany, fossils, husbandry, and the first creation." The chorus was echoed in letters from all over the world and by travelers from abroad and at home. He had made a practical success in a field of operations that few men of that day, if consulted in advance, would have considered possible.

Though he began as a plain farmer and believed in using the land wisely and well for practical purposes he was too saturated with a sense of wonder not to fear the direction too much practicality might take. He would certainly have given a firm assent to Einstein's warning to the students of the California Institute of Technology, though he would have been puzzled by his reference to the Indians. In speaking to the students in 1938, Einstein said, "Just consider a quite uncivilized Indian, whether his experience is less rich and happy than that of the average civilized man. I hardly think so. There lies a deep meaning in the fact that the children of all civilized countries are so fond of playing Indians. Why does this magnificent applied science, which saves work and makes life easier, bring us so little happiness? The simple answer runs— because we have not yet learned to make a sensible use of it. In war, it serves that we may poison and mutilate each other. In peace, it has made our lives hurried and uncertain. . . . It is not enough that you should understand about applied science in order that your work may increase man's blessings. Concern for man himself and his fate must always form the chief interest of all technical endeavors . . . in order that the creations of our mind shall be a blessing and not a curse to mankind. . . ."

The seeds of all this intensive devotion to the practical

aspects of science that Einstein cautioned against so many years later, were being busily sown in Bartram's day. Even the Philosophical Society of which he had been a founder, with Benjamin Franklin, was inclined to deride speculative thought. Under the firm and commonsense direction of Franklin it tended to discount knowledge "as of little use to men when confined to speculation." An accent on comfort was already being sounded when the brochure of the Society announced that: "When speculative truths are reduced to practice, when theories grounded on experiments are applied to common purposes of life, and when thereby, agriculture is improved, trade enlarged, the arts of living made more easy and comfortable, and, of course, the increase and happiness of mankind promoted, then knowledge becomes really useful." The word *useful* had already become a slogan; no one asked "useful for what?" The link between a useful object and happiness was accepted as inevitable; it was part of the philosophy of progress, fate-defying progress, which began to dominate the age. But that philosophy rested in those days on a personal confidence in universal ideals. With the belief in a loving God, a free mind, and the promise of justice, the individual dared more than he ever could before. The individual in the Eighteenth Century felt a basic security that was not primarily economic; scholars and saints had not hesitated to set out on lonely paths, since they were certain of their own direction.

Even in the little world of the Philosophical Society, and in spite of their heavily weighted practical preoccupations, the imagination soared. The technical apparatus had not yet swamped the matter to be observed and the magic wonder of fresh observations brightened every calculation. Though the pages of the Society's reports tend to the intensely useful—or the ludicrous—the editors did not hesitate to give many pages to the inspired watchers who reported "the Transit of Venus over the Sun, June 3, 1769." The cultivation of vines for making wine, observations on silkworms, an account of a machine for pumping vessels at sea without the labor of man, the remarkable case of Lockjaw cured by Opium and the actions of a horizontal windmill were all swept aside on this great occasion.

Different observation posts were set up to check the accounts of the watchers. At Cape Henlopen, at Lewestown, a party headed by Owen Biddle landed on the beach ahead of time to set up their simple and primitive apparatus. Neither the lighthouse nor the shore were suitable for observations; they had difficulty trying to keep their instruments steady and had to devise ways to defend the glasses of the telescopes and the eyes of the watchers from sand and wind. Four days ahead of time they were at their post in cloudy weather with frequent rains. But on the third, Transit Day, the sky was clear without a cloud in view; the air was calm. About twelve o'clock they directed their telescopes to the sun, determined to keep it constantly in the field until the contacts should be passed. In the meantime they set "their boys," whom they had tutored for the purpose, to counting seconds by the clock, each boy counting alternately lest they should be wearied and not perform with sufficient exactness. The watchers had agreed to attend the telescopes one minute by turns until about seven or eight minutes before the expected time so that they might not impair their vision by too steady application.

Biddle had left his telescope the minute preceding the contact, and when he applied his eye to the glass he saw, three seconds later, on that part of the "Sun's limb" where he had expected the contact to take place, a small impression which proved to be the limb of Venus in contact with the sun. All the limb of the sun which appeared at that time in the field of the telescope had small undulatory motions which Biddle believed were caused by the ascent of dense vapors from the sea. "On the first appearance of Venus it was like one of those small waves of the limb of the Sun, enlarged in so small a proportion that I remained doubtful for several seconds whether it was anything besides. It continued making a deeper impression with that tremulous motion for about ten seconds when the tremor disappeared with Venus in contact, and the indenture became truly circular with an even termination. When Venus had entered near one half her diameter on the disc of the Sun, we saw a luminous crescent, which enlightened that part of Venus's circumference which was off the Sun, so that the whole of her circumference was visible, but it did not continue so, until the first internal contact took place. At the time of the internal contact, the eastern limb of Venus seemed to be united to the limb of the Sun by a black protuberance or ligament, which was not broke by the entrance of the thread of light until four seconds after the regular circumference of Venus seemed to coincide with the Sun's."

Benjamin West made a report of the Transit from Providence, Rhode Island, from an elaborate platform constructed ahead of time from "seasoned pine, smooth and level as art can make it and secured from rain or moisture so it would not warp." At Norriton, Pennsylvania, another group took the precaution of putting smoked glass on the eye tube of the telescope with a little beeswax. A large gathering of citizens so thronged the site that the watchers feared their scheme for silence might be defeated. But after being warned of the danger, there was profound silence, "such a solemn pause of expectation as if each individual had been waiting for the sentence that was to give him life or death. We heard no whisper, not even the feet of the counters who passed nearby."

The air in this neighborhood was not tremulous, as it

had been by the sea; "Imagination cannot form anything more beautifully serene and quiet, than was the air during the whole time; nor did I see the Sun's limb more perfectly defined or more free from tremulous motion; to which his great altitude undoubtedly contributed much." Then this watcher continued his observations to say: "When Venus was one half of her diameter advanced on the Sun, I saw distinctly a border of light encompassing that part of her which was yet off the Sun. This was so bright that it rendered that part of Venus visible and pretty well defined although not yet entered on the Sun. But toward the interval of contact, the circular border of light seemed to grow more dusky toward the points where the luminous segments of the Sun's limbs were ready to close around the Planet. This duskiness did not seem to part wholly from the Sun's limb; at the time I apprehended the body of Venus to be wholly entered on the Sun and I judge that at least 16 to 18 seconds more elapsed before I saw the Sun's limb clear of this dusky shadow."

This great union of the Sun God with Venus was reported with all the rapture that devoted amateurs were capable of. They were not only scientifically inclined, they were devotees of a mighty ritual of creation. None of the Bartrams figured in the proceedings but by that time, at the date of publication in 1770, not only John Bartram's name was conspicuous in the list of members but Isaac Bartram is designated as a curator, and Moses and William are listed as members. The father had drawn three of his sons securely to his orbit.

To the very end of John Bartram's life fresh correspondents continued to pour in fresh inquiries. A group of Scottish botanists made an entry in 1765 with a request for some seeds. Scenting new enthusiasts Bartram shipped them a hundred living plants, some rare, with remarks about the habits of each; also a package of "curious seeds," about one hundred different species. This he followed up with about one hundred different young forest trees and shrubs. The shipment tangled up somehow in an Irish port instead of reaching London and took years to unsnarl. Then it turned out the Scotchmen didn't want flower seeds; they didn't even want young trees. Intensely practical, they pined for seeds of *useful* trees. Or they wanted plants used in medicine or dyeing. They even suggested that Bartram make special boxes for each variety of useful tree seeds, the box to be of the identical wood of the tree-to-be. But the trouble came when they asked Bartram to foot half the bill toted up for the extra shipping charge from the Irish port to Scotland. Bartram's share came to seven pounds, ten shillings. He paid but they heard no more from him. Six years later, they seem to have come to the conclusion that if they were ever to hear from him again or receive seeds from him, they must make amends. They politely apologized, said their treasury was now in better shape than it had been and offered to reimburse Bartram for his outlay or, if he chose, to accept a gold medal of the same worth. He chose the medal. It was of gold, weighing 487 grains, and inscribed "to John Bartram from a Society of Gentlemen at Edinburgh, 1772"; on the reverse side was the single word "Merenti."

Time was not so tyrannous in that century; the Scotch had finally come around, handsomely, after six years, and Michael Collinson got around to settling his father's affairs with Bartram three years after Collinson died. Bartram had made no move to apply for the money owing him until Michael put in a request for an accounting. When it was sent the young man was mortified to discover that his father was Bartram's debtor to the sum of two hundred pounds. He had been a total stranger to his father's affairs and had even fancied the balance might lie in his father's favor. He requested Bartram to draw on him at once. The

240

trouble was, he confided, that all such things had been a trouble to his father. Collinson, who had always recommended industry and caution in business affairs to others, had been faithful and industrious, but toward the end of his life his business had totally declined. At the age of seventy-five he had even solicited a small pension from the Crown in recognition of the many services he had performed for his country. He was refused.

Michael Collinson had no reproaches but he was indignant that his father had been humiliated by a rejection which seemed to repudiate the worth of his life. So dilapidated were his fathers' affairs, that his son could not keep Mill Hill as a residence, but was leasing it for two years with the strict proviso that not a single plant was to be moved. But there was little left in the once rare garden. Three brutal robberies had gutted Collinson's great pride almost as savagely as a fire might have done. But Michael had his father's enthusiasm and reported that the great magnolias from the Blue Mountains still towered some thirty feet, foaming with blossom, that as the season moved, "turned each seed pod to a glorious crimson vase."

They continued to write back and forth, Michael Collinson and John Bartram, sharing views about life and nature, creation and destructive forces. Both men seem to have agreed on "the extravagant, confused inventions of men." Both feared that the beauty of the world would be persecuted to the extinction of many of the finer species of vegetables and beasts. It's true that they worried more about the beaver than they did about the fate of man, but Eighteenth Century man was supposed to look out for himself. Michael leaned toward his father's friend in sympathy with his unwillingness to kill a rattler, and he admitted that it was now some years since he had deprived the "minutest individual of life." Like his father he was filled with a mystic awe of the universe, and considered life itself, wherever found, the "heavenly spark, derived from the Great Author and Fountain of all life, which is to be held sacred." They appeared to hold out their hands toward one another from across the sea, for at the close of their correspondence, ending only with the war in 1775, each man was in some way bereaved. Michael had lost his father and John Bartram believed he had lost his son. William had vanished two years before into the wilds of Florida and no word had reached the father of his whereabouts for some time. Bartram believed his son had been killed by the Indians, as his own father had been killed before him.

It had taken John Fothergill almost four years to catch up with his promise to Collinson to rescue Billy Bartram. This intelligent man finally realized that a few commissions to draw snails and turtles was not enough for a talented young man. Gradually he fathomed that Billy's hope was to return to Florida but not as a planter. He wanted to be on his own, at last, and alone to confront the perils which his father had set as the high mountain any pilgrim must cross to reach the tranquil plain. When he received word from Dr. Fothergill that he would back such an expedition, William was off like a shot. It did not take him long to make the great dive into the green fountains of Florida, and in a short time, he ceased to make any attempt to report back home.

If John Bartram was good stout oak he was also highly sensitive. He must have been sorely puzzled over the behavior of this son, the one of all his children upon whom he had set his greatest hopes. If he fretted over a delayed letter from Collinson he must have suffered truly at the silence following William's disappearance into a mysterious wilderness, fraught with perils he knew only too well. But he could hardly have been bowed down. Not John Bartram. There were too many problems yet to be solved. Too many books he wanted to read. His eager mind had reached out for more knowledge from the first, and he had stepped into James Logan's library with its Greek and Roman authors, its Archimedes, Euclid, Newton and Dr. Halley only to walk out with some of those volumes under his arm. The first scientific authors he ever read, so he once wrote to Sir Hans Sloane, were Salmon, Culpeper and Turner, borrowed from Logan. The Philadelphia Library bought solid works and among the first forty-three volumes purchased in London by Collinson for the subscribers were Milton's *Paradise Lost,* Raleigh's *History of the World,* and Locke's *On Education.* Bartram probably had some influence with the managers of the Darby Library for the list of books bought during his lifetime had a secular character not exactly in keeping with Quaker tastes. About 1735 the Darby Library bought Virgil's *Aeneid,* Pope's *Homer,* Cowley's *Works, The Rambler,* Newton's *Optics,* Blackstone's *Commentaries.* In 1773 they were buying *Tom Jones,* Sterne's works, much of Swift, the *Vicar of Wakefield,* Burney's *Evelina,* and Richardson's *Pamela.* Then they added what they could get of Locke, *Don Quixote,* Gibbon's *Decline and Fall of the Roman Empire,* Burns' *Poems* and Adam Smith's *Wealth of Nations.* It was an excellent list and not in the least Quakerish. The official Quaker position toward literature set forth in the London yearly meeting in 1765 was narrow and prudish, reproving the tendencies revealed in new plays, new novels and even in poetry and urging all members to discourage and suppress the same. Such admonitions were not likely to affect the man who had refused to be "disowned" by his Quaker brethren.

What he thought, what he felt, in those last years, we

can only conjecture. It is safe to say he was still agitating for the "truth" and his right to say it. He must have continued to assert that true science may reveal the nature of what men like to call mysteries. He must have continued to whack away at old superstitions in his effort to demolish them. He certainly continued to the end to assert that Negroes are God's creatures; they should not be slaves to free men but themselves freed. Plants like animals do breed and it is possible to improve the species. Animals may feel more than we credit them, and as for plants—who knows—they may have a system more delicate, more complex than the eye of man has yet discerned.

To the very end he was reaching out toward some future, that tantalizing Beyond of which the primeval forest was the great symbol. Knowledge was a bright light; ignorance the thing most to be feared and the prime source of misfortune. If his hatred toward the Indians remains a blot, it makes him in a sense the more comprehensible. Here is the hero, humanly vulnerable. For Bartram was not without his flaws, he was very much a part of the truculent, powerful mass of the New World as he was part of its genius. When the war finally came he must have feared for more than his family. It was his habit to live in a wide universe. Not long before he died he was agitated at the news that the British Army was approaching. It was after the battle of the Brandywine and Bartram feared that the Royal troops now ravaging the countryside might lay waste his beloved garden.

When he was finally struck down with his last illness in September, 1777 he expressed a most characteristic wish. The wish of a man who all his life had been thoroughly self-reliant. He hoped he might not live beyond that moment when he could no longer help himself. His pride held out for that last bargain. His one fear had always been that he might live beyond his usefulness and become a helpless burden. But he had luck. On his last day he cried aloud, "I want to die," and half an hour later, his wish was granted.

Three months later the long lost William returned from his Florida enchantment.

CHAPTER XIV

WILLIAM BARTRAM was now thirty-eight years old. He had returned to his father's house to find that his brother John had inherited the farm and botanical garden. His brother immediately made William a partner in his projects and for the rest of his long life William made no more journeys.

Tempting offers came to him through the years, but he was content to settle down to a simple, quiet life, occupied with his scientific observations, his diary, and his correspondence. In 1782 the University of Pennsylvania offered him the chair of Botany but he declined on account of ill-health. In 1806 Alexander Wilson urged him to accompany him on an ornithological expedition down the Ohio, "from Pittsburgh to the Mississippi, thence to New Orleans," but again he refused, for the same reason. When he was sixty-three he declined a more tempting offer from President Jefferson and one that would have broken his father's heart to refuse; Jefferson urged him to accompany the Lewis and Clark expedition to the Northwest. Dr. Benjamin S. Barton tried to persuade William of the advantages; compensation would be liberal; the journey would not be fatiguing. "Come on. You are not too old," he wrote. "You have sufficient youth, health and strength for this journey. You will render great and new services to Natural Science. Remember that your venerable father continued to make botanical tours long after he had reached your age."

But William Bartram was not John Bartram nor did he try to be. In his five years in the South, he had found himself and his own peculiar relationship to the universe. He had established himself, deep to the core, and he could afford to say, No. His admiration for his father had been profound and everlasting but it had taken five years to break from that thralldom to his own freedom, where, rooted in his own kind of awareness, he could be tough, too, but with a curious delicacy that brought him closer to the poets than to many of the botanists.

He wrote one volume, first printed in Philadelphia by James and Johnson in 1791. It was cumbrously entitled: *Travels through North and South Carolina, Georgia, East and West Florida, the Cherokee country, the extensive territories of the Muscogulges, or Creek confederacy, and the country of the Choctaws, containing an account of the soil and natural productions of those regions, together with observations on the manners of the Indians.* Its frontispiece was a portrait of "Mico Chlucco, the Long Warrior or King of the Siminoles," engraved by T. Trenchard after a drawing by William Bartram. Other drawings by William were scattered through the volume which was picked up by Coleridge in its second London edition of

1794 and praised: "The latest book of travels I know written in the spirit of the old travellers is Bartram's account of his tour in the Floridas. It is a work of high merit in every way." Within ten years of its publication in Philadelphia it went through three editions in America, two in London, one in Dublin, and was translated into German, Dutch and French, going through two editions in France.

The success of his work, the fruit of his years away from home, did not compel him to write another book. Like all the members of the American Philosophical Society he kept a calendar, reporting commonplace observations and seasonable phenomena. William's record is terse and objective, citing March 20, 1802 as the day a flock of geese returned to the north and March 22 as heralding the return of the kingfisher from the south. Apples were ripe on July 21 and on January 8, 1820 he was surprised to hear the voice of the catbird in the garden.

He wrote several papers: *Anecdotes of a Crow* and a *Description of Certhia,* and in 1789, *Observations on the Creek and Cherokee Indians,* published in 1851, after his death. Among his papers were drafts of letters, his opinions on slavery (written on the back of a catalogue of the plants growing in John Bartram's garden) and many scribbled notes expressing his views. He never made the slightest effort to exploit the success of his one work; on the contrary, he was content with a simple, quiet life filled with continuous observations of Nature and joy of living.

The Eighteenth Century was splintering to a new kind of creation; William exemplified the new creative thrust. Practical men were winning out in one great area of the world; in another they were being denied by imaginative men who balked at what began to be made plain: Practical men might very well ruin life and the world for their own gain. It began to be made clear that in the name of "common sense" monstrous advantages were taken by

248

practical men to entrench themselves far into the future. John Bartram had challenged that world of common sense in his own way; he had allied himself with animals and plants against wanton plundering; he had insisted on a mystic's comprehension of an illimitable universe. He had packed boxes and made toilsome journeys, all for the glory of something beyond himself; but he had hated the Indian as an enemy of his vast plans.

On the score of the Indian, William took issue. In a sense, this was the test of his unspoken debate with his father. This, the necessary uprooting of the son. When he was attending the old college in Philadelphia he came under the influence of a tutor, Charles Thomson, who was later to become secretary of the Continental Congress until 1789, and who was described by John Adams as "the Sam Adams of Philadelphia, the life of the cause of liberty." Thomson became known for his work among the Indians; he was honored by everyone who believed they should be dealt with fairly. In 1756 he was adopted into the tribe of Delawares where he was known as "Truth Teller," just as later his pupil was to be adopted by the Indian tribes of Florida. Thomson's attitudes became William's affirmations. To be himself, he could not mimic his father's pattern; division had to begin somewhere. He would not continue to make the journeys esteemed by his father; he would not pack boxes for the ornamentation of the great estates of England. He had contained five perfect years and it was enough. He could live out his existence on that bounty.

He would present the Indian to the world as he had found him during his five years in the southern wilderness. He was no trader among them but "Puc-Puggy," the flower hunter. He had come close enough to Indian bodies to observe the beautiful paintings in vegetable dyes on the skin of their chiefs: the sun, the moon, the planets upon the breast; fanciful scrolls winding around the trunk, thighs, arms and legs, divided the body into tablets of vision, each filled with innumerable figures; animals of the chase, bits of landscape. He had honorably exchanged gifts; their fawn skin filled with honey for his knives, fish-hooks or needles. He had lain on bear skins at their councils, and alone, in a fragrant grove, roasted his trout and stewed their heads in orange juice with a little boiled rice, while he reflected on the Indians secreted in the forests.

His five years alone had counseled him to be sensible, in his own way, and even if he tipped the scale toward special pleading, he would try to show that "to bang away" at the Indians, was no answer. More than his father, in this area, at least, he trusted to impartial investigation and scientific truth; that the Indians, as well as plants, needed to be studied in their native habitats if they were to be understood. He made a plea for men of ability to be sent by the government to live among the Indians, to study them, to learn their languages and, through intimacy, become acquainted with their customs. To touch, to see, to love, was to *know*. Only men who made the attempt to mingle could make true reports and assist in the formation of some judicious plan for the Indians' future, which included the future of the white man more than he knew.

Doubtless he had never argued with his respected father when he was off on a tirade against the perfidious Indian. His answer was delayed; his father never heard his sentiments. But his report would have been as precise, if his father had been alive to hear. For William, belatedly, was his own man. He did not draw the line at this particular branch of Nature because it was Indian; he saw the Indian as part of a glorious landscape; as joyous as the birds; as ferocious as a wildcat when challenged to the death; as able as a plant to further his life's purposes. He took pains to discover that rich tapestry of customs, manners, and profound relatedness that his father was ready ruthlessly to break through. And in taking his stand, with the Indian, he took his stand against most of the colonial world.

He repudiated his father's attitude on other scores. He would not be the obliging humble American botanist, glad to risk his life for the glory of an England that would shortly cease to be the mother country. The leading strings were soon to be cut when Sir Joseph Banks, President of the Royal Society, offered him one shilling sterling for every new plant he might discover in the South. His answer was as proud as his father's diligence had been; "William Bartram, in answer to Joseph Bank's proposal, says, that there are not over five hundred species altogether in the provinces of Virginia, North Carolina, South Carolina, West and East Florida and Georgia, which at one shilling each, amounts only to twenty-five pounds, supposing everything acceptable. It has taken me two years to search only part of the last two provinces, and find by experience it cannot be done with tolerable conveniency for less than one hundred pound a year, therefore it cannot be reasonably expected that he can accept the offer."

He was a little highhanded, too, with his generous patron, Dr. John Fothergill, who had promoted the opportunity for William "to ride through the savannas and the glorious forests of the Creeks and Cherokees with surpassing joy." Dr. Fothergill's original intention had been for the accumulation of "the more hardy plants such as will bear our winters without much shelter." He had tried to steer William to Canada but when that failed the Florida venture was approved. That it took in a vast world beyond Dr. Fothergill's original reckoning and covered not only the intended survey of Georgia and Florida but extended into Alabama and as far as the Mississippi in Louisiana is only a sign of the independence released in a liberated, creative William. On his own, at last, and with funds sufficient to see him through, he intended to explore in his own fashion and to see *everything*.

Even his way of seeing differed from his father's, and, more particularly, from the shallow calculations of the roving reporters of the day who were busy summing up the future mercantile advantages or lightly retelling of wonders which they did not hesitate to exaggerate for credulous readers. John Bartram was inclined to see a single tree, to isolate a plant or a shrub and to get at once at the heart of the structure. William saw plants and birds and Indians, too, in conjunction with all life. Shadow and odor and sound were a resistless trinity that may intoxicate the worshipper with joy. A field was not just a spot of color, nor masses of grasses growing, but a hint of the endless strength of the earth. When he described a bird or an animal he indicated the nature of its existence. These creatures lived as social beings within a society of their own. Birds assembled in squadrons, nations, tribes; horses galloped in troops; fish slid through the water in vast armies. Everything was in motion; birds were in flight; even a contemplative pelican was about to soar; cattle grazed; alligators roared in ferocious battle. The leaves, the bark, the flowers lived in a state of vitality that was never still. They breathed, they felt, they had their immortality in fertility.

He would have agreed with Buffon that the only good science is the knowledge of facts but his type of observation was in itself a challenge. What *were* facts? Appearance was not enough; habitat could not explain behavior. Could we say, for certain, that a plant did not feel? And "We have no certain knowledge that Animals below the order of Mankind have no Intellectual powers." Fact included not only an outer form but sensation. Fact was even a capacity for joy.

Joy was important. William Bartram had found it and was never to lose it. He had celebrated joy when he wrote of the Seminoles that they appeared as blithe and free as the birds of the air. "The visage, action and deportment of a Seminole is the most striking picture of happiness in this life . . . joy seems inherent in them . . . nor does it leave them but with the last breath of life." When William Bartram was an old man and discovered by distinguished visitors in his garden where "with a rake in his hand, he was breaking clods of earth in a tulip bed," he was wearing "an old hat which flapped over his face; a coarse shirt was seen near his neck; he wore no cravat or kerchief; his waistcoat and breeches were both of leather, and his shoes were tied with leather string." But his countenance was "expressive of benignity and happiness."

This man who as a youth had been the despair of his father and Collinson, who had sunk in "sloth," been lost in "obscurity," had learned through that dark time how to love. He went beyond his father when it came to the contemplation of animals; he was not afraid to touch. John Bartram had been squeamish; he could not bear to lay hands on the "disgusting opossum." He not only hated to kill; he did not want to touch. Even insects were repellent to him. But William reached out. He watched a spider pouncing upon a bee; he saw it inflict wounds "like a butcher." He watched with curiosity; this is the creature's cycle of life. But he could be horrified over man's brutality; it was "barbarous sport" to beat out the brains of a young wolf with the butt of a gun. And though a savanna crane made delicious soup, he determined that as long as he could get any other necessary food he prefers "their seraphic music in the ethereal skies." A good horseman, a fine swimmer, an able man with a gun, a good cook, he was equipped to view the world he had chosen.

It had taken time to find that world, but once found it was secure. And enough to last a lifetime. Beauty had its own use; his first impression of a scene is its appearance as a whole with all the play of light and shadow. He pleaded with some hunters, in vain, to spare a herd of deer feasting on a vast savanna. At the sight of the hunters the deer ran off, taking shelter on the opposite side of the spacious meadow. The determined hunters struck off toward them. "On drawing near, we beheld them, thoughtless and secure, flouncing in a sparkling pond . . . some were lying down on their sides in the cool waters, others were prancing like young kids; the young bucks were in playful sport, hooking and spurring the others with their sharp horns, urging them to splash the water . . . Then the hunter fired and laid the old buck prostrate upon the turf as the herd with prodigious speed were led by their chief out toward the savanna; his affrighted followers at that instant sprang off in every direction, streaming away like meteors or phantoms, and we quickly lost sight of them . . . Vultures and crows were ready to pounce upon the entrails."

Nothing was still in that new found world. The very air appeared to be moving; the water shivered. Within that beauty the smallest creature flaunted its brief existence as confidently as the alligator. William describes the minute Ephemera. He asks, isn't its delicate organization as complicated in relation to its scale of creation as the most perfect human being? Perhaps, he adds, in his profound respect for truth, *perhaps*. He enters into the pangs and joys of its entire life cycle, from its tiny birth in deep mud, to its emergence after three hundred and sixty days as a grub, to a brief dance of courtship and death in the sun. He sees these delicate insects in their "awful procession of millions verging on the brink of the grave but insensible of the jaws of the enemy"; the troops of fish and shrimp watching to devour them. It is a universe of preying and preyed upon creatures; but each has its own peculiar set of defenses; each its weapons for survival. A flock of parakeets hover over a swamp alive with otters, snakes and frogs; alligators crowd in a "great sink of water," in such profusion that a man could easily pass from one bank to the other by walking on their heads "which slowly float and turn about like knotty chunks of wood, except when they plunge or shoot forward to beat off their associates, pressing too close; or take up fish which constantly crowd in upon them from the rivers and creeks draining from the great savannas." One alligator could devour tons of fish. He describes the horrid sound of the closing jaws as the great creature snapped up a big trout which flapped about the alligator's nose and eyes before he swallowed it. During a battle between alligators, the very earth shakes with their roars, while cataracts of water stream from their jaws as they charge one another.

The fountains that had so engrossed his father also fascinated him. His journey was in part a retracing of the very country he had explored with John Bartram along the St. John's River. The older man had speculated about these fountains and their underground sources; William was to examine them and track them for miles. He calls one "The Fatal Fountain" where "unspeakable numbers of fish" seek water during the latter part of the summer season when the powerful sun has evaporated the waters off the trickling streams of the savannas. Those who are fortunate enough to escape do so by way of an underground passage, and, if they can get past the fearful jaws of the alligators and armed gar fish, descend into the earth through the wells and cavities in the rocks, and "from thence are carried away by secret subterranean conduits and gloomy vaults to other distant lakes and rivers," to which they ascend through "a rocky, dark door or outlet" to spread over and people the winter lake. Toward autumn when the waters have almost left the plains, "they crowd to the sink in such multitudes, as at times to be seen pressing on in great banks into the basin, being urged by pursuing bands of alligators and gar, and when entering the great basin or sink, are suddenly fallen upon by another army of the same devouring enemy lying in wait for them; thousands are driven on shore where they perish and rot in banks." In the sink called "The Fatal Fountain" by William, there were three great doors or vent holes through the rocks in the sink, two near the center and the other near the rim, much higher up than the other two, which could be clearly seen in the water. Beds of rock lay in horizontal thick strata, one on the other, where the holes or outlets were. These rocks were perforated by perpendicular tubes, four, five or six feet in diameter, "exactly circular as the tube of a cannon or walled well; many of these are broken into one another, forming a great ragged orifice, appearing fluted by alternate jambs and semicircular niches or excavations."

He revisits Mount Royal where his father had measured the great Indian burial mound. It is not much more than ten years since he had seen it, "wild and savage; yet in that uncultivated state it possessed an almost inexpressible air of grandeur, which was now entirely changed." The place now appears as a desert. "All has been cleared away and planted with indigo, corn and cotton," and that too abandoned. His love of nature unmodified by "improvements" led him to behold with "extreme regret, the destruction and devastation which has been committed, or indiscreetly exercised on those extensive, fruitful orange groves, on the banks of the St. Juan, by the new planters under the British government, some hundred acres of which, at a single plantation, has been entirely destroyed to make room for the Indigo, Cotton, Corn, Batatas, etc. or so they say, to extirpate the mosquitoes, alleging that groves near their dwellings are haunts and shelters for these persecuting insects; some plantations have not a single tree standing, and where any have been left, it is only a small coppice or clump, nakedly exposed and destitute . . . exhibiting a mournful, sallow countenance; their native perfectly formed and glossy green foliage, as if violated, defaced and torn to pieces by the bleak winds, scorched by the burning sunbeams in summer, and chilled by the winter frosts."

He was no less saddened at the effect of the trader and "civilization" on the Indian whom he describes as part of the landscape. He relates the myth of the "incomparably beautiful women" on an island of the St. Mary River. The source of this river is a vast lake or marsh called Ouaquaphenogau, lying between the Flint and Oakmulge rivers and occupying a space of near three hundred miles in circumference. This is a vast accumulation of waters seeping from surrounding marshes and in the wet seasons, when it emerges as a lake above the soggy ground, it contains some large islands or knolls of rich high land, one of which the Creek Indians told him was "the most blissful spot on earth." A party of Creek hunters had been rescued from sinking bogs and swamps by a company of beautiful women from one of the isles, who fed them dates, corn cakes and fruits. The Indian hunters call these women "Daughters of the Sun." But when the hunters tried to follow them, they were lost in a perpetual labyrinth and failed to find, ever again, the blessed isle.

Here is the old myth of the magic isles, in the guise of an Indian dream world. The story emerges like a plant from the narration; the Indian women take flight like the birds.

Like his father, William Bartram was precise when it came to details. Camp sites were important and he always reconnoitered before settling down for the night when he "spread his skins and blanket by his cheerful fire, under the protecting shade of the hospitable Live-oak." Or it might be a question of finding a convenient harbor for his little sailboat which was preferably "in a little lagoon, under an elevated bank." A good site was one that could afford a good view as well as protection. When he comes upon "a grassy knoll or eminence, under the cover of spreading Oaks, just by a grotto or sink of the lake, which lay as a sparkling gem on the flowery bosom of the ample savanna" he lingers for several days to range around the delightful country to a great distance.

At night there might be no rest; the mosquitoes could sting ferociously, crocodiles roared, sea fowl were restless and the air so thick with winged creatures that herons, pelicans and spanish curlews were looped together in incredible numbers until the trees were entirely covered. Dawn always brings a fresh blast of sound. "Wild turkey-cocks salute each other from the sunlit tops of lofty cypresses . . . and magnolia. From early dawn to sunrise, from March to April, the watch word is caught and repeated, from one to another, for hundreds of miles around; for an hour or more the country is one universal shout."

He finds color in everything; in the soil, in flowers and leaves, vibrating in the water. Nothing is too small to imitate the rainbow. "The goldfish is about the size of an anchovy . . . of a neat slender form; the head is covered with a falade of an ultramarine blue, the back of a reddish brown, the sides and belly of a flame, or of the color of fine red lead; a dusky line runs along each side, from the

258

gills to the tail; the eyes are large, with the iris of burnished gold.

The world of water is an Orient in which William's favorite fish, the yellow bream, glides in splendor among his attendants and associates; "the whole fish is of a pale gold or burnished brass color, darker on the back and upper sides; the scales . . . are variably powdered with red, russet, silver, blue and green specks, so laid on the scales as to appear like real dust . . . the fins are of an Orange color; and the ultimate angle of the *branchiostega* terminate by a little spatula, the extreme end of which represents a crescent of the finest ultramarine blue, encircled with silver and velvet black, like the eye in the feathers of a peacock's train."

Whether he is observing the eggs of the crane in a tussock of dry grass, "of a pale ash color, speckled with powdery brown," or whether he pauses to worship the dark green of the Laurel, its head forming a perfect cone, "its darkness silvered over with milk-white bloom," or studying the "curious and handsome Snake bird, whose head and neck are extremely small and slender . . . the upper side, the abdomen and thighs, as black and glossy as a raven's . . . the breast and upper part of the belly covered with feathers of a cream colour, the tail, very long, of a deep black, and tipped with a silvery white, and when spread, represents an unfurled fan"; everything that he witnesses is acceptable, even the stealthy tread of bears and foxes in the night when his solitary fire keeps their shining eyes at a distance.

From his father he had learned that nothing is unworthy of notice; the way a plant grows, a bird flies, a fish fights for its life. He was as hospitable to food as John Bartram and as alert to the methods by which the Indians prepared delicious offerings. When the Indians set about to make "hickory milk" he was watching every step of the process, saw how they pounded bushels of nuts to pieces, then cast them into boiling water. This mess they strained five times; then they skimmed from the residue a thick creamy oil, "rich and sweet as cream" and used in cooking, particularly in hominy and corn cakes. But much as he appreciated food, he could content himself with a little rind of cheese when he is suddenly stranded with nothing else to sustain him.

Everything he saw was turned to account. Even an accident. Once his foot slipped going up a steep rocky slope. He reached out to save himself from pitching downward on sharp stones and grabbed up a handful of plants. Their roots filled the air with "the animating scents of cloves and spicey perfumes." He might have been writing a parable of his own life.

In an age when many men sought a Utopia, William Bartram was one of the happy few. He encountered and held fast to the end of his days an actual terrestrial paradise. But again, like his father, he had premonitions. He believed that this marvelous beauty was doomed to pass away and at the hands of a civilization concerning which many men had more than grave doubts. At the very moment when tempting new inventions appeared to open up an entirely new conquest of a world, some had dread. While one faction shouted the glories of inevitable "progress," another faction weighed, hesitated, parried and shuddered.

William Bartram had not fled to the wilderness to escape the sorrows of the world, to find inspiration, or even to seek God. He had entered in full consciousness and with responsibility to bear witness. Nor did he retreat from reason and its just claims to order a saner universe if mankind would only consent to follow. But if he did not lean quite so heavily upon a rational ordering of the universe as his father had done, it was not only because his temperament had other requirements. The mental climate was altering and many thoughtful men were demanding answers which they believed the rationalists could not give. There were imponderables at work; there was an imaginative faculty in man; there was a fine network of mysterious nerves covering the skeleton of man and fish, bird and beast. There was a universe of feeling.

Men were beginning to insist that the brain was not an organ apart; it was fed by the senses. To touch, to see, to feel were particularly important to William Bartram but such an emphasis did not require him to sink into a contemplative stupor divorced from an actual world. On the contrary, it compelled him to act and to speak. He was forthright during the rest of his life on many subjects other men of his day were content to ignore. It was not the opportune moment, they said. But William Bartram had his father's conscience; he spoke clearly for the Indian when the rest of the colonial world, almost without exception, urged nothing less than obliteration. He was as plain as a fence post on the question of slavery, arguing that "God was no respecter of persons and that Black White Red & Yellow People are equally dear to him & under his protection & favour & that sooner or later ye must render full retribution. . . . Americans, ye do not know your own interests by keeping these innocent people in bondage against their will."

Like his father, William was inclined to distrust luxury and accumulations of great wealth with all that might follow in that train. He even distrusted too much industry and mechanics as contrivances geared more for the accumulation of wealth than the welfare of mankind. When a State put too much faith in money, he warned, it signified a distrust of mentality that spelled disaster. The worship of money, in his opinion, led to avarice, contention and in the end, to war. Like the older Bartram, William was inclined to doubt the wisdom of men to guide the world justly. He had witnessed cruelty in men; he feared the tendency toward rank mass judgments. "The more any man or woman approaches to Honesty & Simplicity," he wrote, "the more he is accounted a Fool and he is on the broad road and hastening to Poverty, Contempt and Misery, until death relieves him from oppression and disgrace."

This was no paper sermon. What he had to say burned straight from his younger days. It was the humiliating dreadful truth. He took a crack at those disciples of practicality who might imagine that it was not "profitable" to study the migrations of birds; "there may be some persons . . . who pronounce such attention to natural history merely speculative, and only fit to amuse and entertain the idle virtuoso; however, the ancients thought otherwise, for with them, the knowledge of the passage of birds was the study of their priests and philosophers, and was considered a matter of real and indispensable use to the state."

In this statement he makes another departure from his father. In the first half of the Eighteenth Century men were inclined to be indifferent to history and to look forward, rather than backward, and to glory in full confidence in what was to come. Revolutions in science and the practical affairs of men had worked a ferment which inclined many to insist on a future perpetually geared toward perfection. John Bartram hardly believed in that kind of mechanical progress but his eyes were turned more to the future than to the past. In William's maturity more men began to seek the advice of history, or at least to attempt to try to fathom its secrets. Did primitive peoples have something to teach the world beyond the glittering façade offered by Rousseau? Was there not something to be learned from Plato and Socrates, as Thoreau was to insist when he walked around Walden Pond; can we ignore the wisdom of the Hindus?

Living on in his father's old home, William Bartram was content to pursue a life that altered only with the seasons. He did not lift a finger to refine his existence or to "acquire chairs from Seddons." He was not Janus-faced; preaching one thing, living another. He did not see any reason why he should glorify himself by undertaking any more expeditions. He had absorbed the content he required for his life and would spend the rest of his days digesting his findings and making mental flights. He would communicate what he knew to others as they passed by.

Alexander Wilson lingered in the Bartram gardens for months. As a rebel Paisley weaver in Scotland, he had been in prison and had been forced to burn some of his satires in the public square. Roaming in that country as a pedler with a pack of silks and muslins, he had collected subscriptions for his poems until "feeling a vague terror in the air" he had found his way to America. He had opened a school at Gray's Ferry on the Schuylkill but teaching was a prisoner's life for this born rover. His spirits had sunk as low as William Bartram's in the days of his purgatorial beginnings. It took a William with a familiar suffering experience to befriend and cheer the Scotsman who had found joy the moment he saw a wondrous woodpecker in the Delaware forest. William Bartram had counted two hundred and fifteen birds in his travels, as Jefferson in the *Notes on Virginia* had counted one hundred and nine; and now he hoped this newcomer would rival his list and complete it. Teaching school by day, drawing by candlelight at night, Wilson made rapid progress and in a single summer counted fifty-one birds building their nests. His room was crowded with strange guests; lizards and owls, live hawks and John Bartram's obnoxious opossum. One of his pupils brought him a mouse. Wilson tells how he set about drawing it that same evening, and "all the while the pantings of its little heart showed it to be in the most extreme agonies of fear. I had intended to kill it in order to fix it in the claws of a stuffed owl, but happening to spill a few drops of water near where it was tied, it lapped it up with such eagerness and looked in my face with such an eye of supplicating terror as perfectly overcame me. I untied it and returned it to life and liberty." Freed from his school, he set out on the very trail so much coveted by John Bartram; off to Pittsburgh, on to Ohio and finally down the Mississippi to New Orleans.

William Bartram had been disinterested in sending botanical specimens to England in his father's footsteps. But his book describing his travels through the Cherokee country and the extensive territories of the Muscogulges or Creek Confederacy and the country of the Choctaws had its fruitful effects upon the minds of men. His jetting fountains and incense bearing trees, Indian maids and solitary pelicans, were to open up a fresh scene for imaginative minds at a moment when the prime elements of poetry were already beginning to be dishonored. In *The White Goddess*, Robert Graves has pointed out that the poets "laid hold of the great symbols, the serpent and the fish; they seized the sacred grove before it could be sent to the sawmill." They looked upon the Moon, "not as a burned out satellite, but as a divine and milky deity of the night." They used the great symbols in a period of tremendous transformations, when, for imaginative minds, there was cause to fear as well as to hope. In a world that seemed more and more able to buy anything but truth, the poets laid hold of bird and fish, tree and meadow, in a grand attempt to remind man that he could not live by bread alone.

If Bartram's wondrous fishes, decked out in their gold, green, red and blue spangles emerged in *The Ancient*

Mariner of Coleridge as watersnakes, so much the better for the creative process. In *Kubla Khan* the endless meandering rivers and the fathomless caverns of Bartram's Florida renewed themselves; Bartram's Fatal Fountain was transformed to Coleridge's intention. Wordsworth repeated the green savannas, the azaleas on fire on the hills, the endless lakes and flowering trees in *Ruth*; and in *The Prelude* practically lifted Bartram's pelican which he had described as "a bird who stood alone on the topmost dead cypress tree, his neck contracted or drawn in upon his shoulders, and beak resting like a long scythe upon his breast . . . in this pensive posture . . . they look extremely grave, sorrowful and melancholy, as if in deepest thought."

It is not the aim of this study to particularize, line for line, the effect of Bartram's travels on Coleridge and Wordsworth but rather to indicate how he saturated the imagination of certain minds with a grand array of fertilizing symbols. Bartram's symbols fired these poetic imaginations; but the magic still lies beyond Florida. The doves and snakes, the owls and birds, that Bartram witnessed live again, in Coleridge's own world in *Christabel*, in *Frost at Midnight*. Some of the imagery of Wordsworth's *Ruth* follows almost word for word the descriptions of Bartram, in particular the passage relating how the Indian girls gathered wild strawberries in the wood. Bartram's magnolia and fiery azalea were snatched away to fertilize poetry as surely as John Bartram's seedlings matured and enriched the English countryside.

The grand impact of William Bartram's impressions was felt on many lesser lights. One is reluctant to bring the seed to lowlier ground, but it is interesting to note how far such seed could scatter. Robert Southey is known to have owned a second edition of Bartram's *Travels*, the same edition owned also by Coleridge. In his *William Bar-*

tram, Interpreter of the American Landscape, N. Bryllion Fagin traces lines in *Madoc* directly to Bartram's account of the wild turkey. Southey's owls and magnolias also come from the same source, and even some of his titles in *Songs of the American Indians,* so Mr. Fagin believes, derive straight from Bartram.

William Lisle Bowles, a poet who left his mark on the work of Coleridge, frankly acknowledged his indebtedness to Bartram in a footnote to *Banwell Hill,* and Mr. Fagin seems to think that Bartram's language and symbols infiltrated into more of his work. When we begin to look at Thomas Campbell and Chateaubriand we realize the more how Bartram's trickling streams filtered from strata to strata. Like some best sellers of our day, this work was taken up with a shout of discovery; but with a difference; there was a real source to shout about. Even the poetry of Felicia Hemans seems to have been impregnated with this rich influence. This lady delved into many sources and was generous enough to acknowledge no less than eighteen different fountain heads, among them William Bartram, when she wrote *Lays of Many Lands.* Charles Lamb, the close friend of Coleridge, read Bartram's book and is believed to have commented on it in a contribution to the *Morning Post.*

This field has been thoroughly ploughed by devoted commentators; it is relevant here only to make clear the connection which Bartram's *Travels* finally had with the world. Perhaps the greatest borrower and the one least given to precision was Chateaubriand who boldly filched from Bartram's *Travels*: tulip and magnolia trees, the red cedar, the fiery azalea, white moss, live oaks, the black squirrel, snakes, crocodiles and their nests, Seminole horses, the mocking-bird, cardinals, the humming bird, strawberries and even the hickory milk which had enchanted William. He also blandly took over the physical appearance of the Seminoles, the Indian game of ball, beautiful Indian women, and a view from Occone mountain among other things. Professor Chinard in his introduction to Chateaubriand's *Les Natchez* cites fifty passages which derive directly from Bartram. The French writer even saturated himself in Bartram's style and colored his prose with a "charm" which is unmistakably imitative. That Chateaubriand was influenced by Bartram is not so surprising as he was a visitor to America and gave himself freely to American influences. But scholars in this field, notably Lane Cooper, seem to think that the Bartram influence spread to other countries, not only to France, but through the work of Zimmermann to Germany, and possibly from thence to Holland and Sweden as well.

William Bartram would probably have looked upon all this ferment following in his train modestly. His theme had been felicity itself, the celebration of the things which mankind had set up for glorification or worship since the beginning of recorded time. He would doubtless have considered that the creative transformation by the poets was only Nature at work, in the minds of men, going about her business of the ages.

When he was eighty-five years old, he happily began one afternoon to write an article on the natural history of a plant. A few minutes later a blood vessel in his lungs ruptured and he was dead. It was July 22, 1823. He had never married.

BIBLIOGRAPHY

LAST WORD:

If there was a beginning to a book like this it was in green leaves and happy lingering beside a brook; if there is an ending, the poets should have the final word. What the Bartrams saw and felt in the youthful days of an abundant world may be diminished but not lost. For city dwellers, who may not touch or intimately view, the written word brings this kingdom home. It may be found, richly, in the poems of Marianne Moore where the beasts of fable lie down with the mongoose and the tortoise; where fern seed and field mouse are at ease with ancient beetles and Dürer's benign monsters. "Bird-reptile life is pleasing."

No orthodox bibliography is fitting for work that stems from such diversities as sap and stone, printed page and reveries. But many writings are good guides backward through the woods to the fountains. Poets are best of all. Thoreau knew it to the brim. Emily Dickinson sent tiny bouquets of flowers with notes to friends. And for the dark ground where men's passions find their roots in stone and swamp, Robert Penn Warren's "Brother to Dragons."

The following list is made for those travelers who like to stray from the main highway and who may find within themselves some relic of the Eighteenth Century curiosity that goaded John and William Bartram to their goals. It cannot cover the actual works which helped to nourish this particular study, for the author ranged and fed, made notes and buried bones too long to be precise as to where, or how, the branch, the leaf, the little skeleton was found.

Bartram, John	*Observations on the Inhabitants, Climate, Soil, Rivers, Productions, Animals, and other matters worthy of Notice. By Mr. John Bartram, In His Travels from Pensilvania to Onondago, Oswego and the Lake Ontario, In Canada. To which is annex'd, a Curious Account of the Cataracts of Niagara. By Mr. Peter Kalm, a Swedish Gentleman who travelled there,* London, 1751
	A Description of East-Florida, with a journal kept by John Bartram, of Philadelphia, Botanist to his Majesty for the Floridas; upon a journey from St. Augustine up the river St. John's, as far as the lakes. With Explanatory botanical notes, London, 1766. *Bartram Papers,* Manuscript Division, Pennsylvania Historical Society
Bartram, William	*Anecdotes of an American Crow,* Philadelphia Medical and Physical Journal, I. (1804)
	Bird Migration Records of William Bartram, edited by Witmer Stone, The Auk, Lancaster, Pa., 1913
	Manuscript book on entomology, University of Pennsylvania
	Travels through North & South Carolina, Georgia, East & West Florida, the Cherokee Country, the Extensive Territories of the Muscogules, or Creek Confederacy, and the Country of the Chactaws; containing an Account of the Soil and Natural Produc-

tions of those Regions, together with Ob-
servations on the Manners of the Indians,
Philadelphia, 1791
The Travels of William Bartram, edited by
Mark Van Doren, New York, 1928

Barnhardt, John Hendley   *Significance of John Bartram's work
to botanical and horticultural knowledge,* 1931
Budd, Thomas   *Good Order Established in Pennsylvania and
New Jersey,* 1685
Carver, Jonathan   *Travel through the Interior of North Amer-
ica,* 1789
Chateaubriand, F. A.   *Atala,* Translated by Caleb Bingham,
Reprint, 1930
Chinard, Gilbert   *Chateaubriand en Amérique,* University of
California, Modern Philology IV, 1915
Cooper, Lane   *Methods and Aims in the Study of Literature,*
1940
Cooper, Lane   *The Power of the Eye in Coleridge,* 1910
Collier, John   *The Indians of the Americas,* 1947
Coleridge, S. T.   *Biographia Literaria,* 1817
Colden, Cadwallader   *History of Five Indian Nations in
Canada,* 1747
Darwin, Erasmus   *The Botanic Garden,* 1798
Denton, Thomas   *A Brief Description of New York,* 1670
Duché, Jacob   *Caspipina's Letters,* 1777
Dickinson, John   *Letters from a farmer in Pennsylvania to the
inhabitants of the British Colonies,* 1774
Darlington, W.   *Memorials of John Bartram and Humphrey
Marshall,* 1849
Dixon, William Hepworth, *History of William Penn,* 1872
Earnest, Ernest   *John and William Bartram, Botanists and
Explorers,* 1940
Fox, Richard Hingston   *Botany in the 18th century,* 1919
Franklin, Benjamin   *Plain Truth,* 1747

Fagin, N. Bryllion   *William Bartram, Interpreter of the American Landscape,* 1933

Gerard, John   *The herball, or General historie of plantes,* 1632

Graves, Robert   *The White Goddess,* 1948

Grant, Anne   *Memoirs of an American Lady,* 1808

Harshberger, John William   *The Botanists of Philadelphia and their Work,* 1899

Imlay, Gilbert   *A Description of the Western Territory of North America,* 1793

James, Thomas   *The Strange and Dangerous Voyage of Captain Thomas James,* 1633

Josselyn, John   *New England Rarities,* 1672

Kalm, Peter   *Travels into North America,* 1772

Knight, Sarah   *Journal,* 1704

Lowes, John L.   *The Road to Xanadu,* 1927

Lee, Samuel   *Answers to Queries concerning America,* 1690

Middleton, William S.   *John Bartram, Botanist,* Scientific Monthly, Lancaster, Pa., 1925

Morton, Thomas   *The New England Canaan,* 1637

Pastorius, Francis Daniel   *A New Primer,* 1698

Penn, William   *A Brief Account of the Province of Pennsylvania,* 1690

Peabody, William   *Life of Alexander Wilson,* The Library of American Biography, 1848

Purchas, Samuel   *Hakluytus Posthumus or Purchas his Pilgrims,* Reprint, 1905

Pickering, Charles   *Chronological history of Plants,* 1879

Simpson, Henry   *The Lives of Eminent Philadelphians, now deceased,* 1859

Thoreau, Henry   *Journals,* 14 volumes, 1949

Wansey, Henry   *An Excursion to U. S. A. in the summer of 1794*

Williams, William Carlos   *In the American Grain,* 1927

Youmans, William Jay   *John and William Bartram, Pioneers of Science in America,* 1896

272

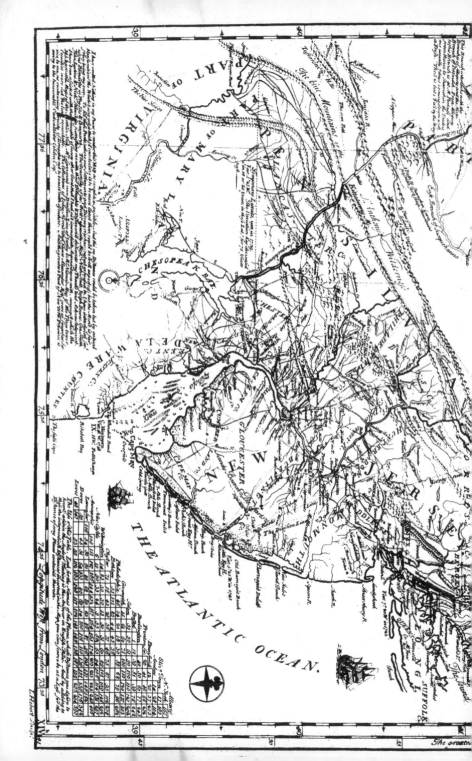